THE AMBER DIARY

THE AMBER DIARY

Janet Gustafson

J. L. GUSTAFSON

TATE PUBLISHING
AND ENTERPRISES, LLC

Published by Tate Publishing & Enterprises, LLC
127 E. Trade Center Terrace | Mustang, Oklahoma 73064 USA
1.888.361.9473 | www.tatepublishing.com

Tate Publishing is committed to excellence in the publishing industry. The company reflects the philosophy established by the founders, based on Psalm 68:11,
"The Lord gave the word and great was the company of those who published it."

Book design copyright © 2014 by Tate Publishing, LLC. All rights reserved.
Cover design by Joseph Emnace
Interior design by Jake Muelle

Published in the United States of America

ISBN: 978-1-63367-397-7
1. Fiction/Thrillers/Espionage
2. Fiction/Mystery&Detective/Historical
14.08.27

For Laura, with the greatest thanks for helping me through every part of this project. Valerie, for teaching me the tools a writer needs. And Keith, for his skeptical mind which spurred me to always ask questions.

HISTORICAL PROLOGUE

The ancient Greeks called it *elektron*. It becomes warm to the touch when held. Ancient shamans carved it. Roman warriors wore it for luck. A small sample in ancient Rome had more value than a slave. At the start of the eighteenth century, artisan Gottfried Wolfram and French jeweler Tusso, under the leadership of architect Andreas Schluter Jr., created an amazing work of art using this fabulous jewel. The organic treasure is amber and the masterpiece was the fabled Amber Study created for the Potsdam palace of King Frederick I.

Select pieces of fossilized tree resin were brilliantly polished. Some were heated to change color. The resulting palette ranged from the typical amber hues of reds, browns, golds, and yellows to the scarcer greens and blues. The walls were saturated with colorful floral mosaics, scroll work, exquisite busts, and symbols of the Prussian monarchy.

Frederick's son, interested more in creating political liaisons than art, gave the Amber Study to Peter the Great of Russia. There it lay in crates, forgotten or ignored until Peter's daughter, Empress Elizabeth, resurrected and enlarged the masterpiece to fit the grand dimensions of the Tsarskoye-Selo palace. The architect, Rastrelli, ordered the original panels framed in a cartouche of carved wood covered with gold leaf. This gilded boiserie, with its accompanying mirrors and Florentine mosaics, enhanced the original size to fit the lofty proportions of the castle's thirty-foot-high walls. Now called the Amber Room, it remained undisturbed until the Nazis looted the Russian palace in 1941.

There weren't many prepared for the aggressive Nazi attack on Leningrad. The palace at Tsarskoye-Selo fell quickly. A small, handpicked group confiscated treasures for the Third Reich. The most exquisite artifacts were stripped and packed. The Amber Room panels were taken down, placed in crates, loaded on trucks, and sent to the East Prussian Capitol of Königsberg, a Baltic port nestled between Lithuania and Poland.

But the end was coming for Hitler's Third Reich. Royal Air Force bombs destroyed the king's castle in August 1944 as well as damaging the surrounding city. It was rumored the crates holding the Amber Room had been moved from the castle and suffered minimal damage.

There were reports of a plan to move the boxes in early January 1945. Before this could take place, the invading Soviets smashed the Nazi Eastern front. Almost all rail communication was cut off from Königsberg and roads were impassable due to troop movements and fleeing refugees.

Gauleiter Erich Koch, who supervised the dismantlement of the Amber Room from the Tsarskoye–Selo palace, was captured and imprisoned. His sentence was commuted due to ill health, although some speculated he was spared because he had knowledge of the Amber Room's location. Erich Koch lived a long life in confinement but the information was never revealed and the crates were never found.

INTRODUCTION

ÖLAND, SWEDEN, 1945

*S*entinel to the island's past, a runestone stood exposed against the
stark landscape. A cold wind and driving rain pushed waves
high against the rocky shore. In the distance, a windmill's creaking
paddles moaned in sympathy. The few cottages scattered on the beach
were patterned after Öland's fortress churches and ancient settlements,
making them well-armored against assaults from the sea. The villagers
knew to stay inside during these storms and went about their weaving
or gathered around the hearth to spin tales of long dead Vikings. One
fisherman chanced riding the sea. Only he saw the immense, dark
hulk slowly rise from the water and then slink again into the darkness
beneath the waves.

1

1989

Feet propped up in relaxation, double agent Ulrik Orensson rubbed a smooth jewel between his fingers. The house was dark, but he didn't need artificial light to recognize amber. It was warm to the touch, bringing memories of younger years and beautiful women.

He knew the history of the Amber Room; the artists who created the jeweled masterpiece, the people who used it as a political pawn, and the nation who claimed it as a trophy of war. Most said it was a treasure lost, destroyed in a fire. Others searched, positive it rested deep in an abandoned bunker. He knew the truth. He was there.

Moving to the kitchen, Ulrik turned on a small light to re-read the recent communiqué from the Capitol. He was anxious at being so close, but he had been close before. There could be no mistakes this time. The split inside the Soviet Union was growing, festering, spreading like a cancer. In his opinion, containment was unlikely this time. The fall would not be in days or months, but it was coming. Smiling at the news, he had already taken the necessary precautions. Turmoil was something he understood and used to his advantage. Chosen ideologies were as common as they were fleeting.

He had served many masters over the years, but those few artistic masterpieces, such as the Amber Room, transcended time and politics. Ulrik had never concerned himself with the typical treasure hunter, who he considered to be motivated by greed and a feigned interest in history. Their ranks were few, resources slim, and techniques sloppy. With the Soviet demise, a different breed would emerge to join the search.

In a new global order, possession of the Amber Room would mean prestige and power to those enmeshed in the political game of global chess. There would be many offers from various factions competing for the world stage, to whoever found this historical treasure. For this reason, his time to find the Amber Room had become limited. It had to be now.

Ulrik had seen the glorious work only once, in the king's castle in Königsberg. He would not allow it to become a pawn for ransom. It should belong to someone who appreciated its beauty, not zealots interested in using the treasure to further a worthless cause.

2

EVANSTON, ILLINOIS, 1989

Lea was numb, her world turned upside down. It had taken one month for Lea's mother to join her father in death. Anna suffered through countless blood cultures, spinal taps, and experimental treatments. Neither parent had been seriously ill before, but autopsies showed evidence of a massive infection that had compromised their immune systems and short-circuited all memory functions.

The specific cause of death had not been identified in either case. In his cramped office in the morgue basement, the pathologist sat with Lea to try and answer her questions.

"Miss Reardon, your parents worked many years in countries all over the world. It's not uncommon for a bacterium or virus to have a latent stage, and then kill its victim in a short period of time. I understand this doesn't give you the definitive answer you want, but it's all I have."

"Ashes to ashes, dust to dust."

Lea heard the minister's words as she stood at her mother's grave. She listened to his description of Anna Reardon's life and saw the mound of flowers heaped on the casket. But she refused to believe her mother was in that box.

Reverend Sedgely finished his service at the gravesite. The minister stood beside Lea as neighbors, friends, and business acquaintances expressed their sympathies. As people left the cemetery, she overheard snatches of conversation about the weather and chances of a Chicago Cub pennant this season. Normal things people like her parents talked about every spring.

The reverend took out his car keys. "Are you going to your apartment or the house?"

She stared at him with blank eyes, not seeming to understand the question. "What? Oh, no, thank you. I don't need a ride. Jake's waiting for me."

"Fine, but please stop by my house later. In fact, stay for dinner."

"I can't. There's so much to do before I leave."

"Lea," the minister said, putting his arm around her shoulder, "just stop by. You don't have to stay and visit. Remember, Mrs. Sedgely and myself are always available if you want to talk or need company."

The offer made her think of how much she had taken her parents for granted, naively assuming Mom and Dad would be around forever. Even though Lea had asserted her independence by moving from Evanston to Chicago's Old Town neighborhood after college, it was only a short trip between the family home and her apartment. She nodded her head in acknowledgment.

"Is eight o'clock okay?"

"Fine. I'll see you at the house." The minister squeezed her hand and walked away to join his wife.

Turning around, she searched for Jake. Lea was ready to escape the churchyard. Unfortunately, the voice calling her name wasn't Jake's.

"Lea, I'm sorry to be late," the tall woman said, trying to catch her breath. "It's too bad what happened. Your father taken, now your mother.

"But, let me tell you, it wasn't right of them to help countries that have forsaken the true God. Those heathens are being punished for what they've done. If your parents would have had the sense to stay out of such places, they'd be alive today."

She stiffened at the woman's words but was determined not to argue or give her the satisfaction of an angry reaction.

"Mrs. Farmer, thank you for coming. Your sympathy over my mother and father is…" She struggled to hold her temper. No matter what, her parents would have expected courtesy from their daughter, not hostility. It was so hard.

"Of all people, Mrs. Farmer, your distress over the loss of my parents is…touching."

Brenda's eyes narrowed. Her mouth formed a strained line in response to Lea's words. Her fingers tightened around a well-used prayer book. "Are sarcastic remarks the thanks I get for coming here with good Christian intentions? Moreover, a consecrated cemetery is no place to use un-Godlike behavior. If you lived in my household, you would have been taught to show proper respect, like my Bradley!" Feeling sick at the mention of Bradley Farmer, Lea walked away.

Her audience gone, Brenda looked for a familiar face, determined that more people would hear news of her only child, his accomplishments since completing law school, and the prestigious firm in New York he would join. Recognizing someone from the neighborhood talking to a tall man, she walked toward the pair, waving her arm in greeting. "Yoo-hoo."

Spotting the advancing woman, the neighbor said a quick goodbye to Jake O'Brien and rushed off. Jake stood and waited.

Brenda hadn't seen Jake since he left for college, and didn't recognize the man he'd become until she was the recipient of his anger.

"Respect, Mrs. Farmer, did I hear you talk about respect? Was it respect that Bradley showed Lea the night she turned fourteen?" Jake hadn't started the conversation with the usual social niceties and ended it the same way. Without a goodbye, he turned to catch up with Lea.

Brenda left the cemetery, muttering about rude hussies and low-caste Irish trash.

Lea had heard the exchange and was grateful for her friend's support. At twenty-eight, Jake O'Brien was considered a success. Outgoing and aggressive in business, he already owned three companies and was looking to gain a fourth. She also considered him one of her best friends. He had been her neighbor since the O'Briens moved two doors down from the Reardon family twenty-five years before. After the death of her grandmother, it had been Jake, his younger sister Sara, and Mr. and Mrs. O'Brien who served as a surrogate family when Lea's parents had to travel.

"Jake, I'm numb. Everything's happened so fast. One day I'm speaking to Mom on the phone teasing about Dad aging so well. The next I'm picking out caskets and a gravesite. Now they're both gone. Do I keep the house or sell it? I'm not sure there's even a reason for me to stay in the area."

Jake reverted to his childhood practice of being a big brother. "Those are important questions. But do you have to run away to Europe to find the answers? Stay here. Spend time around friends. I could take a few days off. We could both relax, plan a short trip. How about it?"

"I need to do this now, Jake," she said quietly.

Lea looked into his worried eyes. He had always been there to listen. She also knew that maintaining his businesses took him out of Chicago for much of the year. It would be selfish to take advantage of their friendship. What little free time he had at home should be spent enjoying his own life, not babysitting her.

"I'll keep busy doing background research for my books and arrive in Sweden for Midsummer. You know my interest in Öland's history. I want to see everything. I want to find all the places Grandpa talked about in his stories. Who knows? I might discover a distant cousin. There's a blank page in my life, Jake. I need to fill in the lines."

He knew when to give up. "Okay. You win. How much time do you need?"

"Honestly, I don't know." She shook her head. "I have so many good memories from the old neighborhood and our home, but right now I don't want to be there."

"I have some book work to finish this afternoon. But if you insist on running away, Lea, how about dinner tonight? We could spend a little time together before you leave." Grinning, he gave her nose a tweak. "And don't forget to leave me keys for the house. I'm getting too old to crawl through basement windows," Jake said, laughing.

Lea saw the concern hidden in his smile and understood the reason. She looked up, hoping for understanding rather than an argument. "It's okay, O'Brien. I'll be fine. Your parents already volunteered to watch the house. As for dinner, I can't. There's more to pack. I have to stop by the reverend's, and the airport limo is picking me up at 4:30 a.m."

The look Jake gave her meant he wasn't convinced.

"Before you ask, I called your sister and stopped by for a last cup of coffee with your mom. And by the way," she said, a rare smile spreading across her face, "your mother leaked the news about the marketing executive who bid for your services at the charity bachelor auction. Is she a blonde, brunette, or redhead? Is it serious?"

"Stop changing the subject." Jake's' cold tone was meant to stop the inquiry into his love life. "We were talking about you, not me. It takes commitment to build up a business. I don't have time to get involved with any woman."

"Your growling didn't scare me when we were kids, O'Brien. What makes you think it will now? Just remember what Sara and I are capable of when your choice falls short of our standards." Lea sobered as she remembered her parents. "It's getting late, I better go."

Jake tried again. "Come on. Humor me, Lea. Cancel the limo. Admit you want my company on the long trip to the airport."

"You're right. I do want your company, very much. But if I let you drive me tomorrow, I'll never have the courage to get on the plane." She gave her friend another hug. "I'll miss you, Jake O'Brien."

3

KALMARSSON INN, 1989

Lea sat at the table in her room at Kalmarsson Inn, finishing her promised letter to Sara. It was hard to keep focused as her eyes wandered around the comfortable space. The walls, pale yellow with blue stencils near the ceiling, made a perfect backdrop for the whitewashed wood floor scattered with rag rugs.

Dear Sara,

It was a long trip! England, Scotland, and Ireland were wonderful, but it was worth the wait to see this beautiful Swedish island. As the natives say, *Pa Öland skiner solen*, or loosely translated, *the sun always shines on Öland*. The island is only eighty-seven and a half miles long and a mere ten miles at its widest, but what a smorgasbord of treasures is packed into such a small area. The north is thick with forests, and the south has a unique area called the alvar—a barren landscape with a rare beauty. In between, I've found ancient strongholds, Viking graves, castle ruins, and picture-postcard villages complete with quaint windmills. I want to spend time exploring them all. Of course, my favorite is the runestones.

I'm staying at a wonderful bed and breakfast in Färjestaden. That name should tug at your memory. Do you remember our plan when we were seven? Run away to Färjestaden and find the little gnomes, the Tomte, that Grandpa always talked about. Why did we have to grow up? The owner of the inn, Sigrid Kalmarsson, is determined that I'm going to have a good time and see everything. She insisted on lending me her car, as she, like most islanders I've met, walks almost everywhere.

Reverend James, Mrs. Sedgely, and the Farmers are traveling Europe for the summer and will be in Denmark by late June and then to Sweden. I know Reverend Sedgely plans to cross over to Öland. He has a room reserved here at the inn. I don't know if he'll be alone or the others will travel with him. Do you remember Mr. Farmer? We didn't see him often growing up, but I remember he was a pleasant man who always took time to say hello to a child. I've always felt a little sorry for him. It can't be easy married to an overwhelming personality like Brenda Farmer. I do recall he spent a lot of time in the hospital. It's nice he was able to make the trip. Well, whoever decides to come with the reverend, it will be enjoyable showing people from home the beauty of this island.

Miss you,
Lea

Finishing her letter, Lea continued an exploration of her room in Kalmarsson Inn. An ornate six-foot-tall porcelain stove, a kakelugn, took up most of one wall. The other three were covered with watercolor scenes of the island. The bed had a feather mattress in blue and white ticking. A handmade ribbon quilt was folded neatly at the end. On the floor, a large painted chest held additional bedding. There were no closets. A large chifforobe had space for everything she brought with room to spare. A practical gate-leg table made a useful desk for her typewriter, which reminded Lea it was time to get back to work.

She wrote a few lines for her latest teen adventure series, and quickly crumpled the page. Scraps of pages were everywhere. Nothing was in order. In a fit of temper, she pushed her papers onto the floor.

"Why don't you admit typewriters are inefficient, and you have to learn how to use a computer," she scolded herself to the empty room. She was determined to attend the local junior college and take a class when she returned home.

"Breakfast is ready. May I come?" Mrs. Kalmarsson asked and hurried in, carrying a loaded tray. The plump, sturdy woman smiled warmly as she stepped over the mess of papers. "I am happy you find the table useful." Putting the tray in front of Lea, Sigrid ran her fingers over the smooth wood. "Mr. Johansson made this for my Ernst and me many years ago. The food is to your liking?"

"How could anyone not like fresh baked bread and homemade lingonberry jam? You're spoiling me, Mrs. Kalmarsson. You don't have to go to so much trouble every morning."

"For me, this is pleasure. After my Ernst died, it was difficult. We never had children. My neighbors say, 'Enough, Sigrid, put on your apron and get busy.' It is good. I always enjoy to bake and cook and tell stories. Now I have reason to clean and fuss and a kind audience for my tales."

"I'd love to hear more of your stories, and maybe you'd share the recipe for those wonderful cookies I haven't been able to stop eating," Lea persuaded.

Sigrid laughed. "That will be good. Soon we have many new guests on the island. They come to celebrate Midsummer." The innkeeper gave Lea a wink. "It is tradition…the night girls will meet their love." Then remembering she still had rooms to clean, food to prepare, and flowers to pick, the innkeeper moved quickly out the door.

The chubby, yellow-striped cat, Gerda, followed close on her mistress's heels.

Lea sat back down at the cleared table. She refused to inhale her food while working as she usually did. Instead, she turned her full attention to her breakfast. She intended to enjoy every bite.

Finished, she straightened the room and piled the dishes onto the tray. Loud words turned her attention to the window. The sentences didn't have to be in English to know someone was being scolded. Looking out, Lea saw Mrs. Kalmarsson take a bottle from the gardener, Gunnar Johansson, place it in her basket, and continue toward the house. She needed little imagination to guess the contents.

Lea liked the old man, and he sure had a special touch when it came to flowers. Blue bachelor buttons, pink roses, and yellow daisies bloomed throughout the garden. The colors were more vibrant, the hues more varied than any flowers she had seen in the States. Lea had asked his secret, expecting some type of homemade fertilizer. Mr. Johansson simply picked up some earth and rubbed it between his hands. "I need only Swedish soil."

Mrs. Kalmarsson had been accurate when she said the island would become crowded for Midsummer. Many people crossed the bridge from the Swedish mainland to Öland for the festivities.

She had been initially surprised when first coming to the island. Even with a partial Scandinavian heritage, Lea had been sucked into the Swedish stereotype so common in the Hollywood media. In reality, she found most people on the island bore little resemblance to that idealized version of the statuesque blond, blue-eyed Swede.

Lea stayed close to the inn her first week on the island. She was content to sit in the big kitchen and listen to the innkeeper's stories of Öland.

The second week, she introduced herself to the townspeople and local farmers.

"Good morning. Can you tell me what day the outdoor market is held?" Lea inquired, speaking slowly and distinctly so the woman would understand. The islanders were approachable and friendly.

"Certainly," the lady answered in perfect English. "It is always on Friday. I hope you will try some of our strawberries. We have the best anywhere in Sweden," she declared.

Unfortunately, no one remembered her grandparents. They were little more than children when both left their island home for America, and too many years had passed. Searching through church records showed no living family members left on Öland.

Lea swallowed her disappointment and began to spend her time seeing Öland with the eyes of a professional. Roll after roll of film was used to capture the unique face of the island and coax its secrets from a timeworn soil.

She was intrigued by the castle ruins of Borgholm, using her writer's imagination to bring life to the cold stone. Looking through crumbled slits, she could almost see thundering horses racing toward the castle, while frantic women scooped up crying children to run into the protection of the keep.

Lea enjoyed the beauty of Solliden, the summer residence of the royal family. After the sparseness of the alvar steppe, she appreciated the garden's green lushness and carpet of flowers.

She walked around old fishing villages and inspected the plaster wall paintings inside fortress churches. Lea intended to spend the rest of her time concentrating on Viking runestones.

4

KALMARSSON INN, 1989

It was early morning when Lea entered the inn kitchen to grab something she could eat while walking. Mrs. Kalmarsson was already in her apron, stoking the fire and getting ready for her day.

"Good morning. You don't have to bother with me for breakfast."

"You are not hungry?"

"I'll grab a cookie and stop later at the market for an apple and coke."

"That is not a breakfast!" Sigrid took out a basket and quickly pulled fruit, cheese, biscuits, and jam from her cupboard shelves.

"Thank you." The woman certainly reminded Lea of her grandmother. As she walked down the quiet road, the soft chirps of waking birds were her only company. The air was a pleasant mixture of fresh-turned earth, horses, cows, chickens, and flowers. Lea headed unerringly toward the water. She never thought to use the car Mrs. Kalmarsson had offered. There was so much more to see, hear, and feel when a bulk of metal didn't surround you. She didn't have a firm destination in mind. The island was filled with spectacular runestones. She would pick up a few books and familiarize herself with the subject.

"Good morning." She waved to one early riser as he walked his cows to pasture and smiled as she noticed his muddy tofflers. Even she had started to wear the practical wooden-soled clogs that were common for both men and women. Lea crossed the area where the outdoor market would soon come to life in celebration of Midsummer. She passed by the large evergreens that surrounded the sleeping campground, and continued farther into the countryside until something caught her eye in the distance. It was a house that looked like it belonged in a painting.

The glen sloped gently down to the clear water. The small, well-tended cottage sat nearby, enclosed by a white picket fence. Wildflowers climbed the arbor. The gate below the wooden arch had a small cutout resembling a swan. Lea had noticed that many island residents had summer homes, even though most cottages were only minutes from their city dwellings. In any case, the place seemed empty of occupants and her stomach decided this was a good spot to eat breakfast.

She stretched out on a large rock that jutted into the water. Ready to eat, she was surprised by the quiet whistles and snorts of a friendly swan expecting a handout.

"Well, hello. Smell something good, did you? Knowing Mrs. Kalmarsson, I'm sure there's enough for both of us." Pulling out strawberry jam, muffins, and farmer's cheese to share, Lea enjoyed the companionship.

She still hadn't opened the package she found from her mother. Lea thought it would be today, but fingering the zipper of her purse, she changed her mind. She wasn't ready yet. It was difficult to accept they were gone. She closed her eyes.

Her father had been a German war orphan. He was named after the soldier who pulled him as a six-year-old out of a burnt-out building. Sent to a Nebraska boy's camp, John ran away in 1949, tired of backbreaking farm labor and constant whippings. He slept in hobo camps, barns, and empty churches, worked odd jobs to survive, and stole when he had no choice. At sixteen, he landed in Chicago. Lea's grandparents owned a small construction company, one of many that popped up after the war to erect needed housing for returning GIs and their families.

Her grandfather took a chance on the brash street kid, gave John a job, and took him under his wing. The money was enough for John Reardon to rent a room, eat at least one good meal a day, and have leftover change to put in the bank. He also had people who cared about him for the first time in his life.

Lea's mother confided that it was love at first sight, and knew it would only be a matter of time until she convinced John they would marry. It happened, but not until he proved his abilities and self-worth to the business. Lea was their only child.

After the death of her grandfather, Lea's father and mother were approached by the State Department to be consultants for joint-venture construction projects. Sent to emerging nations needing practical know-how rather than political promises, her parents were an important link for the government in a rapidly changing world. There was always the possibility of danger, but her parents decided the risk was minimal for the good they accomplished. It was on their return from the Baltics that John and Anna showed the first signs of illness.

Her family lived in Evanston, a suburb just north of Chicago. The house Lea grew up in, a large, sprawling Victorian, was comfortable. There was always room for her to spread out a new project or have a bunch of giggling girls for a sleepover.

She remembered hot nights on the summer porch listening to her grandfather's stories of a mischievous little barn gnome called a Tomtegubben, or Tomte for short, and the days spent in the kitchen learning to bake with MorMor, as her Swedish grandmother was fondly called.

Lea's bedroom was in the tower of the painted lady, the same room her mother had used as a girl. Her parents wanted to redecorate, but she loved the room as it was.

It was not a typical pink, fluffy girl's room. The faded, striped wallpaper with pink cabbage roses and the worn Turkish carpet gave the room character and warmth. Her favorite Lundmark painting of a stormy Lake Superior hung above the four-poster bed. Floor-to-ceiling shelves crammed with books from Stalinism and Shakespeare to Fannie Farmer's 1922 edition cookbook reflected her eclectic taste in reading. She didn't argue when her mother offered to turn what had been a nanny's room into her private bathroom. Those years seemed far away.

It was only after the death of her parents that she realized the extent of her monetary worth. Lea wasn't really surprised to find an investment portfolio that would keep her very comfortable without writing another book. She also knew she wouldn't touch a penny and donated all profits to a neighborhood center that helped abused and battered women. She admired the tenacity and dedication of the staff and the quiet fortitude of the women as they struggled to start a new life.

She thought about her childhood. Her stability was grounded in loving parents and grandparents who gave her the courage and confidence to try many things without worry of failure. They were never disappointed with mistakes, only if she didn't try.

She had the same clothes and toys as everyone else, but money was never spent foolishly. She had friends at school, but Jake and Sara were her only close ones. Then it was 1978, her fourteenth birthday, and the death of her grandmother.

Chilled to the bone in spite of the warming sun, Lea shook herself. This was ridiculous, it had to stop. This mood of uneasiness, of something left unfinished, constantly invaded her thoughts. She hoped coming to Öland would bring fond memories of her grandparents and give her time to research. Instead, the feelings grew stronger until she could think of nothing else. No longer enjoying the water view, Lea hurried back to the inn, accidently leaving the basket behind.

5

Kalmarsson Inn, 1989

As the two sat drinking coffee around the inn's kitchen table, Lea had a sympathetic audience in Mrs. Kalmarsson.

"I feel stupid running away. And from what? There was nothing…I…look at me. I can't even string together a few words without falling over my tongue. I have to go back for the basket."

"Lea, there is nothing wrong in following your intuition. You were uncomfortable and left."

"But Mrs. Kalmarsson, I have no idea what made me feel that way." She didn't add that the nightmare she'd suffered since her grandmother's death had now become a nightly occurrence. She tried to smile as she left the kitchen. Lea didn't want the innkeeper worrying about her.

Upstairs in her room, she pushed back the beginning of a panic attack. Lea hadn't suffered from that sense of choking for years and wasn't about to let that fear creep back into her life. To prove she was in control, she forced herself to resurrect what she had been unwilling to think about for so long, her fourteenth birthday. The time was eleven years ago, but it seemed like yesterday.

Frequently left in the care of MorMor, a special bond developed between grandmother and granddaughter. Many times it was just the two of them hunting weekend bargains on Maxwell Street, or exploring antique shops and auction houses that were in such abundance around the city of Chicago.

One Saturday, the two traveled to Andersonville, a large Swedish American community north of the city. As they looked over old clothes, books, jewelry, and other various items set for auction, she noticed her grandmother examining a large box labeled Contents Unknown. The sole clue of identification was the stamp of origin—Färjestaden, Öland, Sweden.

"Fifty dollars for this box. Come on, folks, who knows what treasures are in here? Who'll give me fifty bucks?" The auctioneer did his best to get people heated up for bidding.

"Here, I will go fifty," waved her grandmother. Lea was excited when the man banged his hammer down on their winning bid. For MorMor, this was a chance to take a step back to the small Swedish village she had left so many years before.

As they drove back home, Lea sat in the cramped rear seat of the two-door automobile, her usual place in front taken by the cumbersome size of MorMor's purchase.

That evening, her grandmother unwrapped the box, hoping to capture fading memories of a homeland separated by miles and years. MorMor sat and watched while Lea looked at what appeared to be the life mementos of a family.

"Look at the beautiful baby clothes." Lea pulled out the small dressing gown banded with handmade lace to show her grandmother. Visible in the top layer of the tightly packed crate were folded baby clothes, embroidered scarves, carved toys, family pictures, and wooden shoes.

Lea gently touched the handcraft, admiring the skills of their creator. She pulled off her sneakers, sliding her feet into the tofflers, and marveling that people wore shoes made of wood.

Drawn to the photographs, she picked up each in turn and wondered what happened to the smiling man and woman in the faded black-and-white pictures. Why would someone rid themselves of such personal keepsakes?

Showing the traits of an author, she looked closely at their surroundings, hoping to find a clue that would tell the story hidden in the box. Perhaps the woman died in childbirth and her grieving husband refused all reminders of what he'd lost.

Gently placing the photos back into the box, her hand brushed a small gold ring that had gone unnoticed under the photographs. Impatient, Lea yanked the length of wool tied around the band to free it. Attached to the other end of the string was a torn page pulled up from the bottom of the box.

Lea looked at the ripped paper as her grandmother frowned. She understood an apology would not be enough. She shared MorMor's love of old books.

"I'm sorry." She handed the torn page to her grandmother for safekeeping.

"We'll fix it together. Always in hurry, just like your grandfather." MorMor smiled and gave her granddaughter a hug.

Lea turned her attention back to the ring, admiring the delicate lines of an eagle inscribed on the gold band. She was intrigued by the trace of red.

Her grandmother saw the girl's interest. "The ring will be your birthday present."

To an impatient thirteen year-old, seven days was a lifetime. "Please, can I…" Lea tried coaxing her grandmother to change her mind and allow her to wear the ring immediately.

The old lady stayed firm. "On your birthday. No sooner."

The two lost track of time in the excitement.

"Look at the clock! It's already past midnight. Off to bed with you," her grandmother scolded.

To Lea's regret, the ring was put back in the crate. She would have to wait until her mother and father's arrival the day of her birthday. She went to bed thinking about the ring and its original owner. She wondered if it was a girl her own age.

The loud crash of thunder and bright patterns of lightning running down her wallpaper woke Lea. Afraid of storms since she was a little girl, Lea padded down the hall to her grandmother's room. She knew MorMor was still awake when she felt the cold air streaming out from under the shut door. No matter the weather, her grandmother insisted on opening the window a few inches to let in some "good fresh air" while she read.

"I can't sleep."

"Crawl in bed with me," her grandmother invited.

Lea saw the bedspread was covered with books. She ignored the mess, climbed into the big bed, and snuggled under the covers. But the night was far from peaceful as strange words and numbers invaded her dreams, making sleep uneasy and restless.

EVANSTON ILLINOIS—LEA'S FOURTEENTH BIRTHDAY, 1978

The special day finally arrived. Lea's parents had spent twenty-four hours traveling to arrive the morning of their daughter's birthday. She loved their gift of a hand-inked sixteenth-century book. Sara gave Lea cosmetics and Jake presented a velvet box. Inside was a gold locket.

In the kitchen helping her grandmother cut the cake, Lea received the present she had been waiting for.

"Happy birthday, *min lilla en*," MorMor said.

"I'm not so little anymore." She smiled. With a nod from her grandmother, Lea opened the small gift and took out the ring.

"It's beautiful. I love it. Thank you." She gave the woman a big squeeze.

"The ring is too large for you," MorMor said, shaking her head. "After your parents leave, I will take you to the jeweler and have it fit to your finger. Take it off before you lose it," she warned.

"I'll hold it in my hand." Lea went into the living room to show friends and family.

After the party, Lea went to her bedroom. Thinking about her grandmother's words, she opened her locket and placed the ring inside. It would be safe there until it could be sized to her finger.

In bed that night, Lea found it hard to sleep. She reached over to turn on a lamp, and grabbed a book from the floor. Unable to concentrate, she got up to check the time. She picked up the locket from her dresser and took out the ring. She admired the delicate cutouts that made up the eagle's wings. She pressed the tiny hinge to open the gold oval and put the ring back inside.

It was no use. She couldn't fall asleep. Instead, she decided to experiment with her new makeup. When Lea took a final look in the mirror she was astonished at the results. She had to show Sara. Creeping down the back stairs, she stood for a moment near the den and listened to her parents discuss an upcoming assignment. She passed by her grandmother's room on her way to the front door.

Slipping outside, Lea ran down the stairs, cut through the backyard, and turned into the alley. Bradley Farmer stood by his car drinking from a bottle hidden in a paper sack. He was a neighbor and the same age as Jake. Lea didn't see him often since he attended military school. She felt uncomfortable, but certainly couldn't pass by without saying hello.

"Lea, you certainly have grown," he slurred.

"Hi, Brad. I can't talk. I promised Sara I'd be over."

"You can take a few minutes to say hello and be a little friendly." He grabbed her by the arm. "Come on, sweetheart. Be nice. Don't tease." He stroked her hair, then yanked at her nightgown as she tried to pull away.

"Brad, don't. Leave me alone. I have to go!" Her heart raced when she realized he was trying to pull her under the dark porch. Lea fought, but she was no match for a six-foot, drunken male.

"Jake, Jake!"

He had just come home from a date when he heard his name. Running into the alley, he saw two figures struggling. Pulling at the larger shadow, his stomach turned when he realized the other was Lea.

"You bastard! Get away from her!" Jake slammed a fist into Bradley's lip and blackened both eyes before Lea was able to stop him. She had never seen Jake so angry.

"Enough. Stop," she pleaded.

"You're lucky, Farmer. A bloodied face is the least of what I'd planned to do," Jake threatened as he stood over Bradley.

Lea's mother and father, hearing the commotion, ran outside. "Lea! No," John Reardon yelled as Anna physically held her husband away from Bradley. She stood close to Brenda Farmer when she spoke. "Bradley should go back to school, now. I don't want to see him near our house or Lea."

Brenda looked at Lea's skimpy clothes. It was girls like her who should be punished for taunting innocent boys. "I'm not saying Bradley is to blame for this. Jake's a bully, and your daughter should know better than to run around outside in a short nightgown. For Bradley's sake, I'll make arrangements for him to stay at school until Christmas."

Bringing herself back to the present, Lea searched for the answer to her question. Who had helped her that night? Everyone took for granted that she had called Jake and she never disagreed with the assumption. In truth, Lea had been so terrified she was unable to force a single word from her throat. She sifted through her memories and placed everyone who was there that night. It was no use, she still couldn't figure out who had called to Jake. She blamed her lacking memory on Bradley's attempted rape and the pain of her grandmother's death.

The one man who could answer that question stood at his file cabinet, a whiskey in one hand, rifling through his folder on the Reardon family with the other. However, in 1978, Ulrik Orensson crouched low behind some bushes watching the unfolding drama just beyond his hiding place. He had been only an hour late for the auction, but the crate was gone. The records had given him the name and address of the purchaser and for the past week he had canvassed the house, watching, listening, learning names and patterns, waiting for the right opportunity to locate the crate.

Now, smiling at the luck of an unplanned diversion, he disguised his voice to mimic a terrified female and called for Jake. Bringing attention to the girl's situation would give him time to search for the diary.

Lea didn't want to hear her parents talk to Brenda Farmer. She didn't want to see Jake. She didn't want help with her torn clothes, to be touched, held, or consoled. Lea wanted to be left alone.

"I want to go home."

She couldn't wait to strip off her clothes and take a shower. Lea felt so ashamed, so dirty. When she got upstairs, she found MorMor on the bedroom floor. Her father called an ambulance. It was too late.

"I'm sorry for your loss," the paramedic had told the family. "Given her age, it was likely cardiac failure."

"Honey, your grandmother lived a long life, a good life. The heart attack was fast. I'm sure she didn't suffer any pain." Lea's mother had tried to give comfort, reminding her MorMor was old, and it was a blessing to have a quick and peaceful death. Lea felt no comfort rationalizing the loss, only pain and guilt. It was her fault everyone was out of the house leaving her grandmother alone.

She thought no more about fitting the gold ring to her finger. After what happened, the thrill of wearing it was gone. She was not interested in the box from Öland or trying to fantasize the story of another family.

After the burial, Lea had refused to enter MorMor's room. Instead, she sat on the floor outside the bathroom and listened to the running dialogue between her mother and father as they sorted through the remnants of her grandmother's life. She wondered how anyone could decide what stayed with the family, what would be relegated to the attic, or which pieces should be packed up and given away to strangers.

Lea didn't want to shove dresses into a cardboard box. She wanted her grandmother back. Eyeing one of the cartons before it was closed, she saw the nightgown MorMor had worn the last evening they spent together. She reached over and pulled it toward her, burying her face in the familiar cloth. A ragged paper fell to her lap. Recognizing the book page she ripped from the auction crate, she tore up the paper. Lea wasn't going to dig through the box looking for a damaged book. Her grandmother was gone.

The world had continued since the night of her fourteenth birthday, but it had changed her in ways she didn't like. She became less trusting, less open, less willing to allow anyone close.

Jake graduated and left for Europe the year she and Sara started college. She enjoyed school but wasn't interested in commitments. Lea was content to stay on the sidelines and watch other people's entanglements. She was popular with the opposite sex and known as a good listener, but it ended there. Any relationship that turned serious she broke off. She would rather write a chapter in one of her books than waste time in the gristmill of dating.

Her baggy jeans and sweaters spelled comfort rather than fashion. Makeup was rarely part of her everyday appearance. It simply took too much time and effort to apply. On special occasions, she dusted her lips and eyes with a light hand. She and Sara had major battles over this issue, but Lea always won out. She sorely missed her friend when Sara decided not to continue classes after meeting Steven Brent II.

Lea had distrusted her friend's serious, twenty-five-year old love from the first.

"I adore him," Sara insisted. "I'm interested in a family and children. He feels the same. He's thoughtful and generous. I've found the man I want to spend the rest of my life with. Be happy for me, Lea."

"You don't know him that well. Finish school, give yourself time. Date some more. Then you'll be sure you've made the right choice. Please think about it," Lea argued.

It was no use. Sara quit school and worked full time for the Brent Foundation. They were married the day Sara turned nineteen. Steven Brent III was born nine months later.

As Sara tried to be the wife Steven wanted, a frustrated Lea watched her friend struggle with gourmet cooking lessons, diction to improve her speech, flower arranging, art, music, and continuous dieting. In the end, it wasn't enough. The divorce was handled in the manner of Brent's business deals—exact, cordial, and expeditious. The papers were signed on their one-year wedding anniversary. Lea hunkered a little more into herself, determined never to allow a man to control her emotions or her life.

"Enough memories," Lea decided. She left her room with a book borrowed from Mrs. Kalmarsson on runestones.

6

ÖLAND, 1989

This time, she walked around Öland with a purpose. Rich in Baltic history and covered with relics from the past, Lea focused on the Nordic runes scattered over the island. She wanted to learn more about the ancient language and she hoped to meet another American who, according to Mrs. Kalmarsson, was also interested in runestones.

Rolf Sundren sat by the water reading another volume on the runic language. He was a man driven by some inner need to challenge the past. He read every book and historical paper he could find on the subject. It was important for him to understand these ancient Norsemen, his ancestors. He knew that most accounts read and understood today were written by the Franks, Irish, English, and other cultures that had been terrorized by these fierce warriors. The tales of brutal pillaging and unmerciful pagan raiders certainly had a content of truth, but runestones were a written page from the Viking's own hand.

Steeped in mystery and magic, the origin, purpose, and alphabet of runic inscriptions were still debated today. The stones spoke not only of Viking raids and testimonials, but also trade, farming, and the introduction of Christianity. This written record gave Rolf an insight to the thinking and strategies from a time of history, when the peoples of Scandinavia—the Danes, Norwegians and Svear—were the focal point of Europe and beyond. This group, known collectively as Vikings, was the middleman in a vast network of commercial traffic between the Orient and Western Europe.

Those who knew the President of Sundren International Industries found many similarities between the ancient men of Svear and this Swedish American descendant. His innate tenacity combined with keen intelligence and stinging wit made Rolf a natural player in the world of international business. He was considered ruthless: a sharp negotiator who refused to suffer fools willingly. His many critics claimed he was without honor, his few friends knew him to be fiercely loyal.

At thirty-one, he was still unmarried but never lacked for female companionship. He made sure the women he associated with understood his strong feelings against legal entanglements and long-term commitments. Some tried to change him, none succeeded. In his world, marriages were nothing more than negotiated contracts.

Rolf had found the basket marked Kalmarsson Inn on the rocks near his cottage. He had seen the young woman and was tempted enough to call his informant.

"Stratton. This is Rolf Sundren. I want information on a woman named Lea Reardon. Be thorough. I want to know her connections to the island, her family, the usual background. Call me with the material as soon as you acquire it. I'll pay the normal fee, nothing more. Goodbye."

Rolf had learned through necessity to be careful. It wouldn't be the first time a woman used imaginative methods to meet the multimillionaire.

He had almost decided he should be the one to bring the basket back to the inn himself, but his common sense prevailed. Instead, he gave a neighbor's son what amounted to a week's wages to return the basket.

"Well, Gussie, old girl," Rolf mused, as he sat overlooking the water beside the nuzzling, mute swan, "an interesting way to start a vacation."

"Lea, someone just dropped off the basket." Sigrid stopped her cleaning to find the young woman sitting on the front porch swing reading the borrowed book on runestones.

"Who returned it?" she asked.

Sigrid smiled at her interest. "A boy came to the back door with the hamper. When I offered a few kronor for his trouble, he informed me Rolf Sundren paid him well. This is the man I told you about, the one interested in Viking runes."

"Rolf Sundren!" Remembering an article from an international business magazine, Lea recalled the description of the successful American magnate. His reputation ran the gamut from devil incarnate, attributed to those who had tried to best him during mergers or hostile takeovers; to womanizer, due to alleged love affairs; to hermit, because in reality, as the magazine noted, he used all resources at his control to keep his business and personal affairs private. The media blurbs were guesswork and hype.

"Do you have his phone number, Mrs. Kalmarsson?"

Lea gathered her thoughts, returned to her room, and telephoned the man. She wanted to thank him for returning the basket, and ask his recommendation for books to read on runestones.

"Sundren speaking."

"Mr. Sundren, this is Lea Reardon. I left the basket on the rocks and...well...I wanted to thank you, and explain—"

"Look, Miss Reardon," he interrupted, "there's no need for thanks or explanations. Goodbye."

"But I..."

Click.

"He hung up on me! The man wouldn't allow me the satisfaction of giving him an apology!" She listened to the dial tone until her temper calmed enough to hang up the receiver without a bang.

7

ÖLAND, 1989

Lea was annoyed by Rolf Sundren's behavior. But after reading about him, it wasn't unexpected. What did trouble her was the continued uneasiness, the anxious feelings she had experienced since her arrival on the island. Her inability to write pages for her latest "Lisa" book was a result of her discomfort. Lea had never encountered writer's block before. Her books were popular, and she enjoyed sending her fictional teenage heroine all over the world for adventures. Maybe her mind needed another direction.

Instead of writing copy for her book, she penned a note to Reverend Sedgely about his upcoming stay on the island. When she visited the couple's Evanston home after her mother's funeral, Lea was surprised at how much she enjoyed the minister's remembrances of her parents, especially her mother. Anna Reardon had known the man, of course, but unlike many from the congregation, patently refused to accept the familiar closeness the popular associate pastor offered to every member of the church. Still, the clergyman was invited to their home for dinner quite often. She knew it was her mother's way.

After the trauma on her fourteenth birthday, other than the O'Briens, Lea had never known her mother to share confidences with anyone outside the family. She was surprised the minister had stories about her mom. Lea remembered her mother as a smiling, friendly woman who had an amazing ability to make interesting conversation while saying absolutely nothing. It was a talent Lea wished she had inherited.

Opening the drawer of the gate-leg table for a stamp to mail her note to Reverend Sedgely, she saw the package. After Lea arrived at Kalmarsson Inn, she had shoved the small, wrapped parcel into the drawer, unable to face anything personal from her mother.

After her mother's funeral, Lea had spent the afternoon in her parent's bedroom going through papers, letters, and books. She had been surprised to find the package from her mother. Her first impulse was to open it, then decided to wait until she reached Sweden. It was time.

Carefully removing the thick layer of paper, she found a worn leather book. Opening to the first page, Lea realized it was a diary written in German. She slowly turned the fragile, stained pages, admiring the neat script. She looked for an explanation from her mom of why the journal was important. There was nothing. Learning a bit of the language as a young teen, time had considerably weakened her grasp, but slowly she was able to translate some of the unsigned entries.

> Königsberg, December 14, 1945
>
> It is December and we must leave soon. Papa gave me one of his journals to write down my thoughts. He knows that pen and paper calm my spirit. The boxes are safe. They stay hidden until this terrible time is over.

> Königsberg, December 15, 1945
>
> Our journey begins in darkness. The transport glides through water with little effort. There are no windows. The oppressive heat and engine smells give me a constant headache.

Lea turned to another entry.

The motors are still. I leave my cot, sliding my hands along braided ropes to find the others. I long to see the rain, hear the wind. I lift my skirts to climb the ladder.

I want to smell and taste the fresh air of the storm.

She skipped the other entries and turned to the last writing. There was no date.

It has been long since I have seen the sky. Tempers are short.

It is hard to breathe. Bells and whistles scream without end.

Papa says we must leave. Water covers the floor. I hurry to finish.

Lea returned to the beginning, gently prying apart two pages. Smoothing out the paper, she saw a detailed picture drawn in what appeared to be pen and ink. Attached to the back cover, wrapped inside a small cloth pouch, was an intricate blue jewel of a substance she couldn't identify. It had been honed into a flower, small and finely crafted.

Lea put the book back in the table drawer. It would be better to wait until she returned home to research the diary. She had never seen or heard of the book, yet it was so close to the nightmare that had plagued her since she turned fourteen: the storm, people screaming…She didn't want to think about it.

"What do you want from me, Mama? What am I supposed to do," she asked aloud.

The next morning, when Mrs. Kalmarsson brought in the breakfast tray to her room, she found a pale girl with dark circles under her eyes.

"Lea, today the men will raise the Midsummer pole. Why not go down to the town square and watch."

"I think I will. Thanks, Mrs. Kalmarsson." Sitting at the table, she took a few bites to satisfy the innkeeper, but as soon as the woman left, she put the cover back over her food. She dressed quickly.

Grabbing her purse, camera, and tape recorder, Lea started out, relieved to concentrate on work again. Almost out the door, she unzipped a separate compartment in the lining of her carryall and dumped her loose change on the sinktop to make room for the diary. If the book was important to her mother, she would keep it close.

The square was already crowded with people setting up their stock for the monthly market. Lea aimed her camera, randomly clicking shots. Bright bolts of fabric, cloth dolls, wooden shoes, embroidered vests, even velvet paintings of Elvis Presley, were proudly displayed in festive stalls. There was something for everyone.

Reaching the area where the celebration would take place, she sat on the sidelines, listening to accordion music and watching a trio of costumed men secure a gaily decorated pole.

She spoke softly into the recorder, describing the scene. "The men are wearing long-sleeved white shirts with red and white buttoned vests, three-quarter-length yellow trousers, white stockings, and black shoes. The women are dressed in white shirts with ankle-length red dresses trimmed with blue and white near the bottom and a solid-blue band at the top." She stopped for a minute to get closer for a better view. "Black shoes and stockings compliment a short, black jacket embroidered with flowers. A white, close-fitting cap finishes the costume," she narrated.

Lea snapped a roll of pictures as musicians practiced their songs, and women weaved intricate crowns of fresh flowers worn for this ancient celebration of summer's return.

Lea tried to focus on the scene, but after tossing and turning all night, she was so tired. The nightmare began in beauty as it always did. There were smiles and laughter. The sea spray tasted salty as she tried to snatch the falling mist from the air. Then the screams started. People were running from something, desperate to get away, but it was always too late. The mist quickly turned into a swirling mass of choking water. She couldn't breathe.

"Help! Help please…" Lea called out.

"Are you all right? Are you ill?" a man asked.

Lea looked up into his face. She frowned and began to struggle. "Leave me alone. Don't touch me!"

The man dropped his hands. "I am sorry, I mean you no harm. I heard you calling for help, and thought there was trouble."

She quickly got up. "I'm fine." She carefully tucked the camera away. "I'm sorry for my rudeness. Thank you."

The man smiled good-naturedly at her obvious discomfort. "Is our island so boring it puts you to sleep, Miss Reardon?"

"How do you know my name?"

"This is a small village and I live near Kalmarsson Inn. I have seen you walking around and meant to introduce myself." He stuck out his hand in greeting. "I'm Per Knudsson."

Feeling comfortable with his explanation, her bout of suspicion disappeared as she accepted Per's handshake.

"I didn't rest well last night," Lea explained. "And to answer your question, I'm enjoying Öland's history and culture very much."

"Then you would enjoy our Midsummer Dance. It is tonight at the re-created village of Eketorp. It would please me to be your escort this afternoon and evening," he invited. "After the pole is raised and the dancing is over, my duties are finished. Why don't you watch the festivities until I'm able to join you?"

"Thank you, Per. I'd like that very much."

"Good." Taking her hand, he brushed her fingers lightly with his lips. Per nodded his head curtly, and walked back to the group of dancers practicing for the event.

She enjoyed the afternoon celebration and watched Per and his partner lightly skip around the Midsummer pole. It looked like the whole town had turned out for the celebration. After the event, Per joined her. They walked the short distance to the park where everyone gathered to enjoy food, drink, and singing. Per was attentive, helping her choose the different Swedish dishes and explaining the names and ingredients.

She enjoyed a taste of herring, smoked flounder, and the national dish of Öland, kroppkakor—a dumpling with a surprise center of salt pork, onion, and allspice. Per handed her a cup of strawberry punch to accompany the food.

"This is wonderful, I've never had anything like this," she exclaimed.

Afterward, Per walked her back to Kalmarsson Inn.

"Good afternoon, Sigrid." He nodded toward the innkeeper sitting on the porch. Looking at Lea, he said, "I will be here at nine this evening. The village is a short distance from here and well…you will be surprised."

Smiling, Sigrid got up and the two went inside. "Lea, I am so happy you will attend our Midsummer Ball. Come upstairs to my sitting room, I have something special for you to wear."

Lea followed, excited about wearing a vintage Swedish dress.

Mrs. Kalmarsson knelt down and pulled a trunk from under the bed. "The clothes we wear on such occasions are handmade with love and pride of our past. A few changes and this will fit you well," she said.

Lea picked up a sleeping Gerda and took her place on a blue-and-yellow padded bench. The cat hardly moved a whisker at the intrusion. Lea watched Sigrid carefully unwrap the bundled tissue paper. Dried flower petals clung to the dress, their faint scent of past gardens still discernible. Standing up quickly to get a better look, the upended cat meowed her displeasure, and crawled under the bench for an undisturbed nap.

"Mrs. Kalmarsson. It's beautiful!" Lea exclaimed, not able to contain her excitement.

After fitting the dress to her smaller frame, the older woman helped Lea into her special outfit for the evening. Long stockings first, then the dress followed. Made of handwoven cloth, it had an embroidered red apron and a simple white blouse. A short jacket fit snugly over the bodice and showcased her small waist. The black shoes with buckles were too large. She solved the problem wearing her patent flats.

A smiling Mrs. Kalmarsson answered a knock on the door and escorted Gunnar Johansson into the sitting room. Instead of using the cutting beds, the old gardener had searched for his prize blooms. It had been over forty years, but his fingers had not lost their skill. He held out the exquisite crown of blue, pink, purple, and white flowers to Sigrid, who placed the wreath on Lea's dark hair.

"Thank you both so much." Lea gave each a hug. She was ready for the evening.

8

ÖLAND, 1989

A s he got out of the car to pick up his date, Rolf buttoned his tuxedo jacket. He frowned at the teenage term. This was business, not enjoyment. He didn't want to go to the party. If this hadn't been an important fundraiser for the National Antiquities Board, Rolf would have stayed home and gone to bed.

"Good evening. Would you prefer to come in for an aperitif before we leave?" Her smiling face greeted him in the doorway. She was a self-assured, beautiful woman.

"Will Morgan be joining us?" Rolf inquired.

He always enjoyed talking business and politics with Kristin's father, an international banker with a talent for putting together consortiums of investors. Unfortunately, his daughter was another matter. After meeting Kristin, Rolf thought it too bad the banker was incapable of managing his spoiled offspring as well as his portfolios.

"No. As usual, Father is working on some deal and can't join us." In truth, she had told him to stay away. Trailing her hand down Rolf's arm, in what she considered a sensuous move, Kristin continued, "Besides, we've never had a chance to get properly acquainted. Now, how about that drink?"

"We're running late." He wasn't about to fall into that trap.

"As you wish. What do you think of my dress?" Turning a slow pirouette, Kristin was annoyed at having to push for compliments. She had purposely decided not to wear the traditional folk outfit, choosing instead a fitted, turquoise sheath she knew shaped her curves to their best advantage.

With her blonde hair swept up into a tight chignon, leaving her neck and shoulders bare, Kristin hoped the obvious absence of jewelry would give Rolf ideas. This was the first time she had finagled time alone with the rich American and she intended to take advantage of the situation.

"I think you should find something to cover your shoulders. It'll be cold when we return," he answered. She tried to hand Rolf the matching velvet stole but he had already opened the door to the outside. Walking to the limo, he hustled Kristin into the back seat. During the ride to the party, she dropped all subtlety.

"I know it will be a late evening. I have everything I need," she said, patting her purse, "if we spend the night at one of the hotels. A cozy dinner, a hot shower before bed..." Kristin wanted to be clear she would not be averse to a much closer relationship. Rolf ignored her overtures.

Per was correct when he said Lea would be surprised. An open carriage was their transport to the *Midsommar Dansa.* As the team of horses made their way up a cobblestone path, Lea felt like a storybook character come to life. The scene looked like an illustration from a Grimm's fairy tale. Rows of windmills sparkled from the light of hundreds of hanging lanterns. The animals, with flowers and colorful ribbons woven into their manes and harnesses, pulled wagons filled with costumed revelers to the annual dance.

The small village had been constructed to evoke Öland's past. Hand-cut stone walls and roofs thick with turf were copies of the Iron Age ringed fortress of Eketorp. The large size of the main building was perfect for the annual *Midsommar Dansa.*

"Beautiful," murmured Lea.

"This is only the beginning. The night is young." Per laughed at her obvious enjoyment. He gently lifted Lea from the wagon and took her arm as they walked into the dance. She wasn't beautiful in the classic sense, but her appearance met with his approval. Her makeup was minimal, only lipstick and a small amount of blush, simplicity that marked her as a lady. That afternoon, Lea had told him all about her family and her ties to the island. He listened carefully, not willing to miss a sentence. He was sure the evening would bring more disclosures.

Lea smiled at her escort. Per was comfortable to be with, like an old friend, someone you could trust and confide secrets in. Maybe sometimes his manner was a little too smooth, but she pushed away feelings of doubt. It was just the European way. Per had done nothing to cause her any concern.

Lea heard the name Rolf Sundren announced and turned to see the man enter the garden with a stunning woman. The two made a striking couple as they stepped under the rose arbor for a photograph before continuing through a door into the main room. Interesting lines and angles, she thought, very good looking, but with a perpetual frown. Rolf Sundren did not look happy to be there.

He spotted her immediately. Even as Rolf had hiked around the island, he noticed Lea. He saw her walking around the alvar, taking rubbings from grave markers and photos of fortress churches. Thinking about the woman was a discomfiting sensation for someone who considered self-control essential.

When the musicians began a Swedish waltz, Per brought Lea onto the dance floor, the time had come for him to act. He had spent a long day removing barriers and reservations with the knowing ease of a man who had done this many times before. It was necessary to have her trust. For the drug to work at maximum efficiency, Lea needed to be relaxed. She would soon give answers to whatever questions he asked.

He had started the mixture slowly that afternoon to calculate the strength needed. Per wanted the woman completely alert until late evening so as not to arouse anyone's concern or suspicion. At Ulrik's direction, he had injected a mild form of an irritating stomach bacteria, known to vacationers as "the traveler's trots," into a small batch of food during the afternoon celebration. It would be difficult to detect, and the source of contamination hard to find.

He smiled to himself at the misery some of his friends would soon experience. It should keep the locals busy for the next week with bouts of headache, fever, nausea, and diarrhea, and the American's illness would not appear an anomaly. He had been carefully slipping Lea his formula in her strawberry punch. It wasn't the simple stomach irritant, but a potent, mind-altering drug.

She had told him much about her life already, but still spoke nothing of the book. Lea had a strong, independent mind and her system had shown an amazing tolerance. Per had increased the strength for the evening, but she stubbornly refused more drink.

"Come, Lea, have more punch," he commanded with a smile. "You have hardly touched your drink all evening. This is a celebration, Skol!" Per raised his glass in salute.

"I've had enough." Her stomach was beginning to feel queasy.

This was not working. Per decided it was time to change tactics. He deliberately maneuvered her away from nearby couples toward a dark patio.

"I want to be alone with you, Lea. I want…No, I need to show you how I feel, what you do to me as a man." Per's tone matched his words in intensity.

Taken by surprise and unnerved by his sudden change of demeanor, it became obvious to Lea, as he pushed her closer to the patio door, that Per would not take no for an answer. Lea's inner defenses screamed danger.

"Brad, I want to go back…" Lea called out with the high pitch of fear in her voice. It was her fourteenth birthday again and the attack by Bradley Farmer.

Continuing his calculated threat, Per enveloped her body, swallowing her outburst with a deep, intimate kiss. He released Lea to pour a glass of punch, giving himself time to judge her response and to compose his features into a mask of apology. His eyes narrowed speculatively at the obvious pain and gripping fright put there by someone named Brad. Bad memories and strong fears were tools of his trade. The East German Stasi was known for their use of mind-altering drugs and psychological terror to effectively break one's spirit. Per intended on using these skills in his search for answers. His superiors were growing impatient.

"Forgive me, Lea. I am sorry for any unpleasantness. For your comfort, we will have a night of eating, drinking punch, and talking about Sweden."

She felt ridiculous and uncomfortable at her overreaction. Still, Lea was unable to relax again. She reminded herself not all men were like Brad. She tried to rationalize Per's behavior, but old fears lingered. She couldn't tolerate a man holding her tight or pulling at her, even under the guise of fun.

As a teenager, she kept boys at arm's length. As she matured, she learned to control her dates by using humor, tears, and fury, whatever it took to stop unwanted pawing. She hoped in time this fear would lessen. Jake sympathized but always supported her skittish sense. Lea decided now was the time to shed her past. She was confident in her ability to handle Per.

"I'm the one who should apologize. Sometimes bad memories are hard to shake."

Per held the glass to her lips, playfully forcing her to drink the liquid. He had to be there when the drug stripped the answers from her mind. He liked this reticent American, and hoped the high dosage he intended for her to ingest would leave no permanent damage. Ultimately, however, he would complete his job whatever the cost.

Lea felt a prickle at the back of her neck and turned to face a frowning Rolf Sundren.

"What the hell are you doing?" he demanded. Ignoring Lea, Rolf grabbed Per by the shirt, pulling him to the nearest corner. Rolf had been blindsided when he noticed Per's blatant manhandling.

Her good humor gone, Lea pushed herself between the men and turned to face Rolf.

"Who do you think you are? Go away and leave us alone," she demanded.

Determined to make her listen to reason, Rolf made the mistake of forcefully holding her still to get his point across.

"Don't you understand what he's doing?" He didn't like bullies, and seeing Lea's frantic response as Per pulled her toward the patio, Rolf had barreled through the dancers and was close enough to hear her apologies and note the private smirk on her partner's face.

Instinctively, Lea turned her body to gain leverage as she had been taught in defense class.

"Let me go. Now!" She looked into Rolf's surprised face as she flipped him upside down. He landed on the ground showered with roses and a splintered arbor.

Lea had had enough. After apologizing to the people around her, she searched for Per. She wanted to go back to the inn.

"If you are looking for your partner, he left," Rolf said as he got slowly up from the floor.

Lea ignored him and walked outside to find her escort. Rolf followed.

Kristin watched them leave. She wasn't jealous of the other woman. She knew the value of her beauty and that there were few women who could match it. Rather, she was humiliated by the scene and furious at being abandoned. It wouldn't be difficult to find a replacement until Rolf's return, but Kristin would make sure he remembered this unconscionable slight and paid accordingly. She smiled at the thought of a day together shopping, at his expense.

9

ÖLAND, 1989

Rolf waited while a stone-faced Lea searched for Per. Her date and ride home were gone.

"Look, I know it's my fault you're stranded. I'll take you back to the inn."

"It seems I have no choice." Lea's sour answer matched the feeling in her stomach.

Remembering with hindsight his date, Rolf made arrangements. "Wait for Miss Johnsson and take her home," he instructed his driver. "Afterward, take the car back to the garage. I won't need you anymore this evening."

"Yes, sir, Mr. Sundren." His wife would be surprised to see him home early and with a generous tip.

Rolf walked over to the nearby stable and arranged for a horse and small buggy. After lifting Lea up onto the passenger seat, he quickly climbed up next to her.

Picking up the reins, he started the horse at a slow trot. For a time they drove in silence, the rustle of wind their only vocal companion. Rolf then turned to the matter at hand.

"I'm sorry. It wasn't my intention to strong arm you away from the dance, or your date." He really wanted to believe what he was saying. "It seemed to me that you were out of your element and needed some help. You know, it might be a good idea to pick your companions with a little more care."

Lea clenched her teeth, determined to keep her composure. But after hearing what he considered an explanation and apology, she lost the battle. "Out of my element, Sundren! It was you who ended up sitting on the floor, not me. Besides, what I do and whom I do it with is none of your business. You couldn't be bothered with me when I called to try and thank you for bringing back the basket. What changed your mind tonight?"

She wanted a response, but ran out of patience. "Oh, forget it. Let's not talk."

Pulling up to the inn, Rolf offered Lea his hand to help her down. Lea stood and waited while he found the gardener to take the horse and buggy.

"What I did was out of line. It was a knee-jerk reaction. How many times do you want me to apologize?" She drove him crazy with her arguing. The woman had a retort for everything he said.

Lea ignored his words and offer of help. "It's not necessary to go any farther."

"I'll walk you to your room." His jaw hurt from clenching it shut. He didn't want to say more and make matters worse.

Her stomach cramping, she didn't argue.

Lea opened her door to chaos. Her clothes were scattered everywhere. Pages from her story were ripped out of the binder and thrown around the room. Feathers from the torn mattress and pillow covered every surface.

"Why would someone do this?" Shaking, she sank to the floor.

Rolf called out to anyone who might hear him through the open doorway. He didn't want to leave her.

Sigrid hurried to Lea's room, saw the mess, and quickly knocked on Inspector Youngmark's door. It took only minutes for Lars to get dressed and walk the short distance to Lea's room after Sigrid alerted him of a break-in. He was staying the night at the request of the innkeeper. After introducing himself to Rolf and Lea, the detective walked slowly around the room, scowling at no one in particular as he took off his glasses, and rubbed the red marks on the bridge of his nose. There was very little crime on Öland, even with the growing number of tourists every year.

After adjusting his lenses once more, the detective scribbled on a small pad taken from his shirt pocket. A thorough man, he covered the area, opening drawers, sifting through the remains of her dumped suitcase, and reading those parts of her book that were scattered across the floor.

"Miss Reardon, did you bring any valuables to the island?"

"I have little jewelry, not a great amount of cash, and one credit card. The most expensive item I own is my camera."

Inspector Youngmark next focused on Sigrid Kalmarsson; the gardener, Gunnar Johansson; and the American, Rolf Sundren. He handed each a pencil and paper.

"Please give details of what you did this evening." The inspector put his glasses away and waited for the lists to be complete. "Miss Reardon, I need names of persons you have had contact with while on Öland. I will expect you in my office in Kalmar tomorrow forenoon." Almost as an afterthought, he continued, "When you sort through your belongings, please mark what was moved about, and if anything remained untouched." He walked out the door, talking to the gardener and Sigrid, and then stopped again.

"It might be wise if someone stayed with you for the rest of the night," he recommended.

"No, I'll be fine." Lea didn't want company. Her stomach was feeling worse.

With Gunnar's help, it didn't take long to bring a new feather mattress and pillow to the room. Smoothing fresh linens on the bed, Mrs. Kalmarsson shooed Gerda off the clean duvet. Lea picked up the insulted cat, finding comfort stroking her fur.

"If there is more you need tonight, you call me." Mrs. Kalmarsson gave Lea a gentle hug before leaving the room.

"Thank you." She allowed the squirming tabby to follow her mistress.

Rolf waited until everyone else was gone before he spoke.

"I'll sit outside in the hall for a while. Consider it a friendly gesture after what I did. Then we'll call it even. I'll stay out of your way."

She shut the door behind him and purposely locked it. Slowly, she sifted through the mess, trying to make some sense of what had happened. She put her papers back in order, picked up her clothes, went through her suitcase, drawers, the chifforobe, and bathroom cabinet. It soon became obvious that every personal object, including underwear, nightclothes, even the hand cream on the bathroom shelf, had been moved, thrown about, or taken apart. But only one object was missing, her camera.

Almost finished putting her things back in order, Lea heard three chimes from the hall clock when the nagging headache and nausea had her running for the bathroom. The loud moan had Rolf pounding on the door.

"Open up now, Lea!"

He watched as she swayed on her feet, pale and white-lipped. "What's wrong?"

"I don't know. I feel sick and faint."

A run to the toilet underlined the problem with her stomach. He followed and sat on the floor as she heaved, wiping her face with a wet cloth between muscle spasms.

"Lea, I'm going to hold you in the shower." He lifted her carefully.

With nothing left to come up, she nodded and let the warm water wash over her.

"That feels good."

He held her until she closed her eyes. Wrapping her in towels to stave off chills, he grabbed a nightgown from behind the bathroom door. He set her down on a stool and turned his back as Lea managed to get out of her wet clothes and pull the gown on. Rolf helped her into bed and covered her with a warm quilt.

"I'll be right back. I'm going down to the kitchen."

"I don't want anything."

Ignoring the protest, he returned with some weak tea and soda crackers. While Lea considered putting something in her stomach, Rolf walked to the bathroom, stripped off his soaked clothes, and wrapped a bath towel around himself. He didn't feel comfortable leaving her alone.

"Come on, just a little," he coaxed with patience he didn't know he possessed. It took a long while for Lea to fall asleep.

Ulrik Orensson paced the room waiting for Knudsson's phone call. The developed negatives proved the necessity of the theft. It had been clumsy to be caught on film by Lea Reardon. Fortunately, the stolen camera fit with his overall plan. He had been careful to leave a faint trail for the detective to find, enough to spark the man's curiosity. His success depended on the inspector.

Ulrik looked forward to their first visit together in many years and hoped his old friend had recovered from the loss of his wife. It had been a distasteful chore silencing Hulda, but the woman proved all too astute at reading his character. It would have been only a matter of time until she confided her suspicions to Lars.

He had waited for Lea to leave for Europe before breaking into the Reardon family home to search for information. Empty of occupants, Ulrik had the needed time to be thorough. He examined the old lady's room and rummaged through boxes in the attic where her belongings had been stored. There was no trace of the diary page. The loud ring of the phone brought his mind back. He sat down at the table and picked up the phone.

"Knudsson. Did you find information?" Ulrik snapped.

"Nothing of importance, yet. Unfortunately, there was a disturbance created by an American, Rolf Sundren, before enough drug was taken by the woman."

"Any disruption is a risk to the operation," Ulrik warned.

"I am convinced the interference was the result of a former disagreement between the two Americans, nothing more."

"Do you still have her trust or is she aware you are Stasi?" Ulrik asked.

"She trusts me," Knudsson answered.

"Contact me when you have more information." He had to know if the missing diary page still existed. If the paper had been destroyed, there was only one option left.

Getting up, Ulrik took the shredded camera film and tossed it into the flames of the stove. He took another roll of film he had snapped at the festival. In his closet darkroom, Ulrik carefully isolated the last frame. He brushed it with a coating created specifically to protect an image from accidental exposure. After drying, he purposely exposed the entire roll to a bright light making every frame worthless, except the one he had doctored.

The developed and magnified photo would reveal Per Knudsson's hand around a small vial of liquid, standing next to the buffet table at the Midsummer celebration. The camera and film would be found hidden in a secret compartment in Knudsson's flat along with other incriminating documents, including photographs of Lea's parents taken in the Baltics shortly before their deaths. The damming evidence would be uncovered at the appropriate time. Ulrik needed a scapegoat. Knudsson's fall from Stasi grace would be long and painful, and end only when the man had stopped being useful.

Returning to the table, he examined the Reardon file one page at a time. Mulling over Knudsson's report, he made a note to find information on Rolf Sundren. He would not allow the American's untimely appearance to threaten his long-arranged plans.

As usual, Lea woke early. She sat up quickly, regretting the action when a sharp pain jabbed the top of her head. She gingerly reached into the bedside drawer for aspirins, taking two with the remains of her cold tea. Holding her aching head, Lea carefully slid out of bed, eager for a hot shower. She saw Rolf's clothes hanging over the shower pole, but left them where they were.

As steam filled the bathroom, she took off the flannel nightgown, and hung up the wet Swedish clothes in the sink. Puzzled by her choice of nightwear, her pajamas and robe were still hanging on the hook behind the door. Lea didn't remember changing into the heavy gown her grandmother had sewn for the cold nights of a Chicago winter. She had packed it as a sentimental afterthought, something of MorMor to bring back to Öland.

After her shower, she tried to focus on the events of the previous night. *The Swedes certainly served a strong brew with a nasty afterkick*, she thought. Wrapped in her robe and toweling her hair, she was startled at the loud grunt. She turned and saw Rolf sprawled out in the bedroom chair.

Frowning even in sleep, she wondered if the man ever smiled or laughed. She remembered his astonishment at sitting on the ground covered with a broken trellis, and doubted there were many who argued with the owner of Sundren Industry International. This was a man who clearly expected to have his own way.

He surprised Lea by his compassion, refusing to leave her side when she was too sick to help herself. Rolf Sundren was a man of contrasts. He thought she was naïve. Maybe she was, a little. She wondered why he was bothering with her. What did he want?

The phone rang. She caught it on the first ring. Lea spoke softly not willing to wake Rolf yet.

"Hello. Lea Reardon."

"Lea, this is Per. I wanted to make sure you were safe after the disturbance last night. I'm sorry. I was called away and wasn't able to take you home. I blame myself…"

"Everything is okay, Per. The misunderstanding has been worked out."

"Is it possible to spend some time together, maybe tomorrow?" Hearing Rolf move around, Lea decided to end the conversation. "I can't talk right now. Tomorrow is fine. We'll speak then."

Rolf got up, slammed the bathroom door, and dressed in his damp clothes. Lea knew he had heard the conversation.

"How are you after last night?" he asked, emerging fully clothed.

"Much better. Thanks for your concern."

Her stilted rhetoric did nothing to improve his mood.

"I don't mean to hurry you, but obviously you have to change out of those damp clothes, and I have to get dressed and drive to the inspector's office in Kalmar. I appreciate your staying with me when I was sick."

"You're welcome. If you need anything else, this is my private number." He handed her a card.

Rolf walked to the porch of his cottage. He needed to put the events of last night and early morning into perspective. The smell of earth and water always gave him a peace he never felt when he was in a city. He scattered some crumbs for Gussie and sat down to sort things out.

He had always solved problems by using logic. Rolf looked at life in the distinct sharpness of black and white. Problems were never amorphous, without definition; never gray or muddy. Solutions were calculated, boxed, and set aside until needed, but not this time. He couldn't find a clear answer. Rolf admitted a growing attraction to Lea Reardon. It was something he wasn't sure how to handle. The ringing phone brought him back inside.

"Sundren."

"This is Leonard Stratton. It took some serious digging to get information on the Reardon woman. She wasn't an easy profile like the other dames you had me check out, but I finally got some background. It wasn't my fault the news was buried so deep."

"You'll get the money if the information is worth it. What do you have?"

"Her parents worked for the State Department. And the latest news running through the agency, their deaths weren't an accident, although no one outside the loop would know that. It also looks like they're sniffing around the heart attack the grandmother suffered eleven years earlier. The bet is her death was also a homicide. I couldn't get any more, except that the Department figures the Stasi were involved in some way."

"The Stasi! What was her family involved in that the East German Secret Police would kill for?"

"At this point, there aren't any answers floating around, but if something becomes available, I'll try to get it for you."

"I'm not interested in 'ifs.' Contact me when you get the rest of the material. I've also sent a list of additional individuals I want you to find." Ready to end the exchange, he thought of one last question. "Stratton, is Lea Reardon aware of the information on her family?"

"It's doubtful."

He hung up the phone and quickly got dressed. Lea was entitled to know the truth, what little he knew, concerning the deaths of her family. On the other hand, the theft last night now took on more complexities. If Stasi agents were behind the break-in, she could be in real danger. Until he had a more detailed report, it might be better to say nothing and stay close to her. Considering how they left one another, that would be a challenge.

10

KALMAR POLICE STATION, 1989

True to her word, Lea arrived at the inspector's office in Kalmar. She looked around the small room as she waited for the detective to appear. The walls were oddly empty. No family pictures, no citations, no "thank you" letters. Nothing. A metal case was crammed with books. On the large desk were piles of magazines, foreign newspapers, stacks of correspondence, and file folders. She noticed one side drawer was pulled out to accommodate a telephone.

Bending to put her purse down, she was hit by pungent odors. Lea noticed a large metal ashtray filled with cigar butts and a delicate flowered bowl set on the floor. The mixture inside it seemed to be the remains of several past meals. A water dish and a large bone lay nearby.

Startled when the door opened, she turned around to see the inspector enter the room carrying a cut glass vase filled with deep pink roses.

"Good morning." He set the vase down gently on the littered desk, trying not to spill any water. "Would you like any coffee, tea or juice?"

"No, thank you."

"Does Knute bother you?"

"Knute? I don't know what…"

Hearing his named called, the large black dog got up from his resting spot under the desk and lumbered out to greet Lea. Tail thumping, he sat directly in front of her and offered his paw.

"Hello, boy." She bent over and stroked his big head.

"Knute, over here. Stay!" Lars pointed to the floor. The station's guard dog stopped to pick up his bone before disappearing under the desk.

Lea opened her purse, pulled out the requested list of places she visited and people she met. She also detailed what objects were gone through and what was missing from her room.

"This is everything."

Watching the detective scan the list, she wondered if he would pick out a suspect and quickly solve the crime in the manner of the 1930s serial detective movies that she enjoyed so much. Inspector Youngmark's manner remained unchanged as he penciled notations on her paperwork. Stopping for a moment to search for the pad on his desk, the detective looked at Lea and frowned.

"Are you ill, Miss Reardon?"

"I drank too much strawberry punch at the midsummer festival. I'm not used to alcohol and was sick all night."

"There was no alcohol served at any of the activities. Maybe it was something you ate." He paused and picked up his phone to the outer office.

"Check and see if any people attending Midsummer became ill from eating or drinking something. If the answer is yes, I want to know how many, their names, and if any treatment is needed." Lars wrote himself a reminder then continued his questions.

"There were no other acquaintances, you are sure? Someone you met briefly that you overlooked?"

"No," she replied.

"When you went through your things, you found only the camera missing. Is this correct?"

"Yes."

"Yet, you said the camera was sitting in clear view on the table. Why would someone go to so much trouble to tear apart your room? Your clothes, shoes, and bag are not overly expensive. Your jewelry simple." He admired her sole decoration, a gold locket. "A thief would assume credit cards would be with you. Since your arrival in Öland, have you received any mail or purchased an object that someone might want?"

"No, not really."

"Not really? Please explain."

"The only thing was a package from my mother. I found it among my parents' things right before my trip, and waited until I was here on Öland to open it."

"Were you alone when you unwrapped the package?"

"In my room at the inn, yes."

Lea didn't feel it necessary to mention that she briefly showed one page of the diary to the gardener, Mr. Johansson. She didn't want the inspector focusing on the harmless old man.

"Was this package in your room when it was ransacked?"

"No."

"Can you tell me what was inside?"

"Why would it matter, Inspector? I see no connection."

"Is it personal writings from your family?"

"No."

"Then I don't understand."

"I've learned not to be a trusting person." Lea knew her remarks were rude but that was the intent. Experience had taught her that being polite and friendly encouraged people to get personal. Unwanted stories were pushed by those determined to get Lea to tell about herself. If bounds were set from the beginning, she was left alone.

"Miss Reardon, as a policeman, I give you my word that anything we talk about will not leave this room without your permission. The choice is yours."

It was hard to break old habits. There were very few who inspired Lea's trust, but her instincts told her Lars Youngmark should be one of them. She opened her purse for the diary and handed it to the detective.

"The package held this book. I'd never seen it before, and my parents never mentioned it. My mother enclosed no explanations or instructions. I was going to do some research when I returned home."

Lars looked with interest at the blue stone nestled in the pouch attached to the book. Living near the Baltic all his life, he recognized the material as amber. The quality of the flower carving was exceptional. There were very few artisans who had this ability. Carefully replacing the stone, he gave the writing a cursory glance before turning his attention to the ink drawing. It was a curious scenario of death. An eagle, claws outstretched for attack, swooped down on a group of ravens feeding on the human remains of an ancient battle.

"Do you read German, Miss Reardon?"

"Not well. I was able to pick up enough words for a basic understanding, nothing more. I haven't a clue about the picture or jewel. What do you think?"

The inspector ignored her question and turned to examine the picture again.

The pen strokes were dissimilar. It seemed that the shading was meant to disguise rather than enhance. It was more than just a drawing.

"With your permission, I would like an associate of mine to look at your book. My suspicion is that someone searched your room not to steal your camera but to find this diary. My friend is an expert in Nordic history. He may be able to tell us the reason someone might be interested. I would make a copy of the pages but that would not give the quality needed for documentation. Will you leave it?"

"I'd rather keep it with me." Lea tucked the book into her bag.

"Before you go, I have something you can use until your missing property is found." He handed Lea a small camera.

"Thank you very much." Lea put the unexpected gift in her bag with the journal. "I'll bring the diary back whenever you say."

"You're welcome. And Miss Reardon, your things were thrown around, but no one was hurt. Until I'm able to speak with everyone on your list, please be careful. If anything out of the ordinary happens, call me immediately. Good day."

Lars Youngmark leaned against the window frame watching the young woman leave the building. He saw her stop to talk with a passing Romanish family before pulling out the replacement camera he had just provided. Lars could see her unguarded animation and laughter as she knelt at eye level, talking to the children as she snapped pictures. She gave the boy and girl a hug when she was through. Looking to their parents for approval, Lea offered the youngsters a few pieces of candy from her purse. This was a side of the young American he had not noticed before.

Sometimes, he wished he had a small part of his wife's ability to see through words and find the real person hiding behind them. He relied on hard work and the experience of almost forty years of being a policeman. Some people called it detective intuition; but any in the police department knew it was the long hours, days, and months of methodical research, and sometimes luck, that uncovered the truth. After witnessing Lea's easy manner with the Roma children, Lars realized the rigid attitude she displayed was an attempt to disguise her real problem.

For whatever reasons, Lea Reardon kept people at arm's length. He should have understood. Many years ago, he remembered being the recipient of that same disdainful manner from a young girl he asked to dance. Aloof disapproval only spurred his determination to break down her barriers. Lars laughed to himself as he recalled those difficult, long-ago days of courtship with Hulda, and the wonderful years that followed.

He automatically picked up the vase of roses, inhaling their sweet fragrance. His beloved wife had been gone ten years and he missed her more every day. He sat down at his desk and looked over his notes, but his mind strayed. He pulled out his wallet and looked at the picture of his wife.

11

KALMAR, SWEDEN 1977

The tragedy happened during the winter festival. As an agent for the Swedish government, Lars spent long periods away from home. To be together for a holiday was a rare opportunity. It began as a happy occasion. He had asked his associate and friend, Ulrik Orensson, to share their celebration. The holidays could be a lonely time for a man without a wife and child.

Father and daughter were ready to leave early in the morning for a few hours of shopping.

"Ulrik, we are ready to go." Lars called out. Ulrik was scheduled to join them but was nowhere to be found. The disappearance hadn't surprised Lars. The man likely made himself scarce, unhappy at the thought of spending a few kroner to buy a holiday gift for his host.

To be fair, Lars doubted that Ulrik recognized his stingy behavior. Both men were the product of a generation that experienced the hard years of a depression followed by the shortages that accompanied a war. It left an indelible impression. When times improved, people were careful with what they had. Even so, Orensson was still more spartan than most. Many times when the men ate out together, a lost wallet, forgotten money, or some such excuse had Ulrik saying "thank you" as he pushed the check to Lars.

Hulda wasn't as accepting of Ulrik, but she would have never been outwardly rude. Whenever the man visited their home, he was made to feel welcome and treated to the best cooking her budget would allow because it made Lars happy. It was the reason Hulda hadn't accompanied her family that morning.

"You go shopping," Hulda had said. "I need time to prepare a special dinner in honor of the holiday and our guest."

The certificate marked his wife's time of death as early morning. By the time Ulrik walked into the kitchen searching for lunch, Hulda was slumped over the table and nothing could be done to help her. Tired and happy from a day of sloshing through the wet snow of Kalmar, Lars entered the house, his arms loaded with packages, to find the coroner covering his wife with a blanket.

Ulrik had stayed to help and Lars appreciated his friend's support. Taking control of the household, Ulrik handled the many details that accompanied death. He informed Swedish authorities, made the necessary calls to friends, and went with Lars to pick a burial site. He nagged Lars and Margretta to eat the meals he prepared, and spent numerous nights helping the pair work through the grief of losing a wife and mother.

KALMAR POLICE STATION, 1989

Even after so many years, Lars felt the abject loneliness of Hulda's absence. Only the sweet-smelling flowers he kept on his desk seemed to bring memories of their life a little closer. He remembered nights sitting together at the dining room table planning a retirement cruise through the fjords, or maybe a trip to the United States.

Policemen don't make a lot of money, but Hulda always managed to slip a little away each month to make sure they would be comfortable during what she laughingly called their "golden years." The money she carefully saved still sat in a dresser drawer, upstairs in their modest home.

After her death, Lars left his job as a security officer and moved back to Öland where life was slower, less complicated.

He shook his head as he glanced at the calendar. It was almost time to leave for vacation at his daughter's farm. His two-year-old grandson enjoyed playing with Knute, and Lars was anxious to try out a new fishing pole. He had already dug up one of Hulda's prized rose bushes to transplant into Margretta's kitchen garden. His wife would have liked that. She always said the smell of roses were a gift from the angels to remind mortals what delights they would find in heaven.

He recalled the only serious disagreement in their long marriage was his abandonment of religion. When you spend your life with the dregs of mankind unraveling the horrors committed by the human race, it was hard to believe in a conscious God. Hulda tried over the years, urging him to attend church services. He always refused.

However, when visiting her grave to bring flowers, Lars would stop inside the empty church to sit and think. Looking at the altar, the pictures, the candles, and other trappings of the Christian faith, he tried to understand why being in this room had brought Hulda peace and strength of mind. He hoped if there was such a thing as an afterlife, a merciful God would understand his grief and allow him to reunite with his wife.

Shifting his thinking back to the Reardon case, the inspector ran his finger down the names on Lea's list and compared them to those he had received last night. He would investigate everyone at Kalmarsson Inn, but three names stood out; the American, Rolf Sundren, and two locals, Per Knudsson and Gunnar Johansson. All had several encounters with Lea Reardon, but did one of the men have knowledge of the journal's existence and possible importance? The inspector knew little about Sundren or Knudsson, but he was very aware of the troubling background of Kalmarsson Inn's gardener, Gunnar Johansson.

It was last year when Sigrid first called him out to the inn. For some reason, Gunnar's tenuous hold on reality had loosened, sending the man back to the past.

Fighting specters only he could see, Gunnar spit curses and threats at imagined enemies. Inspector Youngmark might not have condoned the man's actions of rage, but recalling the inhuman conditions Gunnar survived, Lars could understand the reason. Overall, the man had done well since his release from the various hospitals, and had been happy working at the inn. The detective didn't feel one lapse warranted sending him away again.

Instead of writing an official report, Lars took the gardener back to his room and stayed by his side during that difficult night. He began spending a few nights during the week at the inn instead of returning to his own apartment in town. He hoped his leniency had not been a mistake. As for the other two men, he decided to call in some favors. Official channels were too slow and sloppy. Lars wanted information quick, and the inquiry kept confidential. The response didn't take long.

"Inspector, Erik Swansson. It certainly has been long since I've heard from you. This call is to answer your inquiry pertaining to Rolf Sundren and Per Knudsson. I will give a verbal summary. This conversation will not be listed in the agency logbook.

"Rolf Sundren is thirty-one, American by birth, unmarried, and the sole owner of Sundren Industry International, a business that specializes in security. He resides in New York and owns property on Öland. He is considered an amateur authority on the runic language. There is nothing in his background or current status that would raise red flags at this time. Per Knudsson is another story. He is unmarried and a Swedish citizen. We believe he is a Stasi operative, but there is no conclusive evidence. There have been complaints by neighbors of abnormal behavior. We consider him dangerous, Lars, with a short temper. His home is on Öland but he rarely spends time there."

"Thank you, Swansson. Your help is appreciated."

While in town that morning asking questions about the inn theft, Lars spoke to many who had attended the festival. Some suggested the thief would be found in the marketplace among their own kind. The remark had not come as a surprise. Throughout history, this group of people made many uncomfortable just by their presence. They stood apart while selling their wares from brightly decorated stalls, their ancient language of Romanish as idiomatic as the people themselves.

It was possible, he supposed, that a Gypsy broke into the room and stole the American's camera, but he didn't think it likely. While the camera would be easy to sell and bring a good price on the black market, he also knew the same people who pointed to the nomads as thieves were known to hold intolerant views. Gypsies provided a convenient cover for their own indiscretions, or were blanket scapegoats for any trouble that came to the island.

Next, he considered Lea's illness and how it might fit into a plan to steal the journal. He called the local doctor for answers.

"Inspector, at this time, I have many people showing flu-like symptoms. The common denominator seems to be Mrs. Sundersson's *janssons frestelse*. There are additional tests to try and isolate the cause. I should know more tomorrow. Good day."

Lars had already checked the food from the Midsummer buffet table. Mrs. Sundersson's recipe was one of the festival favorites. Her version contained potato, anchovy, cream, butter, onion, and the unusual addition of dill.

The inspector hung up the phone slowly. By all outward accounts, it seemed a straightforward case of theft and food poisoning. Maybe, he thought, or maybe someone went to a lot of trouble to make it appear that way. The drawing in the diary and the amber carving gave him reasons to search for answers in another direction.

During the Second World War, as a lad of fifteen, Lars secretly patrolled a section of the island's coastline, looking for signs of a Nazi assault. He reported his findings to undercover British agents. Lars knew some in Öland sympathized with the Germans while others, like himself, wanted Hitler's defeat.

The war had infused a hatred of aggression as he watched countries all over Europe crushed under Hitler's boot. Lars took his job seriously, memorizing all the bumps and curves of the island's perimeter under his watch. He recognized many of those features rendered in the drawing from Lea's journal.

World War II was long over. Today people in Sweden were concerned with the reality of communism, not foolish stories told by old men over a glass of schnapps. But a good policeman watched, listened, and remembered.

Nations, like people, hide information when the truth is damaging. The inspector knew no government publicly admitted playing a role in the many treasures stolen and hidden during WWII.

He wondered if the amber piece uncovered in the book, might have come from one of those lost artworks.

However, if treasure seekers dared to dream, the journal was a door to reach what many considered the pinnacle of stolen World War II masterpieces.

As the invading Red Army destroyed Nazi strongholds in the waning days of the war, an important man was captured. His mission was to guard a large number of boxes as they moved from Königsberg—his name, Erich Koch. The boxes contained the Amber Room, a treasure missing to the present day. Lars picked up the phone. His visit to Margretta would have to wait. There were too many incidents, and all seemed to center around Miss Reardon and her diary. He didn't know the motives of Rolf Sundren, but if the Stasi was interested in the diary, Lea Reardon was in danger.

12

ÖLAND, 1989

After a long morning at the police station, Lea drove back to the inn. She smiled, remembering the inspector's obvious attempts to gain information while giving nothing in return. But then weren't those the hallmarks of a smart detective? She didn't regret her decision to show him the journal.

Lea looked around her room. Everything was back in place. It still brought a measure of discomfort to know a stranger had gone through her things. She thought about what the inspector said. She would be careful.

After changing into the comfort of a worn pair of jeans and a T-shirt, Lea walked into the kitchen, smiling as she listened to Mrs. Kalmarsson sing in garbled English "Mammas Don't Let Let Your Babies Grow Up to Be Cowboys."

Sigrid stopped her vocals when she saw Lea. "Ah, you are back." Sigrid mixed the dough for her pancakes. "You are not to worry." She used the wooden spoon for better emphasis. "Lars Youngmark is a good man. He will find who did this."

Lea smiled and wondered if the inspector knew Sigrid regarded him as more than a friend. "What are you making, Mrs. Kalmarsson?"

"*Jast pannkakor.*"

"May I help?"

"Of course. Take the large green bowl from the shelf, butter the inside, and pour the batter in. All of it. Now cover the bowl with this towel, and place it, here," Sigrid said, pointing to the shelf above the stove.

She watched as Lea followed her directions. "In about thirty minutes, the mixture will double in size and we will start the yeast pancakes." When the timer went off, Sigrid pulled out the black cast iron pan, buttered each of the six indented, round impressions, and put it on the stove to heat.

"Pour batter into each circle. When you see bubbles form, run your knife around the edge and turn them over." Sigrid put a plate over a pot of water simmering on the stove. "When each pancake is done, put it on this plate to keep them warm." The two women working together finished the bowl of batter in a half hour.

Sigrid wiped her floured hands on a towel before pouring two cups of coffee from the fresh pot sitting on the back of the stove. For Lea, she added a large plate of anise cookies.

"These are for you and the guests in the garden. And before I forget, a message came." The innkeeper reached for the paper in her apron pocket and handed it to Lea.

Balancing the plate of cookies and her coffee, Lea walked toward the flower garden where she heard talking and laughter. Her eyes widened as she saw two women stretched out on beach towels. Both were wearing monokinis, scant bottoms with no tops.

Smiling as she walked through the gate, Lea wondered if she would ever get over her prudishness, which for many Europeans stamped her as distinctly American. Her smile faded as she heard a third voice. Relaxing in a chair, bottle in hand was Rolf Sundren.

"Hello. You must be Lea. It's nice to meet you. I'm Margit. My friend and I are visiting Sigrid for the day. We were just trying to find a mutual subject for conversation with Rolf."

"I don't think that's a problem. The subject is obvious. The man has eyes," Lea sniped. Her manners had disappeared with her good humor.

It wasn't that she was jealous, she tried to convince herself. What hurt was their ability to make Rolf smile and laugh. Lea was envious at his easy camaraderie with the women. Everything she said or did had met with his anger or caused an argument.

She stopped, shamed by her rudeness. "I'm sorry. That was uncalled for." Her glare aimed at Rolf made clear he was not included in the apology.

She turned around, went inside up to her room embarrassed by the petty explosion. Lea set the dishes aside, no longer interested in eating cookies. She grabbed the large bed pillow and cried with her face buried in its thickness.

Rolf had followed and stood watching from the hallway. He rapped lightly on the door before treading carefully into her room.

"What's this all about?" He turned Lea around to face him. "Is it the theft?"

She shook her head. "I don't want to talk to you. Go away."

He ignored the request. "I'm sorry for losing my temper earlier and for the words I used." For him, that was a generous apology.

Lea didn't answer. A hot streak of jealousy controlled her emotions, and he was the reason. It was hard to face the truth. Throwing the pillow on the bed, she walked out of her room into the hall.

Normally, a woman's tears meant nothing to him. He had watched his mother use them as a tool to control his father. Her episodes were always public, well-orchestrated, and successful. This was different. He figured Lea was entitled to tears. What she went through the night before would unsettle anyone.

While Rolf credited himself with a level disposition and temperament, it seemed around Lea, every conversation provoked a fiery disagreement. However, until the inspector's investigation was complete, and he received the background details he requested from Stratton, he wouldn't relax or let his guard down. Once he was certain Lea was in no danger, they could go their separate ways.

Rolf knew, unlike the fictional James Bond movies with fast cars and beautiful women, the most effective agents fit into their targeted population with ease, living simply and calling no attention to themselves. Anyone, from a local shopkeeper, her friends at Kalmarsson Inn, to the police inspector himself, could be a Stasi operative. He had to find the words to make her cautious without revealing the reason.

"Wait. I'd like to talk to you alone."

"No, Rolf, no privacy. Say what you want here in the hallway and then leave me alone."

She continued walking until he turned her around in his arms, and pinned her to the wall. For Rolf, the subject of her safety, as well as any thoughts of calm, dispassionate explanations had disappeared.

"You're going to listen to me. I admit when I left this morning, my intention was to continue my vacation and forget I ever met you. It didn't happen. I need you to understand." He softened his voice. "You're not a game to me, Lea. And your actions tell me you're not as disinterested as you insist."

She was ready to lay it all on the line. Dancing around adjectives was a waste of time.

"Okay, I admit it bothers me. You bother me! I've always stayed away from serious relationships. I direct my own life and make my own decisions. Now, the simplest things have become complicated. I can't concentrate, and it's impossible to have any self-control. If you feel the same, and I'm not a game to you, then exactly what am I?"

She watched his eyes turn cold. He stepped back, distancing himself emotionally and physically. "Don't try to put words in my mouth, Lea. I admit you're important to me, but I won't lie. I can't give you what isn't there."

There was nothing left to say. It hadn't been her intention to push or try to pin Rolf down. Her frustrations simply boiled over. She had made a complete fool of herself by admitting her feelings. For someone who took pride in keeping her emotions tucked inside, she was living the script of a soap opera queen.

"What do you want from me?" she asked.

"Stay with me at the beach house, spend the time we have left on the island together. Accept me as I am. Don't expect me to offer empty promises simply to get you into my bed. It won't happen. Be honest with yourself. Do you want to ignore this attraction we have for one another?" he challenged.

Though the candor of Rolf's statement didn't take her unaware, she had a hard time forming an answer as he moved closer. Damn, what was wrong with her? Men had these carnal cravings, not women. She was a freak.

Lea admitted her vulnerability. It wasn't propriety or other people's opinions that gave her pause. That peculiarity went to a nagging inner voice, uneasy at the thought of becoming dependent on any man.

"I don't know. I need to think about it."

"I'll come back this evening." He felt the uneven beat of her heart, as his mouth brushed softly across her eyelids before gently pulling away. He watched her eyes open slowly, narrowing in judgment before she turned and walked back to her room.

Had she guessed his calm, detached manner was a sham? He knew Lea had been disappointed with his answer, but he could have said nothing else. He might be his father's son, but Rolf was determined not to make the same mistakes.

The voice behind made him made Rolf turn in surprise. "I am sorry I overheard your words. I did not mean to listen. I will say, Mr. Sundren, I am ashamed for you. You might have a Swedish name, but you don't have Swedish heart." Mrs. Karlmarsson walked away, leaving Rolf alone.

Lea entered the bathroom, shedding her clothes as she walked. Turning on the water, she shivered as icy needles hit her skin. Apparently, it wasn't only men who needed the quelling effects of a cold shower. After toweling off, she decided to call Per.

"Per, it's Lea. I can't see you tomorrow. Something has come up." *Actually someone, named Rolf.* "Maybe another time." She knew there would never be another time. "I'll talk to you later."

"I understand. I will call again." The soothing tone lasted until he hung up the phone. "Do not make things difficult for me, Lea. It will be harder for you, in the end," he ground out the words.

Lea bit into one of the anise cookies, oblivious that her appetite for food and work had returned. Remembering the note from Mrs. Kalmarsson, she stopped to look at the message.

The Farmers and Mrs. Sedgely have decided to stay in Denmark. Only the Reverend would travel to Öland. He had reserved a small room at the inn. It still amazed Lea that Susan Sedgely and Brenda Farmer were sisters. The reverend's wife was shy, soft-spoken, and gracious. Her sister was ill-tempered and sharp-tongued.

Lea didn't know Mr. Farmer well, but then few people from the neighborhood or church did. It had been years since she last saw the man, and doubted an ability to recognize him on the street unless Brenda was with him. What she did recall was a man who was hospitalized a lot with a bad stomach. A man who earned contempt from neighbors for his long absences from home and alcoholic benders. Her few memories were of a thin, wiry man with vivid blue eyes and a pleasant smile. During childhood summers of making money with lemonade stands, it was Mr. Farmer who always stopped to buy the watery liquid.

As a salesman, Benjamin Farmer traveled a lot. The brunt of childrearing fell to Brenda. Gossip attributed Benjamin's choice of job and his love of alcohol to a shrewish wife, a spoiled son, and the thought that no one could stand living under the same roof with either one for very long. In time, that story died as most do when replaced by fresh fuel.

Unfortunately, the attack on young Lea and the death of her grandmother provided the fodder. Unlike the Reardon family and their friends, who kept the details private refusing to speak on the subject, Brenda Farmer sought any sympathetic ear willing to hear her views on the topic.

Though Pastor Sedgely had not been in the congregation at the time, Lea was sure he had heard some variation of the story of her fourteenth birthday, the attack by Bradley Farmer, and the death of her grandmother.

13

KALMAR POLICE STATION, 1989

Inspector Youngmark pulled his reference material out of the desk drawer, preparing for Ulrik Orensson. Lars had said little over the telephone, but his old partner agreed to leave for Kalmar right away. The two had been friends for over thirty years. They met in 1953 when both worked for the Swedish government. Lars analyzed information interpreting data from outside sources while Ulrik excelled in counterintelligence using his skills to break codes. The jobs resulted in a close relationship between the two men.

Working for the government, it was difficult to make or maintain outside friendships. The job meant long hours and sometimes days or weeks away from home and family. As a result, strong bonds were formed between many of the agents. Lars had a few friends in the agency, but Ulrik was a loner. The one person he talked with was the detective.

Ulrik was one of the few who understood Lars's grief and helped him after the death of Hulda. They met many times to talk. Ulrik supported Lars's decision to become a policeman at the Kalmar Station after he left Swedish security. The agency considered Lars unstable after Hulda's death. It was later he found out Ulrik had become a field operator, leaving the home office as well. In time, Lars became head inspector, but he kept his home on Öland, the small island off Sweden's east coast. He didn't mind his trip across the water to the bustling city of Kalmar every day.

Over the years, Ulrik made sporadic visits to visit Lars, but mostly the friends kept in touch by letter and telephone. Recently, Ulrik had written, sharing plans for his visit during the Midsummer festivities.

KALMARSSON INN, 1989

Lea answered the phone in her room. "Miss Reardon, if it is convenient, a police car will pick you up in one hour and bring you to my office in Kalmar."

"Inspector, I'm perfectly capable of driving myself," she argued.

"I insist, Miss Reardon." Lars hung up the phone. Until he knew the exact circumstances of the theft, her illness, and Stasi involvement, it was better to be cautious.

When the car arrived, Lea kept the driver waiting while she taped a note for Rolf on the door explaining her absence. She stopped in the kitchen to make sure Mrs. Kalmarsson wouldn't worry when she missed dinner.

Waiting in the reception area of the police station, Lea's stomach growled with hunger. Hearing sounds of laughter coming from the inspector's office, she resigned herself to sitting for a time. She dug into her purse, intent on finding a candy bar stuffed in her bag. The chocolate bar was half eaten when Inspector Youngmark walked out of his office.

"Miss Reardon, I apologize for your wait," he said, and eyeing the candy bar in her hand, added, "and for apparently making you miss a proper meal. I'll have food brought in." He called out to an assistant at the main desk. "Please bring a sandwich and drink to my office. Now, Miss Reardon, please come and meet Professor Ulrik Orensson. Many years ago, we worked together. Today," he said, turning to his friend, "Ulrik is a professor of Swedish history."

As Ulrik stood for the introduction, Lea noted a thin man with faded blonde hair, light blue eyes, medium height, and was clean-shaven. There was nothing unusual about Ulrik's appearance or dress. This was someone who could easily blend into a crowd, she thought, until Lea noticed his gloves. As she held out her hand for the accustomed handshake, Ulrik pointedly refused the gesture and greeted her with a formal bow.

"Miss Reardon, it is good to meet you."

"Thank you, Professor Orensson. It's nice to meet you as well."

Noticing Ulrik's unease during the introduction, the inspector remembered his friend's discomfort at having his hands touched. Lars was accustomed to the cotton gloves the man wore to hide his extensive scarring, and was sorry he had forgotten to mention the condition to Miss Reardon. Anxious to get past their uncomfortable beginning, the detective was glad when the aide interrupted with a sandwich and drink. He took the tray from the young man and closed the door.

"Shall we begin?"

Lea reached into the zip side of her purse, handing the book to Orensson before biting into the open-faced sandwich. She recognized the taste immediately, stopped eating, and pushed the plate away. The swelling and congestion she would suffer as a reaction to the popular herb wasn't worth a second bite.

"Miss Reardon, the food is not to your liking? Do you wish something else?"

"It's not that, Inspector. My allergy makes it impossible to eat anything with dill. It's something I always avoid. Please don't bother about me. I'll eat when I get back to the inn." Lea sat back as the professor began his inspection of the journal.

Ulrik turned the pages slowly from beginning to end. Reaching into his briefcase, he pulled out a magnifying glass and held the drawing up to the overhead light in the office. He stared at the picture a short time before turning his attention to the amber. Holding the fossilized tree resin in his hand, Ulrik noted the rare color and scrutinized its intricate carving from every angle. Satisfied, he replaced the object in its protective pouch and closed the journal. Leaning forward in his chair, he picked up a pencil and paper drawing what looked to be a series of lines and angles. Some were similar to modern letters, most weren't.

"Miss Reardon, do you know what this is?" Ulrik inquired.

"They look something like the writings I've seen on the runestones around Öland," she replied.

He nodded his head. "That is correct. It is writing. You are looking at an ancient language, one that has not been actively used in Sweden for centuries."

She looked closer at the lines and noticed that Orensson had put corresponding letters under the first six runes along with short explanations and the word *futhark*.

"The writings of this alphabetic script are so ancient, their origins have been lost to time. One definition of the word 'rune' comes from a Gothic term and translates as 'secret.' Some of the most primitive forms date back to the earliest centuries and were likely used in casting spells of magic, protection on a sea voyage, or words to help a warrior find his way after death. Few instances exist of this early form. It is thought that examples of this rare script might be found on Öland."

Ulrik stopped talking and shook his head. "Forgive me. Even to my ears, I sound like a lecturing professor. You did not come here for a lesson on our ancient history."

"You're wrong, I'd really like to know more. You have…"

"I am sorry to interrupt," an officer opened the door. "There is a phone call for you, Inspector."

"Excuse me." The detective got up and left his office for a more private space.

"Inspector Youngmark speaking."

"Inspector, this is Agent Swansson from Military Intelligence. I wanted tell you personally that the department intercepted a letter meant for Ulrik Orensson. It referred to a cover letter for an official report from Berlin, dated 1945. Our interest is a reference made to a set of papers known collectively as the *Hitler Document*. This compendium lists foreign nations and corporations that dealt with Hitler and the Third Reich. To avoid seizure by the Russians, the document was removed from Königsberg by water transport to an island off Sweden's coast. That is the sum of our information.

"Ulrik has been under surveillance and was followed to your office. Our agency is interested in a trade. If Orensson has the *Hitler Document*, and agrees to defect, we will provide money and protection. If he mentions anything about these papers, contact me immediately."

"I understand." Lars hung up the phone slowly. He had just found out one of his oldest friends was a traitor.

Lars knew from his post-World War II work in security that any records linking corporations to Nazi Germany were invaluable in their worth. He was familiar with the *Hitler Document*. In 1974, an investigator contacted his office looking for information indicating prominent companies had dealings with industries connected to the Third Reich. For those businesses, it would be critical to keep past embarrassing allegiances quiet. As problematic were hints connecting neutral nations to Hitler's regime. While overtly pleading nonalignment and peace, these same nations covertly dealt with Nazi Germany. For those involved, any proof supporting these claims would open a Pandora's box. How much would those countries pay to keep the lid closed?

He could guess what type of protection Swedish authorities would offer if Ulrik agreed to their terms. A new identity, a false resume, and a "safe house" would be provided until a mutually agreed permanent location was found. The money would match the importance of the information.

However, Security mentioned nothing about Lea Reardon or her diary. Lars thought they would be interested and want to inspect the book before the young woman took the journal back to the United States.

He remembered Ulrik's avid interest when he called his friend and told him about the book. It was possible that the diary hid the *Hitler Document*. He looked at his watch. Fifteen minutes had passed. It was too late. Even with Miss Reardon sitting in the room, Ulrik would have had sufficient time and skill to remove the papers from the journal. Lars centered his thoughts. He could not allow Ulrik to see anything in his face or manner to make him suspicious. If he realized Swedish authorities knew he was a traitor, Ulrik would disappear underground with the papers and shop the document and terms of asylum to competing factions.

"Please excuse me, Professor Orensson. I'd like to stretch my legs and get a drink of water. Please tell Inspector Youngmark I won't be long." Lea left the office.

Ulrik was alone. He had quit smoking years ago, an accomplishment readily bragged about to Lars in past letters. Unfortunately, the fierce pressures of being this close to his goal had robbed his mind of focus and it had not taken much to slip back into a habit that had always provided calm for his edgy temperament.

Sitting in Lars's office, the smell from the inspector's tobacco had filled the air and made his fingers itch for the cigarettes in his pocket. He knew his friend would graciously accept the lapse and understand his need for a smoke. But not to remove his gloves, a habit consistently practiced by Ulrik to avoid the brown stains of tobacco on white cotton, would cause too many questions that he couldn't answer.

Still, things were different now. He was not the same person. This time he would control the urge that once controlled him.

If he rationed the cigarettes to one a day, he wouldn't become dependent again.

Searching through pockets with his clumsy gloves proved too frustrating; he was out of practice. It had been a long time since he had been forced to wear the damned things. Looking out the glass door panels to make sure no one was around, he pulled them off.

Turning his back to the door, Ulrik felt in his pocket until he found the box of English cigarettes. Opening the top, he took out one, rolled it between his fingers, and tapped the end against the desktop to firm the tobacco. Scratching a match against his shoe, he lit the cigarette, pulling the smoke in deeply before expelling with an audible breath of satisfaction.

Hearing the inspector's voice, Orensson snuffed the tip and shoved the half-smoked stub back into the pack for later. Quickly pulling his gloves back on, he turned around as Lars walked in followed by Lea. The inspector closed the door, signaling the break was over. "We're ready to begin," he said.

Looking closely at the series of penned lines showing the runic alphabet, a question occurred to Lea. "How many different symbols are there in the script?"

"In the original Germanic, there were twenty-four. But sometime before the beginning of the Viking Age, the script was reduced to sixteen symbols," Ulrik replied and smiled. "It's unusual, eh, Lars, to have a young person interested in something most people consider a dull subject. Erecting large runestones celebrating the old gods, beliefs, and customs declined around the eleventh century. With the expansion of the Roman Catholic Church, Latin began to replace what the missionaries considered heathen script and pagan idolatry." Orensson's blue eyes twinkled.

"But the Swedes are a stubborn group, Miss Reardon. The people simply adapted the writing to fit this new religion. Instead of giant stones commemorating war, men's bravery, or something as simple as listing household goods, the stones, now mainly erected in church yards, spoke of baptisms, prayers, and saving souls. Today it is a dead language, of interest to a few academics like myself, and a curiosity to tourists."

Ulrik held up the drawing to the light again. "Whoever drew the picture in your journal was someone well-versed in the runic alphabet. This person went to a lot of trouble to communicate using this script, and see here," he pointed to the pen and ink, "he cleverly hid the message among the various lines and shadows of the drawing. The deception is well done. If I am correct, and your journal is authentic, we are looking at some type of map leading to a treasure from the World War II era.

"Considering the dates and the description of the surroundings, I would guess the original owner of the diary was aboard a submarine trying to escape the Allied invasion. The jewel found in your book is a rare form of amber, the carving very fine.

"Placing everything in context, in other words, the map, the amber, and the time period, the clues point to one of the many artworks stolen by the Nazis almost fifty years ago and never recovered.

"Unfortunately, as the means to identify or find this treasure, the book is of no real value without more information. The runic transcript is incomplete and one page from the diary is missing." Orensson pointed to evidence of a ragged tear. "So the drawing alone is not enough to understand what was hidden, or where it is located.

"I also agree with the inspector. Whoever ransacked your room was certainly looking for this book and might try again. Even with what we know, it is difficult to track and apprehend a person obsessed with finding a treasure. You must be careful to protect yourself."

As Lea turned, Inspector Youngmark noticed her face had lost color. "Are you feeling unwell?"

"I'm tired. It's been a long day for me with a lot of information to digest. I'd like to go back to the inn."

"Take Miss Reardon back to Kalmarsson Inn," the inspector called downstairs to his driver.

"I must leave too, Lars. Mark your appointment book for lunch tomorrow at the Brewhouse tavern. We can talk old times together."

Lars sat in his office, thinking about his meeting with Ulrik and Miss Reardon. Knute came out from under the desk. "Good dog," he said, scratching behind his ears. Lars took his calendar and penciled in his lunch with Ulrik. He would have preferred a more private setting, but Ulrik liked the outdoor space of the tavern. He put the calendar down. Something was puzzling him. Lars speculated about Lea Reardon's sudden change of attitude. After showing such interest in the diary, now she had no comment, no questions on the translation of the diary. *Why not*, he wondered.

He thought about the one answer the American had inadvertently given him. The strong smell of dill would have caused her to avoid Mrs. Sundersson's *janssons frestelse* served during Midsummer. Those who reported cramps, nausea, and diarrhea had all eaten Mrs. Sundersson's dish and only she added dill to the casserole. Something else had made Lea Reardon ill. Lars gathered his notes and left alone for his apartment. He had a lot of questions to find answers for.

14

KALMARSSON INN, ÖLAND, 1989

Rolf knocked on the door at Kalmarsson Inn. He waited a short time and rapped harder. Patience had never been his virtue. Finally the innkeeper opened the door.

"Good evening, Mrs. Kalmarsson. I'd like to see Lea Reardon."

"I'm sorry, she is gone." The old woman tried to shut the front door and go back to clearing the dinner table, but Rolf stepped across the threshold, effectively blocking the door.

"Do you know where she went? Who she went out with?" His voice took on the icy tone of a demanding executive who expected immediate answers from those he perceived subordinate.

Sigrid Kalmarsson raised one eyebrow. She was not the type of woman to be intimidated, especially when it concerned the well-being of one of her guests.

"When Miss Reardon left, I was in the kitchen. Goodbye." Sigrid shook her head and pushed the door firmly. It was not a lie she convinced herself, just not the whole truth. Remembering his words and Lea's tears that afternoon, she decided the man deserved nothing more.

Rolf walked back and forth in front of the inn. "Where are you, Lea?" he asked himself. It was getting late. He returned to his car and took some work from his briefcase. At least he could use the time productively. Unlike other women he knew, Lea didn't like to talk about herself. He smiled as he thought of the familiar childhood retort, "It takes one to know one". It was the reason he intuitively understood one aspect of the woman. She bruised easily.

Rolf enjoyed his past relationships because they were reciprocal as well as superficial. The women enjoyed the media attention that followed the unmarried CEO of Sundren Industry International, as well as his generosity. He enjoyed the noncommittal companionship they offered. Lea was different.

She hadn't asked him the expected questions about his business and monetary worth, nor had she hinted for presents in a coy manner. He looked at his watch. It had been almost two hours. "Where could you be for two hours?" He was getting worried.

Rolf had justified the reason for not sharing the knowledge he bought from Stratton, but now acknowledged his motives stemmed more from jealousy than altruism. He was fully aware of the strong sexual chemistry that existed between them, and had purposely stirred the mixture that afternoon. Sharpening the tension would keep her close. His excuse had been her safety, but that was only part of it.

He had to move, at least feel like he was doing something. He got out of the car and began to walk. Lea had been open with him. She explained the turmoil of trying to understand and deal with her feelings. He answered her honesty with distrust, manipulation, and coercion, determined to continue their relationship on his terms. Now, he wasn't sure what her decision would be.

He could have explained why he refused commitments. Rolf still fought battles from his childhood. He knew his father as a harsh, angry man who solved problems by burying himself in business. Rolf remembered the loud arguments between his parents concerning one of his mother's frequent companions. He watched his father endure his mother's numerous lovers in order to keep her home. But a time came when tolerance and expensive gifts lost their appeal. Raina Sundren wanted freedom, not the constraints of a husband and son. Like many children, Rolf blamed himself for the breakup. As he grew older, he realized both his parents were far from ideal.

In time, the names Raina and Erik Sundren represented nothing more than printing on his birth certificate. It was as an adult that he recognized the qualities his parents instilled in him by their desertion. Besides the deep, piercing aversion toward the double trappings of love and marriage, he learned to be tough and resilient at a young age.

Rolf set his own rules and walked a narrow line on the side of legitimate. He wasn't a team player. He prided his independence, trusted his instincts, kept his own council, and in important matters, depended solely on himself. He considered these necessary traits in the business world he inhabited.

He understood how love had weakened Erik Sundren. Unfortunately, when he thought of Lea Reardon, he saw too many similarities between himself and his father. Rolf admitted long ago that like the elder Sundren, business had become the guiding force of his life. Now he feared one more vestige of difference between father and son was erased.

He shook his head at the rambling string of thoughts that stormed through his mind. Rolf got back into the car just as a black vehicle pulled up in front of the inn. He didn't recognize the man who got out and walked Lea to the door before driving away.

It can be seen where twenty-four meets sixteen
In an ancient place where scalds still speak
Of earth scarring battles and blood stains deep
Brave warriors lost and treasure taken
Separate the eagle's dance with the raven
Old gods speak tales of foreboding
Evil stalks the lines unbroken.

Lea spoke the words aloud, repeating them until the entire verse flooded back into conscious memory. For the first time since intruding into her dreams as a teenager, she was able to remember the complete rhyme when awake.

She sat on the porch in the cool air trying to remember where she learned the meaningless rhyme which always signaled the beginning of her nightmare. That part was still a blank. After listening to Professor Orensson, she realized the verse might have something to do with Nordic runes. It made no sense. She knew nothing of the ancient language.

Unfortunately, what did make sense was her mother's reason to keep the journal private. Were the trips her parents took all over the world simply a cover for hunting Nazi treasure?

Lea lowered her forehead to rest on the wood railing. Her head felt as heavy as her heart.

Rolf heard her speak the rhyme as he walked up the porch steps, but in that moment, he wanted to know where she had been and with who. Ironic, he admitted, since he was the one insisting there be no pledges, no guarantees in their relationship.

"Lea," he said her name softly.

She looked up. She didn't know when he had come and it didn't matter. Her resolve was gone.

Mrs. Kalmarsson opened the door when she heard voices.

"Lea, everything is good?"

"Yes. Everything is fine," she replied.

Rolf felt a weight lift and smiled to himself at the protective instincts of a Swedish innkeeper toward her young guest.

Sigrid frowned when she noticed Rolf on the porch. "Come now, there is pannkakor left from dinner."

"No, thank you." Seeing concern in the woman's face, Lea added, "You can go to bed. Don't worry about me." She gave Sigrid a hug. "I'll be spending the night with Rolf."

The innkeeper stood for a moment, giving the young girl a measuring look and nodded her head in acceptance. "Good night." She shut and locked the door, and turned off the house lights.

Rolf and Lea walked toward the water. The couple followed the path that ended at the beach near Rolf's cottage. The wind whipped around them. A storm was coming. Lea turned to the roar of breaking waves. Stopping to look over the foaming waters of Kalmar Sound, the moon gave off just enough light for her to see Rolf's solid strength.

Understanding her apprehension, he bent his head to gently brush his lips across her neck. They arrived at the house, and Rolf opened the door to a three-room cabin. A massive fireplace dominated the large wood and stone living room. Lea looked at the cavernous opening, picturing whole pigs turning on an iron spit next to a bubbling cauldron of Viking ale.

At the opposite end, in front of a row of windows, a grand piano overlooked the sea. A large wooden desk flanked by open cubbies held a phone, fax, and computer equipment. Lighted shelving filled with books and professional journals lined the wall. Planked floors were covered with the thick sheepskin rugs common to the island.

She recognized the iconic furniture from reading her father's architecture magazines. The elegant lines of the steel and leather Barcelona chairs created by Ludwig Mies van der Rohe in 1929 blended perfectly with two sets of Florence chairs, pushed together to form a pair of couches. A modern look created in the past.

Unlike her home in Evanston, which offered no surprises, the polar opposites between the stark inside and the whimsical exterior of Rolf's cottage were a contradiction, like the man.

The approaching storm brought a chill to the house. Having already laid wood in the fireplace, Rolf reached for the matches to start a blaze. He left Lea staring into the flames while he walked into the small, well-equipped kitchen.

He had designed every aspect of the cottage except for this room. That task he left to the one woman who traveled with him everywhere, his housekeeper of many years, Frieda Benton.

Hanging stainless steel racks held all cooking utensils. The stove, refrigerator, and sink formed a triangle for economic movement. Dishes were stacked on open shelves.

He opened the refrigerator to find the cut of roast beef Frieda prepared before leaving. Rolf hoped his housekeeper enjoyed the two-week visit to her daughter.

He spread homemade bread with a spicy horseradish, piling on slices of beef for two sandwiches. Adding a couple bottles of American beer, he placed everything onto a wooden tray and returned to the living room.

Rolf stared at Lea curled up in the oversized chair. Her dark curls were windblown and her skin glowed from the warmth of the fire. He set down the tray on the butler's table and pulled up a chair for himself. Shadows from the firelight danced around them. The crackle and popping sounds of burning wood filled the room along with the smell of resin, as the heat forced the branches to release their last scent of the forest.

Reaching for a sandwich, Lea tried to hide her nervousness and calm her thoughts. Becoming increasingly uncomfortable with the silence between them, as well as Rolf's watchful gaze, she forced herself to consume an entire sandwich.

"I've never been particularly adept or comfortable at showing my feelings, Rolf. And up until now, it hasn't mattered. But it's important to me that you understand."

He watched her face, her amber eyes aglow. Her body hid the cool, graceful lines of a dancer. Rolf had never allowed sentiment or emotions, which he considered synonymous for weakness, to factor into decisions. It was not his intention to start now.

Lea moved toward him. She felt the odds improbable that Rolf would ever return her feelings. He had made his attitude clear and warned her not to expect any commitments. Her intentions were more basic. She was going to make the next move and take a risk.

15

ÖLAND, 1978

In 1978, thirty-three years after the tragedy of losing his wife and baby, Ragnar still lived in the house of his birth on the island of Öland, south of the ruins of Borgholm castle, close to his beloved sea, and the heavy stones under which his family lay.

Ragnar watched an aging Saab jog along the ruts to where he was mending his nets. The fisherman's hands, twisted and torn by years of battling the sea, were still steady, his eyes clear. He stood silently waiting until Ulrik, who always wanted to speak of the past, got out of the car. Ragnar didn't want to remember what happened all those years earlier, but Ulrik was persuasive.

Except for his brother-in-law, there were few who drank with him and talked. They came to buy his fish, but to most of the superstitious villagers, Ragnar was someone to be avoided, a pariah. Ulrik understood his problems and sympathized. He always brought along the one tool capable of loosening Ragnar's tongue—aquavit. Over the years, when Ragnar could not stand the torture of memory, only this Scandinavian vodka helped dull his suffering for a short while.

"Come into the house. Sit and eat," he invited Ulrik. After washing at the pump, Ragnar went about the ritual of setting the table with china taken from his wife's cupboard. "Have some bread and cheese," he offered. The hard loaf Ragnar placed on the table had broad patches of green mold spreading from the brown crust. The chunks of cheese were dry and bitter with age. But neither man cared as they sat down to eat and drink together.

Ragnar was aware this time Ulrik appeared anxious and impatient to get started. He had always refused to speak of the serpent during past visits. He gave hints as he danced around the subject, coming closer with each story. This day, he would give the visitor what he wanted.

"The villagers do not want to hear my story of the monster. No one from town visits my home. Not one of them will talk to me, except on the beach to buy my fish. You are the only person who eats with me under my roof. You bring me vodka. Today, I have something for you." The fisherman knelt on the wooden floor to remove a loose brick from the hearth. He reached in and grasped an object obscured by dank wrappings. He thought of his beautiful wife and child as he slowly unwrapped a glorious amber box. Ragnar cleared his mind to remember the events of a winter day in 1945.

ÖLAND, REMEMBERING 1945

"The omens were bad. The storm was fierce, even for December. The beaches were covered with debris thrown from the angry water. I hurried my fishing boat, battling to reach the open water of the Baltic." Ragnar took another swallow of vodka.

"My storehouse held large provisions of smoked roe deer and harvest vegetables, but my cache of fish was small. A break in the weather was a chance for a good catch. My Inga's belly was swollen with our first child." Ragnar put down the glass and stared out the window at the water.

"Go on, man. What happened?" Ulrich urged.

"Inga begged me not to chance the storm, but I wanted my wife and baby to lack for nothing during the cold months. She was only twenty years old and not a strong girl. Like my father, grandfather, and those ancestors who went before me to venture into these ancient waters, I have seen many strange creatures. This time, the churning and spitting water in the distance took on the form of a giant sea monster. Hissing bubbles shooting toward the sky, the screaming sounds from the animal, a death cry."

The man listened intently and brought his chair closer to Ragnar.

"The black shape pushed itself higher out of the roiling waves, and then slowly sank beneath the surface. I waited to see if the devil would show itself again. Then I saw it, something floating in the water. As my boat got closer, I saw clumps of light hair spreading outward like silky strands of seaweed. I looked down at the still form torn from the bowels of the creature and threw a net to catch the lifeless mannequin and pulled it into the boat. It wasn't a doll. The girl was young, no older than twelve or thirteen years of life. Her face did not show the signs of death yet. I pried open the child's hands clutched tightly around a package." Ragnar stopped again and poured another drink.

"Finish your story! What did the girl hold?"

"Wrapped in layers of oiled cloth to protect against the water, was a small box inlaid with amber. When I removed the box from her grip, I saw she wore a gold ring. I struggled to remove the band from her swollen finger.

"The storm worsened. Waves lashed, tearing at the sides of my boat. I knew if I didn't get away quickly, my boat could go down. I wrapped the child tightly in blankets and secured them with several lengths of rope. I weighted her with ballast so nothing would disturb her last sleep." Ragnar stopped again and lifted his head.

"Is that it? Is that the end of your story?"

"I slid the girl back into the water." He remembered calling on the gods of the sea to protect and watch over the child in death, and recited a Norse poem, recalled from his father, about the sea bringing sorrow and misery, as well as life and sustenance.

"I decided the ring would be a gift for Inga, but the amber box would bring a good price in the city, maybe enough for a new stove. I headed for shore, thoughts of netting codfish forgotten. But Inga was not there to greet me."

He found the bloated, fish-ravaged body of his wife washed ashore three days later. "The gods struck down my family because I was greedy and stole from the dead," Ragnar said quietly. The burden and blame for the death of his wife and child replayed in his dreams every night. Time would never lessen his guilt and sorrow.

"I attached the ring to a book I found inside this box, and stuck everything here." He pointed to the hiding place. He opened the amber box to show a glimpse of the book.

As the fisherman told his story, Ulrik also remembered that day. He had pulled himself out of the freezing water, barely able to crawl onto the beach. The raft had punctured a few yards out from land, forcing him to swim the rest of the way. He rested, sprawled on the sand, until brightness from the lightning revealed the outline of a cottage. As he neared the house, Ulrik could see the flickering lights of a fire through a window. A woman was in a small back room sitting at a spinning wheel. He looked around but saw no one else in the house.

Ulrik needed dry clothes and provisions before he could continue his journey to the Swedish mainland. He had made sure there would be no others in competition for the Amber Room. Those who had the knowledge were at the bottom of the sea. He held a small notebook, folded maps, and charts in a waterproof sack tied around his waist.

He entered the house quietly, intending to secure what he needed and be gone before anyone was aware of his presence. The woman saw his shadow as he passed. She turned around, calling her husband's name. Ulrik quickly snapped her neck.

He found a small wooden boat anchored near the beach, put the woman inside, paddled out from shore, and dumped the body into the water. Back on land, he pushed the empty skiff away from the beach, into the waves.

ÖLAND, REMEMBERING 1978

After so many years of searching, following blind trails, he considered it a deserved opportunity that a tale he overheard in a local tavern about a cursed fisherman, a sea monster, and a dead girl, led him back to the same cabin he came upon in 1945, Ragnar's cottage.

As the two men ate in silent companionship, Ulrik knew it was time to help the tormented Ragnar join his wife and child. Afterward, he washed the dishes and carefully put the cabin back into proper order. While fitting the brick back in place, he heard the sounds of a villager.

"Ragnar, what fish are you selling today?" A woman called out.

Bundling his prize together, Ulrik ran out the back door.

When the fisherman's body was discovered hanging from the cottage rafters, no one questioned the suicide. Most had expected it long ago. The townspeople gathered together to mourn the fisherman. He was buried with his wife and child using the prayers and ceremony of the Christian church. But a small group of fishermen, believing in the ancient ways, did what was necessary to honor their many gods. They waited until nightfall, dug his body up, placed the corpse upright in his fishing skiff, filled the boat with food, drink, and tools, and set it afire. The ashes were covered with dirt, and a wooden stick inscribed with Ragnar's name was stuck into the ground.

A few villagers emptied Ragnar's cottage of all worthy goods sending the contents to relatives living in Andersonville, Illinois. The possessions were to be sold for the benefit of the poor. No one from town was tempted with curiosity to read the book found on the floor by the door, nor greedy enough to take the gold ring attached to it by a narrow length of wool.

Even in 1978, not one villager was willing to risk the anger of the old gods. No words were spoken of the drowned girl found so many years before, or the goods Ragnar stole from her. There was no mention of the curse, only silent thoughts of what happens to those who take from the dead.

16

ÖLAND, 1989

R olf woke with a start at 2:00 a.m. The other side of the bed was empty. The warmth he had folded into the curve of his body during the night was gone. He remembered how right it felt as her shape curled into his. Getting up to reach for his jeans, he noticed Lea's clothes missing from the pile left on the floor. After a quick search, he realized she was not in the house. Opening the door, the moonlight cast a shadow on a lone figure.

He brought a wrap to the woman sitting on the cold, wet beach, but she seemed oblivious to the dampness. Back stiff, knees drawn up tight. Whatever unhappiness disturbed her slumber came from inside.

"Can't sleep?"

Lea turned as she heard Rolf. "No. I didn't mean to wake you. I have something on my mind."

He didn't want to think about it, but had to ask the question. "Are you sorry you came?"

She stood up and shook her head. "I have no regrets, Rolf. This is about my family."

Lea walked closer to the water. "Sometime before my parents' death, my mother left a package in the bedroom bookcase that said 'To Lea from Mom' on the front. I didn't find it until the night before I left for Europe. I stuck it in my bag, intending to open it here. None of it made sense to me. It was completely unlike my mother to leave something like that."

"What was inside?"

"A World War II German diary." Lea couldn't help smiling for a moment as she shared her mother's eccentricity with Rolf. "The joke in our family had always been my mother's notes. She wrote pages of explicit instructions just to go to the grocery store. Yet, for something as important as this book obviously was to her, she left nothing."

Lea stopped talking. Bending to pick up a wave-polished rock, she rubbed the smoothness against her cheek before throwing it into the sea. She looked over the dark water at the silent flashes of lightning, as the distance swallowed the sound. Her thoughts centered on her mother, and the days spent at the hospital sitting by her bedside.

Infection had raged through Anna Reardon's body, but unlike Lea's father, who died almost immediately after coming back from Europe, her mother lingered. There was no consciousness. The incoherent speech pattern that both parents showed on their return quickly progressed to a coma. Only the heart machine's quiet blip gave any assurance her mother was still alive.

The hospital staff came and went with sterile efficiency to check IVs or draw blood. Lea understood the difficulty of trying to talk when wearing the required mask, gown, boots, cap, and gloves put on before entering the room. The entire outfit was discarded in a special bag before leaving.

When her mother had a particularly bad spell, it was all she could do not to remove her mask and try to comfort her. The staff had warned her of the necessity for protection.

The large sign on the door gave the reason: Isolation. Not only would her mother's weak immune system not survive the introduction of another bacterium or virus, but there were fears of spreading the unknown organism responsible for her mother's sickness and father's death.

The doctors had counseled Lea that her mother would likely not survive. She refused to accept their certainty, as if by not acknowledging the words, it would not be allowed to happen.

"You're strong, Mama," she remembered saying. "You won't let this beat you."

The young doctor who came to check warned the end would be soon. Still, Lea went home for a change of clothes, stubbornly determined death would not take her mother. When she returned, the bed was empty, the room already disinfected for the next patient. She never had a chance to say goodbye to her mother.

Rolf moved to Lea, taking her hand as she stood staring at the water. "Whatever it is, if I can help…"

Jerked back from her memories, she turned away from him. "No. Talking about my mother…I…" She shook her head to clear away the tears. "When I was at the inspector's office, he told me that whoever tore apart my room was very thorough."

He said nothing about her changing the subject. Lea had begun to open up, and trusted him enough to confide about the diary. Whatever happened concerning Lea's mother, she wasn't ready to talk about it.

"The inspector thought the thief was looking for something specific. He asked if I had any idea what the person might be after. I told him about the diary. He thought the book unusual enough to call one of his colleagues, Ulrik Orensson, a specialist in Nordic history. That's the man I met at his office yesterday.

"After examining the book, drawing, and stone, Professor Orensson…"

"What do you mean? The diary has a drawing and stone inside?"

"The picture is a battlefield scene. The stone, he said, was a rare form of amber. After studying the drawing, the professor decided it was a map that contained hidden codes using runes, and it was probably written by someone trying to escape the Allied invasion in a submarine. The translation of the book pointed to a treasure stolen by the Nazis, but he said there wasn't enough information to identify the object, or where it had been hidden."

Lea's voice was an unemotional monotone. She ran her hands through the sand, continuously sliding the grains through her fingers.

"Both men agreed whoever broke into my room was probably after the book and stole my camera to throw off any investigation."

She walked to the water to wash the sand from her fingers. "Rolf, I don't want to believe my family was involved in a Nazi theft." She pulled up a corner of her shirt to dry her hands. "But I need to know." Lea looked up at him. "I need to know why my mother was so secretive. Why would she leave the diary for me? My parents worked for the government, providing knowledge and opportunities for underdeveloped countries. They would know the right people to give the diary to. Why didn't they?"

The pieces were coming together. He now understood the reason Stasi agents were interested in Lea's family. If the diary gave answers to the whereabouts of a priceless artifact from World War II, that would be motive enough to commit murder. It was time to tell her what he knew about her family. Putting his hands on her shoulders, he turned her to face him. "Lea, I have information you should know."

Per strained to hear their conversation from his hiding place outside the cottage. He had kept an eye on their movements all evening. He had relaxed and dozed after sensing no movement from the couple after the bedroom light went out.

A small shelter of underbrush had kept him relatively dry during the short storm. The frequency of bad weather made this an unusual June. Öland was normally dry during the summer months. The angry weather matched his mood.

Taken by surprise when Lea walked out to the beach with Sundren following, Per had to scramble to recalibrate his electronic hearing device. Unfortunately, clarity of the conversation remained weak.

As Per tried to adjust the headset, all sound from his earphones ceased. In an attempt to regain transmission, he woke a sleeping bird. The resulting screech was loud and long.

The sound was enough for Rolf to forget about his intended explanation about her family. Instead, he moved quickly toward the trees. Per noted his advance and waited for the American, his knife ready.

Rolf stopped to listen again. Hearing nothing more, he turned and walked back to Lea. Wrapping his arms around her, he smiled, not wanting to worry her. However, the thought that someone might be out there stayed with him.

"Sorry, I thought I heard something."

She saw the brief look of concern, but Rolf revealed nothing.

"What's wrong?"

"Nothing."

Lea didn't believe him. Pulling away, she looked at him directly. "Is it only women you mistrust?"

Her question took him by surprise and he answered with a tone colder than he intended.

"Is that what you call the hours we've spent together, an example of my mistrust?"

Her face reddened, but she pushed forward, determined to get an answer. She knew what happened in his past was none of her business, and thinking of her sharing her own personal confidences, she understood.

But, if this was going to be more than a shallow affair, she had to take the chance and try to find out what caused such bitterness, even at the risk of ending their relationship. Lea assumed it was from a failed love affair. It never crossed her mind that asking about his past would open doors in her own life.

"It's obvious you love women, but for some reason, I don't think you like us. Am I right?"

His face hardened, thinking of his mother.

Lea saw the change, but kept to the subject, hoping he would open up. "I understand very well how things from the past can affect your life, and how hard you try to keep them inside. When I was fourteen, a boy from my neighborhood tried to rape me." She stopped talking, stunned by her unintentional confession.

Rolf had no words of comfort great enough to offer. All he could do was hold her tight. She stiffened and pushed him away.

"I'm fine. What happened is long over." The words came too fast. Even as she tried to smile, Lea searched for a safer topic.

"Tell me about your mom and dad. Do you come from a big family? Any brothers or sisters?"

Hearing the anxious tone in her voice, he understood she was not fine, and that night from her past was far from over or forgotten. His mind turned to anger and retribution aimed at the person who did this to her. Though in reality, as much as pummeling this jerk might soothe his temper, it would gain Lea nothing. If he wanted to help her, Rolf knew he had to let her in. He searched for the right words to begin.

"In my life, I've had many acquaintances, but very few friends. I have no brothers, sisters, grandparents, aunts, or uncles. I haven't seen or heard from my mother since I was twelve. That's when she ran away to Europe with her latest lover. After that, my father abandoned any pretense of family."

Rolf spoke in a cold, sterile tone, describing his mother and father which underlined how difficult those years had been. They had both spent years erecting barriers. Rolf had taken the first step. Now it was her turn.

Lea knew the thoughts she kept on the surface would be easy to share. Those she had purposely set apart would be much harder to put into words. "Walk with me," she said.

As the couple set out, Per decided to return to his apartment. Ulrik had ordered their surveillance and would be anxious for a report. First, he cleaned the site, making sure nothing remained that could link him to the area.

Stasi elite had an unforgiving attitude toward ineptness, and he had already made embarrassing mistakes. This was all Lea's fault. She had tricked him to look like a fool. Rolf Sundren clearly meant more to her than she led him to believe. Now his careful planning and preparation had to be altered. He would be forced to ask Stasi permission to eliminate Sundren.

Per felt an odd sense of disappointment. Had Lea purposely misled him? Now, after Sundren, she was just another man's soiled leftover. They would both pay.

As Per moved away, a second man emerged from hiding. Walking over to the site the young Stasi had just swept, he placed a smudged footprint where the American was sure to find it.

Holding Rolf's hand tightly as they walked, Lea again dredged up the memories of her fourteenth birthday. She told the story of her grandmother's death, and the fear and humiliation of her encounter with Brad. She talked about her nightmare and the enigmatic words that began the rhyme.

After finishing the last sentence, she was surprised to feel relief. It was the first time she recognized the extent to which her life had been disrupted. Because of that night, or maybe in spite of it, Lea had chosen a narrow, safe life, determined to keep her shame and guilt private.

"Until now, I never understood how much of myself I lost. Besides my grandmother's death, I didn't realize hidden somewhere in the back of my mind, I blamed myself for Brad's attack. Somehow, I must have encouraged him."

"You've punished yourself for actions and circumstances that were never your fault. Why didn't you tell someone how you felt?"

She couldn't control the tears as she recalled the pain of her parents.

"My mother and father were so upset at what happened to me. They both cried. And then to lose my grandmother." Lea shook her head. "I just wanted to make everything right for them again. I couldn't bring back MorMor, but I could stop their worry over me."

She closed her eyes briefly. "I convinced myself and my parents that since nothing happened, I was fine. The uncomfortable feeling around boys...normal teenage anxiety." She stopped for a moment and tried to smile. "Writing stories helped take away some of the pain, but my distrust never went away...I..." Lea struggled to regain her composure and continue. "When I got older, there were a few men who wanted to get serious. When talk turned to commitment or marriage, I made sure the relationship ended."

She looked at Rolf. "Then I met you. And you forced me to reconsider everything I thought I knew about men."

17

ÖLAND, 1989

Per felt a familiar rush of energy as he entered his apartment. Striding back and forth through the cramped rooms, he allowed the intensity to wash through him. There would be no sleep while this force controlled his motions, this passion that fused mind and body into a synergy of power and destruction, the excitement that was death.

He planned the attack to take place in the Brewhouse tavern on Öland. Per had learned the time and place of a meeting between Inspector Youngmark and Rolf Sundren from Ulrik. He would be waiting for the American.

A passing brush would deliver a single prick from a poisonous stick hidden among the stems of a flower bouquet. The neurotoxin he planned to use was a particularly nasty substance found on the skin, liver, and ovaries of the puffer fish. Added to another compound of his own invention, the completed mixture would immediately paralyze the target's nervous system. The dose intended would keep Rolf alive and aware, but outwardly give every appearance of death. In the confusion, he would slip close to the fallen American, making sure he understood every detail of what was about to take place, and who was responsible for his terror. Per rehearsed his speech to Sundren.

"You will hear the siren of the ambulance. A death bag will be zipped over your body. You will feel the cold of the morgue, the hardness of the stainless steel dissection table, the smell of rotting flesh. You will suffer every slice of the pathologist's scalpel, every pull and jerk of the saw as it cuts through your bone. You will scream for death as a release from pain, but no sounds will come. Only when your heart is removed, or your skull sliced open and scalp peeled back to extract the brain, will your suffering end."

It was a fitting demise to the interfering American, he thought. Inspector Youngmark would initially be suspicious, questioning the coincidence of Rolf Sundren's death and Per's own timely disappearance for a week. But the sophisticated poison dissipates quickly after death, and such an obscure cause would be overlooked by a small-town detective. Even if the inspector proved clever enough to ship the body to the forensic lab in Linkoping for analysis, it would be too late. Murder is bad for any tourist trade. In a short time, the episode would be forgotten.

The phone rang. Per quickly answered the call from Ulrik.

"The break-in to Lea Reardon's room has caused the inspector to become suspicious of you. He is asking too many questions about your background. Our network of agents in Sweden is at risk. One week away from the island is not enough. Your use on Öland is over, Knudsson."

Per accepted the judgment without argument. "What are my orders?" he asked.

"Your written instructions from headquarters will arrive shortly. After they are carried out, you will return to Germany." Ulrik hung up the phone.

Per sat back, thinking over what Ulrik said. Sundren's death would not change his situation. If he had been able to locate the Gypsy responsible for the petty thievery of Lea's camera, he would be dead. Per would obey. However, before he left, there was unfinished business. Willingly or unwillingly, Lea would accompany him to Berlin. Lea had told him that she had no set itinerary. There was no family, and her few close friends had no idea when she would return. People who embraced isolation made his job easier.

A brief note would be left at Kalmarsson Inn, giving Sundren's death as a reason for getting away by herself. It would be a long while before anyone questioned her prolonged absence. By then it would be too late. Thinking of her tethered and helpless made him smile in anticipation.

"I like it slow and rough," she would say. It was what women always said.

"I will give you everything you want," he would reply. Per intended to pleasure her first, knowing his gratification would come later. He pictured the bag holding his instruments. His loins hardened when he thought about his skinning tool, with its sweeping blade and curved tip. He didn't use the typical stainless steel. Those were too difficult to sharpen. He preferred the older carbon steel blade which he kept honed in readiness.

"What are you doing…?" Her voice would be tinged with fear as he grabbed her. One fast hit and Lea would be unconscious. "What happened?" she would say upon awakening. "Oh my God! Get these ropes off me." Then she would scream.

Per would open his bag and pull out his knife. "I'm going to skin you from top to bottom. First, I will separate your skin from the tender meat underneath." He would enjoy her begging as he started the process. "Then I will use the curved tip of the knife to gut your abdomen without damaging your internal organs. It won't take long," he would assure Lea.

When he was finished, the neighborhood dogs would enjoy her organs. The rest he would cut up and dispose in the Baltic. It was what whores deserved. Now that Ulrik had access to the diary, Per was confident Stasi interest in Lea had ended, and she would be his. Exhausted, his body covered with sweat, he sank into a cushioned chair and called Ulrik's line. He would relay his elimination method for Sundren, but keep his plans for Lea to himself.

After listening to Knudsson's surveillance report of the couple's movements and the graphic description of Per's planned assassination of Rolf Sundren, Ulrik set a time for the two men to meet and hung up the phone. He would give Per the suitcase. The young agent expected the bag to contain his orders and other needed documents for a new life. Knudsson was eager for his identification papers and coordinates of the submarine that would take him to safety after Sundren's death.

Experience had taught Ulrik that there were many types of men, including those like Per, who took great joy in death. This was neither an aberration nor an anomaly, simply fact. Torture and murder were acceptable tools used to facilitate a planned directive, but never to increase one's own pleasure. Initially he had been concerned at using a man with such perversions.

Stories of Per's sexual deviations and torture of women were known in Berlin, but this predilection was considered a minor flaw, unless it compromised a mission. It was more important the person accept the righteousness of the cause and be programmed to follow orders without question. Ulrik believed other modern covert agencies, whether democratic or communist, agreed with this line of thinking.

Budget constraints dictated the bulk of money allotted to espionage be spent on high-tech electronics, not the people trained to gather information. Training agents takes time and patience. Temptations are many in the covert field. In today's world, Ulrik saw too many operators whose loyalty could be compromised by money and women, among other things.

In Ulrik's opinion, a mind molded in obedience and a straight line of thinking, rather than the broader realm of logic and deduction, was a dangerous flaw in this methodology. However, in the end, he needed someone to take responsibility. Knudsson's behavior during a 1988 operation made him the chosen candidate. It had been rumored that the selection of music, during the Estonian festival, would include songs encouraging national pride. The trend toward nationalism was a danger to the unity of the USSR. Ulrik needed to keep a close eye on the situation as well as get information from Mr. and Mrs. Reardon concerning the diary.

ESTONIA, 1988 MUSIC FESTIVAL

"Your mission," Ulrik had told Knudsson, "is to observe the Reardons during the Festival, and look for an opportunity to kidnap them." Ulrik wanted to know what information, if any, the couple had about the diary. "Once you have secured the Reardons, you will wait for me to arrive at the hotel.

"In preparation, I want you to mix a mild drug that will ensure confusion and temporary memory loss to Mr. and Mrs. Reardon," Ulrik ordered. While under its influence, he would be able to extract the couple's thoughts.

"No invasive torture, Knudsson! It is possible I will have to interview the couple again. I want no lasting effects, mental or physical. The abduction is to be wiped from their memory. Do you understand your orders?" Ulrik had asked.

"Yes. I will follow them exactly," Knudsson affirmed.

Arriving at the hotel first, Per decided to prove his expertise to Ulrik. The combination of drugs and electric shock peeled knowledge from the Reardons' brains like the skin of a ripe banana. Their information became useless babble. Whatever insight the two might have possessed about the diary was lost; the damage to their intellect and sanity, irreversible.

To avoid an investigation, Ulrik had been forced to administer a lethal virus to mask Knudsson's error. It would take months, but the couple would die. It was a mistake he would not forget.

ÖLAND, 1989

He smiled to himself. He had purposely not reported the transgression to Stasi headquarters. "Knudsson, you have shown your ability to me and the organization. I have sent a message praising your loyalty and efforts," Ulrik had said. That report effectively saved the young agent's life. To Ulrik, a quick death was a waste of resources. He had arranged to use Per's talents, while making sure the young Stasi paid for his indiscretion.

The knowledge Ulrik gleaned from Knudsson's personality file proved to be an invaluable tool for the successful manipulation of the young agent. Like a grand puppeteer, Ulrik maneuvered events and people to suit his purpose.

"Knudsson, I have no current report on your surveillance of Sundren and Lea Reardon. Is there a problem?" he had asked.

As Ulrik anticipated, Per became increasingly frustrated with the constant glitches in his electronic equipment, and the inability of his poisonous brew to have the desired effect on the young woman.

"No," he assured Ulrik. "I am working on adjusting my equipment to get maximum coverage of their conversations."

"Knudsson, I need answers, not excuses," Ulrik had stated bluntly. Per faced his mounting failures with an anger escalating to fury, promoting more mistakes.

Ulrik enjoyed magnifying the young agent's errors. It pushed his total loss of control closer. The young Stasi had no idea his apparatus was modified to fail, and the drug he had administered to Lea—a harmless purgative.

Sundren's unexpected presence proved a bonus. Over the years, he had dealt with men like Rolf Sundren, greedy men who used any and all methods to accumulate wealth. He considered them no better than vermin, although in this case, beneficial vermin. It was the American's romantic interference that had the egoistic Per teetering on the edge, and ripe for a grand finish.

Ulrik looked over research on the American. The man's interest and amateur expertise in Scandinavian runes would prove useful. If Lea asked Sundren to examine the diary, he was confident Sundren would accept his doctoring of the drawing without question.

It would send Sundren, and anyone he confided in, looking in the wrong direction. The man's life had contributed to Ulrik's purpose, as would his death, courtesy of Per.

For Knudsson, there would be no escape to Germany. Following his assassination of Sundren in the Brewhouse on Öland, Ulrik planned for Per to be apprehended by the inspector.

To be certain Knudsson's encounter with the detective had lethal results, he had replaced the young Stasi's weapon with a broken copy. If by chance Lars's aim only maimed Per, Ulrik calculated with comfortable surety that the indoctrinated agent would choose a swift death by his own hand, rather than capture.

Earlier that day, Ulrik had packed the suitcase he would give Per. There was only one other paper he had to insert. Knudsson would be instructed not to open the case. And following protocol, Ulrik was confident Lars would not tamper with the bag turning it directly over to Swedish agents.

Ulrik rolled up all the papers used to create and perfect his forgeries. He kept one separate, which he intended for Per's case. Ulrik placed the group of papers in the stove and made sure the bundle was consumed in flames until only ashes remained. The single paper he set aside would buy him a new life. He was very proud of his efforts. It had taken many sheets and countless hours to craft his flawless work. The documents Ulrik considered his greatest forgeries were the last piece of an elaborate hoax of his own design.

The possibility of incriminating Nazi records and the capture of a double agent had served as the perfect decoy to tempt Swedish intelligence. Unlike many forgers, Ulrik considered himself a perfectionist. There was no steaming combination of coffee and tea to give the paper age. That ploy was for amateurs. He had always been one to think ahead. Before leaving Königsberg in 1945, he had been clever enough to take samples of writing paper with official letterheads, as well as a Reich seal to ink any papers needed in the future. Anything he made would satisfy the most stringent inspection.

Ulrik had known that Swedish intelligence would not ignore the report on the *Hitler Document*. He made sure they intercepted the cover letter addressed to him and likely reported the incident to Lars Youngmark. Ulrik knew they would be watching to find out more. He would not disappoint them.

He had been careful to be as authentic as possible, making sure the fraudulent document would not be uncovered until he was ready. There were no mistakes. An examination in detail would show no anomalies in the Nazi documents. The pulp composition of the paper, the ink, the seal, everything was genuine, only the content was fake.

The end would come when Swedish authorities found the paper he had placed in Per's suitcase. That paper was identical to the *Hitler Document*, the text he was supposed to broker for his immunity package, but with one critical difference. The paper in the briefcase had the author's marks along one side, showing the manner in which the phony document was created. It was the forger's practice sheet. Recovery of this paper would prove the document he had allegedly removed from the diary was unquestionably a fake. It would stop agents from any further searches and effectively kill all interest in the book.

With Sundren's death, Lea Reardon would again endure the loss of a loved one. Ulrik considered that a prime opportunity to exploit her vulnerability. With her family gone, she was the only person alive who knew the words from the missing diary page.

Over the years, using various methods, he had been able to discern enough parts of the story to learn about the rhyme and grasp its importance. He felt sure being in Sweden would trigger the woman's memory of the verse.

Opening the door to his hiding place, Ulrik carefully unwrapped the exquisite amber box he had taken from Ragnar's cottage. Picking it up, he stroked the resin enjoying the feeling of warmth that spread through his fingers. He removed the scholar's ring from inside the box and was struck by its superb craftsmanship. He slid the band on and off his middle finger. It fit as though it were made for him.

Looking at these two articles reminded him of the years lost to this single-minded obsession. Finding the Amber Room had become an all-consuming passion. At first, he had focused on finding the missing diary page. When he concluded the paper had been destroyed, he concentrated on Mr. and Mrs. Reardon, and finally Lea. The trap had been set, the bait was taken, and the chosen players were acting out their parts. All he had to do was wait. The woman had the answer. This time it would be his.

Ulrik looked at the time judging how long it would take to walk downtown to meet the inspector, but first, the meeting with Per. There was still more to do. He checked his book, making sure last-minute details had been completed.

Military records lost or amended, hospital information displaced, photographs removed or altered. Ulrik knew how this operation would end, but he had to leave enough room to maneuver changes.

As a seasoned operative, he knew the value of careful planning and patience. Unfortunately, those traits had previously failed to secure the Amber Room. Some would blame bad luck. The superstitious would attribute his lack of success to the curse. He knew it had been his own repeated carelessness that resulted in the years of delay, frustration, and disappointment.

It would be different this time. He refused to think of another failure. When this was over, he would have the life he deserved.

Ulrik looked down at the smooth skin of his hands before sliding on the gloves. The plastic surgeon had finished what the acid had started on his hands and fingertips. His prints were gone. Soon this part of his life would be over. Ulrik would no longer have to play cat and mouse with the KGB and Swedish agents keeping him under watch. The building holding files on citizen and agent alike would fall quickly when the Soviet bloc collapsed like a house of cards. People would be hungry for vengeance. Agents of the Soviet state, who had created such fear in the populace, would know fear themselves, as the hunters became the hunted.

Once he secured the boxes holding the Amber Room, Ulrik planned to seek legal protection and right of possession under salvage laws. He understood the fight would be long and riddled with opposition concerning ownership, especially by the Soviet Union. With the support of the West, he suspected his chance of obtaining the masterpiece was good. If Russia was allowed to legally claim the treasure as the last owner of record, it would open the door to a spate of lawsuits.

Any nation guilty of looting artifacts in time of war would be liable for reparations to the legal owner. Would the stolen treasures be returned? The legal and moral questions were as twisted as they were undeniable.

Even if the unthinkable happened, and one day nations temporarily turned their back on war, embraced old enemies, and in good conscience returned stolen artworks to their proper owners; many of the institutions, collectors, and museums that received their rightful property would discover, upon close examination and testing, just how many looted artifacts were fake. How many stolen masterpieces had been scrupulously duplicated by master forgers? How long would it take the original owners to find that some their returned masterpieces were copies?

Ulrik laughed at the scenario, wondering who would get blamed for the forgeries, and how many international incidents, law suits, and threats of retaliation would emerge from such a debacle? He had no sympathy for fools.

On the other hand, for those who had aided in his search for the Amber Room, he would be generous. The public would become aware of those individual heroes, like the Reardon family, whose tragic deaths played a role in his recovery of this magnificent treasure. A book would be a certainty, maybe a movie. It had been long in coming, years of hiding and searching in too many countries. He had abandoned his allegiance to British intelligence immediately after his escape from Königsberg, choosing to work in Sweden, and for the communists as a double agent. That had given him the needed mobility to continue his quest, and a lucrative side operation for an agent willing to take the risk of selling classified information. The buyers who contracted his services were worldwide and not interested in how their material was obtained, only that it was accurate.

It didn't matter to Ulrik whether a client was a communist regime, a democratic nation, or an aspiring dictator. Corporations came to him, and their competitors sought him out as well. It seemed everyone had something to hide. As long as they paid his fees, it made no difference who got the information or how it was used. The game was wearing thin, however, and he would be glad when this part of the charade was finished.

Initially, he had been able to understand many of the scholar's notes, the academic who treated the Amber Room as his own. The scholar's writings enabled Ulrik to recover a few minor art pieces for Moscow, as well as selling a number to black market dealers. But it was only after the death of Stalin that Ulrik sought Moscow's backing and protection for his search to locate the Amber Room. Until then, he considered it healthy to remain anonymous to the schizophrenic personality that had dominated the Soviet State.

Ulrik knew well the results of Stalin's terror, the purge that had dominated the Soviet Union when the Georgian ascended to power. Totalitarianism became a way of life. Vast numbers of friends from Stalin's early days, military leaders and officers, politicians, and the intellectual elite, were shot or sent to work in gulags. The few who escaped were tracked down and assassinated. When Stalin started his blood bath on the peasants, it became understood that no one was safe.

The fear diminished only after the dictator's death, but the "big brother watching syndrome" remained a way of life for anyone under the domination of the Soviet Union.

As the years passed, the Cold War heated up. The NKGD became the KGB; the old leaders inside the Kremlin aged and died, and new ones took their place. However, the return of the stolen Amber Room to Mother Russia was always a priority.

Ulrik knew his value to the Soviet State. The KGB covertly placed him as their direct operative in the Stasi elite. With such credentials, he had the power and leverage to work independently.

As a double agent working in Sweden, Ulrik used the years to build a false identity and a secure home base. He was able to pass reams of confidential material from his position as an intelligence operative to East Germany and the Soviet Union.

To keep the rope of intrigue pulled tight, Ulrik made sure Swedish counterintelligence gained critical information concerning the Soviet subs silently patrolling the channels between Sweden and the Soviet nation.

Ulrik smiled at his reflection in the hall mirror as he passed by. It was time to meet Per, and then have his meeting with the inspector. His memories took him back to the beginning, back to the city of Königsberg. He whistled a jaunty tune as he walked toward town.

18

KÖNIGSBERG, 1942–1945

A specialist in breaking codes, with a knowledge of navigation and fluent in German, Ulrik had been the first choice by the British to be smuggled into Nazi Königsberg as an operative. Sometimes, Ulrik remembered him with fondness, the man he called the scholar, the man who nurtured and cared for the crates of amber like they were his children. The two had become friends—one trained in espionage, the other a scholar of classical art. They were drawn together by a mutual love for chess, an interest in ancient languages, and a passion for the Amber Room.

It was the scholar who tried to stop Ulrik from dipping his hands into concentrated acid in a drunken attempt to obliterate tobacco stains, but he had understood his reasons. Anyone in this city who gained entrance into the upper echelons of Nazi trust was likely a nonsmoker, unless their status or profession made them indispensable to the cause.

Forms of addiction were considered an abnormality and threat. Usually, the average person ignored Nazi attempts at indoctrination and accompanying decrees unless it affected them directly.

It was dangerous for anyone to use a substance the Reich declared a hereditary contamination and a menace to racial purity. In the beginning, many in Germany considered the Fuhrer's declarations as nothing more than propaganda. Ulrik did not. Recalling the dictator's earlier writings, he believed every word.

To secure the pureness of the Aryan race, the Reich chose the science of eugenics as one way to reach their objective. Those

Germans who embodied the finest examples of the desired mental and physical attributes were selected to copulate and breed. Conversely, any group that threatened the expansion of this correct genetic disposition was removed from the population and eliminated.

The end result would perpetuate those traits decreed to make German Aryans superior to all others, while distilling out any examples that diluted this perfection. The idea took on genocide proportions when six million men, women, and children were annihilated for being Jewish. And the numbers swelled like the bloated corpses they represented, when the murders of Roma, those with mental and physical impediments, drug users, and homosexuals were counted.

A heavy tobacco user since age twelve, Ulrik's stained skin and fingertips had been chemically treated and sanded by pumice stone before leaving Britain. Unfortunately, his craving for nicotine had not been erased.

Promising himself to smoke only a few, smuggling the British cigarettes had almost proved his undoing. Both hands became discolored with the telltale evidence of cigarette smoking once again. An amateur attempt to bleach his skin with acid had caused deep patches of mottled scarring, ragged fingertips, and prompted an official inquiry.

He had been surprised by the scholar's support for his story of being burned in a chemical accident. It would be three years before he found out what favor the man expected in return.

The scholar admitted to Ulrik a growing concern for the safety of the Amber Room at the hands of Nazi loyalists. The automatons carried out the dictator's every whim, and would likely never question an order to destroy many of the world's greatest artifacts if the word came from their Fuhrer. Those in the top ranks of the Reich, who planned to save the Nazi movement by escaping with enough treasure to finance a new invasion, were just as dangerous.

These were the men who knew the worth of the looted art works, where they were located, and had the means to appropriate the masterpieces. If the war was lost, this group would disappear into the ranks of civilians escaping to the shores of a sympathetic country. The Amber Room would go a long way to help pay for the future creation of a fourth Reich.

With the escalation of Allied bombing, a timely move to an open courtyard saved the crates from destruction. As the castle lay in ruins, the Amber Room was put under the protection of Gauleiter Erich Koch. Some assumed it would be transported to Saxony–Wechselburg in early January. The Soviets broke through the Eastern Front before this could take place, making travel difficult. Most believed the crates were moved to an underground bunker beneath a local tavern. Only the scholar knew the truth. He planned an escape and trusted no one but himself with the final hiding place of the masterpiece.

Those last weeks proved a chaotic mixture of frightened citizens abandoning the area, and German troops trying to mobilize men and equipment. In the frenzied confusion, no one questioned the movement of numerous crates.

Using a handful of his trusted friends, the boxes were removed from the bunker at night, one at a time, to avert suspicion. The crates were taken to a barn close to the docks and hidden under large piles of hay and cow dung.

The scholar's note was slipped under Ulrik's door, early on December 16, 1945. A submarine was waiting. Instructions were to leave everything behind, talk to no one, and depart for the docks immediately. Remuneration would be considerable for assistance.

Ulrik watched crewmembers drag one last crate down to the deserted pier to be loaded on the submarine. He noticed the cadre of soldiers usually on guard near the warehouses was nowhere to be seen. He assumed someone paid the group handsomely to abandon their posts for a nearby beer hall.

When the heavy work was over, Ulrik joined the group. The crew was just sufficient to man the submarine. The passengers numbered twelve, including company executives, party officials, and assorted family members. Their common denominator was money. Forged documents were expensive, and the crew, even though friends of the scholar, had to be well paid to ensure loyalty and silence.

Ulrik took his place to help navigate the U-boat, avoiding the underwater minefields and vengeful Russian subs.

"Scholar, it is time. I need your maps and charts."

The man spread the papers in front of Ulrik. The small journal he always carried in his shirt pocket remained private.

"The plan is simple, Orensson. You are to sail across the Baltic to this small, sparsely populated island, off the Swedish coast," he pointed to Öland. "Steer around the south end to the west side of the island. You will remain in charge of the crew. I will give a change of clothes, false passports, and money in Swedish kronor to your men. For your expertise, the compensation will be very generous," he added.

"What about the passengers?" Ulrik asked.

"I will take care of the passengers," the scholar asserted. "Once it is dark, we will leave the submarine in small groups, and paddle by raft to an isolated area of Öland." He pointed to the place on the map. "From the island," he drew a line across the water with red pen, "we cross Kalmar Sound, here, to reach the Swedish mainland." He put a red dot to show the place. "After that, each person will make their own way.

"Ulrik, you will make sure the charges are activated before you abandon the sub. The Amber Room will be safe at the bottom of the Baltic until we are able to recover the crates."

It was a difficult voyage for the uninitiated. The submarine ran submerged until it was forced to ventilate and recharge batteries.

"Mama, my stomach is sick. The smell is terrible," Clara cried.

"I am sick as well. Be brave, it will end soon," her mother assured. The claustrophobic conditions took its toll on the group. The stench of diesel fuel and unwashed bodies caused many to become ill. The scholar had chosen his crew with care, but he would soon learn not carefully enough. There was a traitor on board.

Everything went as planned until Öland was spotted through the periscope. It was time. Ulrik had poisoned the drinking water, but he planned for the crew to feel the effects before the passengers. Already incapacitated, the men would die within minutes. The others were surprised when a gun was raised.

Orensson smiled at the youngsters, calming their fears. "Children, it's time to play pirate. While I tie everyone up, I want the boys to search through your fathers' pockets and take all their money. Girls, you look for jewelry. Your mothers have secret hiding places. Don't let them fool you," he taunted. "We'll put everything in a big pile and you can play with your booty. When our voyage is over, the game will end," Ulrik said. The children laughed at their new diversion and leeringly threatened their parents with consequences if they didn't cooperate.

"You will walk the plank," one boy threatened.

"And hang from the yardarm," a girl chimed in.

The little ones enjoyed their new amusement. Orensson knew it gave the adults a false hope for life, a reason to cooperate, and time for the chemical to work. As an agent, Ulrik used death as a last resort. During war, there were too many operatives who dispatched men, women, and children without conscience. Unfortunately in this case, there was no alternative. No one could be left alive who knew the resting place of the Amber Room.

Ulrik searched the scholar's pockets himself and removed his notebook. He leaned close to whisper sympathetically, "Your discomfort will soon end."

He spoke to the youngsters. "We are almost at our final destination. It is time to put all your booty into the captain's treasure bag." He held out the sack and the children followed his orders willingly.

Leaving the group, he returned to the helm. Ulrik brought the submarine to the surface one last time. He disabled the boat, but only activated specific timers. He didn't want a loud spectacle. He damaged the buoyancy tanks to prevent resurfacing and flooded compartments for a quiet death. He wasn't sure how long it would take to recover the Amber Room from its sunken home, but he wasn't worried. The treasure was well packed. If by chance water intruded, Ulrik was confident there would be little damage. He remembered seeing amber pieces floating on the waves of the Baltic Sea until they washed on shore.

The passengers remained quiet, confident of their safety until Ulrik returned with canvas bags tied around his waist. Only then did they recognize his intent to sink the submarine and abandon them to the floor of the Baltic.

As an afterthought, he remembered a ring the scholar wore. It was a piece he always admired, and a corpse needed no jewelry. He hadn't noticed it as the ropes were tied and it wasn't in the pirate bag. He decided to take a second look.

"Where is your ring?" he asked. Ulrik yanked the ropes of the scholar to gain better access, but the man's fingers were empty. He eyed the daughter's closed fist.

"Open your hand, now," he commanded.

"No. I do not want to," answered the child.

Ulrik forced her fingers apart and wrenched the ring away. "This is something you will have no use for."

"Don't do this, Orensson. If you refuse to save us, think of the children," the scholar begged.

"I cannot help you," he said. Ignoring the plea for life, Ulrik tipped his hand in a goodbye salute. He knew the man's ropes had been loosened enough to escape his bonds, but it didn't matter. Even if he managed to escape and open the cover; anyone making it out of the hatch before the explosion would be dead from the poison before the numbing cold of the water claimed a victim.

Ulrik grabbed the bag, climbed the ladder and unlocked the outside hatch. The victim's screams stopped only as the cover slammed. He threw the raft into the rough sea and jumped away from the U-boat.

European peace was at hand, but the military intentions of the victorious Allies were still unclear. It was common knowledge that relations were strained between the United States and the Soviet leader, Stalin. Instability and unease brought confusion and new players to the international table. Those who celebrated the end of war would prove premature. Ulrik considered himself a patient man. He could wait for his reward. He wondered what his tolerance level would have been, if he had known how many years this quest would control.

He had gained needed supplies from a fisherman's cottage before making his way to the Swedish mainland. Ulrik still remembered clearly the moment he opened the bag to look at the scholar's book. He expected charts, names of contacts, and a list of various art treasures that he knew the man had kept concealed from the Russians. He wanted to find everything. Ulrik planned on selling the smaller items to various European and American buyers who hungered for fine pieces of classical art.

Looking through the notebook, his error became obvious. There were no names, no contacts. The boxes on board the U-boat did not contain the Amber Room. The scholar had tricked them.

At some unknown time and place, he had removed the panels from the original crates, and had commissioned a woodworker to make a number of smaller, water-tight containers. Those boxes were then moved to a new location. The scholar made sure that the few drunken lackeys he recruited for the job of repacking and moving the Amber Room were eliminated when they reached their final destination.

The original boxes that were laboriously moved to the barn and then to the submarine contained nothing more than trash.

The notebook referred to the scholar's distrust of those aboard the submarine and their promises to keep the hiding place of the

Amber Room secret. He understood the motivation of greed and ambition. If anyone from the group betrayed the information, only worthless industrial scrap would be found on the sea floor. Only the scholar knew where the treasure was located; and he noted that in case his map fell into the wrong hands, or something happened to him, the answer to finding the masterpiece rested with his daughter's diary.

Ulrik had been furious with himself. Allowing the children to keep their assorted trinkets had cost him the hiding place of the Amber Room. For many years, he had searched other avenues for clues, believing the diary, along with its author, rotted in the dark waters of the Baltic. Then one night in 1978, as he sat in a bar soliciting information on a suspect, he overheard a tale told by a tavern patron about a strange creature that had surfaced off the coast of Öland at the end of World War II.

"I tell you the story of the sea serpent is true. I know Ragnar. He is a good man and a good fisherman. He found a dead girl burped up from the belly of a beast. She held an amber box in her hand." The bar patron looked around to make sure no one except his friend paid attention to his words. "Ragnar stole the box from the child. He took what was given to the gods of the sea." The man shook his head. "He was punished. Ragnar found his wife drowned."

The appearance of the monster had been taken as a bad omen by the fearful islanders. For those susceptible to ancient beliefs connecting amber and magic, the sighting had ignited old fears among the superstitious. Now, whenever a catch was meager or a boat lost to unusual circumstances, that ominous day was resurrected and the legend retold, of Ragnar, the sea monster, the young girl he found floating in the water, and the amber box she held.

Ulrik smiled to himself. He had been given a second chance.

19

ROLF SUNDREN'S COTTAGE, ÖLAND, 1989

U sually an early riser, this morning came too fast for Rolf. He was used to waking up alone. In the past, whatever time he spent with ladies, hotels were used for any pleasures he and his companion had during an evening. He never invited a woman to his home. That was an intimacy he refused, until Lea.

Not wanting to wake her, he got up quietly, dressed, and set the coffee to brew. He wanted a look at Lea's journal. With a steaming cup in one hand, the diary, and a few reference books on runes under his arm, he walked out to the porch.

One of the reasons the runic language intrigued him was the difficulty of translation. In his business, information was synonymous with money. Technology was fallible and easily breached from both a human and mechanical standpoint. It was not difficult for an accomplished industrial spy to gain sensitive material.

Unknowing employees threw out enough information to complete the first step. With discarded manuals, a few names, and common phrases to work from, the spy would chat with random workers on the telephone until gaining a good understanding of work groups and employee absence lists.

After that, it was only a matter of time until an employee, working on an experimental or protected project, took time off. Using the familiarities and clichés common to a company insider, the spy focused on an unsuspecting worker, intent on tricking the person into providing vital information and codes. The scam worked more often than not.

In the early years of his company, a competitor using this ploy managed to obtain phone and computer logs. The spy gained access to Rolf's protected business sources and unpublished technology. Discovering the thief was in his father's employ pushed him to develop new techniques that would protect his company from outside intrusion.

There was no such thing as a single, perfect formula to store, connect, and transmit data. In industrial espionage, someone would always find a way to break through barriers and gain information. Instead, he used complicated cryptograms, varied his methods of storage, and used a series of links to make it more difficult and costly to steal his files. It would be a game of seek and find for the intruder.

As he sat on the front porch steps, Rolf took his first good look at the diary. He set aside the stone, being more interested in the pages of the work itself. After looking at each page, he gave his total attention to the picture. He wanted to examine the rune symbols that Ulrik Orensson found embedded in the drawing. He hoped to have a few answers by the time Lea got up. He knew she would not stop looking until the connection between the diary and her family was found. He understood and respected her tenacity.

After staring for forty-five minutes at the battle scene that made up the foreground of the drawing, Rolf found the first symbols. Considering how well the runes had been hidden, he considered that record time. He had already been told where to look and was well-versed in the language. For someone not expecting the concealment or familiar with the script, the camouflaged letters would be almost impossible to discern.

After taking more time to search out additional symbols, Rolf reached a few conclusions. If the artist intended to convey a message, the method used was unlike anything he was familiar with. The writing was not set in typical runic fashion of symbols grouped together in a linear fashion. And the script itself originated from different eras. Two of the runes came from the sixteen-symbol alphabet used during the Viking period, while two others appeared to belong to the more ancient form containing twenty-four.

A challenging language to comprehend under the best of conditions, this could prove unreadable if the drawing contained only these isolated fragments. On the other hand, it might be the author's first clue. He knew there were very few areas in Scandinavia that contained examples of the more primitive runic tongue. There was no evidence that Öland contained examples of the ancient Elder Futhark, but he had heard rumors of the possibility. In other words, a place where twenty-four, the number of symbols in the old language, meets sixteen, the number of symbols during the Viking age. It was also the first line in Lea's rhyme.

Next, he held the paper to sunlight. Normally his first step, Rolf didn't want to use the common technique until he found and examined the rune script already discovered by Orensson. Examining the drawing for any curious change in light displacement, one small area near the battle scene looked promising. Carefully tracing the lines that appeared somewhat darker than others, another view appeared. Instead of the individual runic symbols he expected, the shadowy rendering was of a place.

Located near the eastern shore of the island, Rolf recognized the outline of Sandby churchyard. It could be a logical connection to the hidden script in the journal since the churchyard contained two fine runestones. Everything was falling neatly into place and that bothered him. It had been too easy to find, too perfect.

Emilio Arganza had been the caretaker of the family summer house. Working with animals had been Emilio's way to teach Rolf patience. But it was his introduction to jigsaw puzzles that honed the young teen's insight and perception. He remembered one summer afternoon, sprawled on his stomach in the barn, trying to fit together pieces of a puzzle he initially thought simple.

Emilio offered only one comment, "Sometimes, my young friend, you miss the magnificence of a forest, by focusing on the beauty of a single tree."

Instead of narrowing his vision to concentrate on lines and symbols, Rolf widened his scope to scan the entire picture. For the first time, he noticed the image had a clear, intricately penned foreground compared to a horizon that was a jumble of hastily drawn stone fences, trees, bushes, and rocks.

The artist had intentionally designed the pen and ink to pull the eye away from the unsettling background and focus instead on the distinct battle scene in the near view.

Why," he mused aloud, "would someone set up a picture in this manner?

"The obvious," he answered himself, "was that the artist centered on the concealed runes and hidden rendering, in order to relay a message.

"Except you don't strike me as obvious or apparent," he said to the person who had skillfully integrated the runic symbols into the pen and ink. He searched the chaotic background for another answer.

Rolf concentrated on the trees and bushes. Skimming with a magnifying glass, he found only a confusing hodgepodge of meaningless lines. He rubbed his eyes to relieve the strain.

Again holding the paper to light, Rolf looked for any subtle variation, more of a whisper than a shout. He centered on a pile of rocks crowded against a stone fence. Comparing it to the other forms, the area appeared somewhat more opaque. The magnifying glass yielded no clue. It was too difficult to visually separate the many shapes layered together. He had to find a way to peel them apart.

Rolf carefully traced every contour and line onto another paper. Slowly he isolated each rock outline, looking for a recognizable shape. Close to the bottom of the layer, he stopped.

It had taken an hour and a half to find, but there it was. Thumbing through the reference book, Rolf confirmed his guess. The illustrated silhouette of the magnificent, granite Karlevi runestone was identical to the rock he had just isolated from the drawing. The famous landmark was virtually indistinguishable when buried among the congested rubble of various size and shaped stones. Rolf's measure of respect grew for the intelligence and talent of the artist. It was a brilliant job of camouflage and deception, but how did it fit into the mystery of the diary?

Taking out a map, he drew a pencil line from Sandby to Karlevi. Sandby was located near the coast, on the east side of the island, while Karlevi was situated on the west coast. Rolf concluded if someone stopped looking for clues after the more obvious view of Sandby appeared, that person would be searching about ten miles away from what he considered the intended site of the author, Karlevi.

The storm had cleansed the air, and the vitality of a reenergized earth surrounded him. Remembering his pocketful of crackers, he whistled for his friend. "Gussie, come on, girl. I have crackers for you." She was always waiting for her handout in the morning.

Rolf walked halfway down the path to the beach when he noticed white feathers. He continued farther to the sheltered copse of trees he knew the pen favored. Some of the ground plants were covered with blood. He looked around for evidence to resolve what had attacked the bird. The area was clean of tracks, but one. He saw the faint outline of a shoe, and remembered the noise he heard last night.

Lea opened groggy eyes to a bright sun shining through the bedroom windows. After a shower, she could accept the light and cheerful attitude of the yellow rays flooding the room. She was a night person. Lea's thoughts were clearer and more creative in the late hours. She forced herself out of bed and into the bathroom. She was thankful for the new toothbrush waiting on the stone vanity.

The toothpaste was half out of the tube, when her hand stopped in midsqueeze. On an open shelf next to the cabinet sat a small marble sculpture of a woman holding a delicate crystal ball. But it was the much larger version of the glass "seeing" crystal eye holding an abundant supply of packaged condoms that made her laugh.

"I like discovering this irreverent sense of humor in you, Rolf. It makes you a little more approachable, more human."

Lea had many reasons to be grateful to him. Without Rolf, she would never have confronted the guilt she had considered unimportant.

It was when the pain of her fourteenth birthday became overwhelming that she initially found comfort in writing. It was her mother who encouraged her to put thoughts on paper as a way to push away fears and regain control over her life.

Lea soon realized she enjoyed the process of creating a story; taking a basic idea, shaping it, forming her characters, adding and subtracting quirks and personalities. She was thankful her books became popular and the money she earned was enough to be independent. Although, when did being an author become an excuse to stay in the house and exclude friends?

She had refused to see anyone during her mother's illness. Instead, when not at the hospital, she sat at home, immersed in pity feeding an anger at her inability to put a sentence on paper. Only now did she recognize her behavior as guilt and depression.

After her shower, she tried to shake out the wrinkles in her clothes. Realizing it was a lost battle, she rummaged around in Rolf's closet, finding a long shirt. She would go back to the inn later for some clothes, then laughed at the thought. She had no intention of leaving. She wanted this time with Rolf, just the two of them alone, no interruptions.

With that in mind, she washed out her clothes in the sink. Looking for a place to hang them, she noticed he had lit the wood in the fireplace. After taking a minute to enjoy the warmth of the flames, she found a length of butcher string in the kitchen and secured the line in front of the fire to hang her wet clothes.

Where is he, she wondered. The coffee in the pot had been sitting for quite a time. Lea dumped the bitter dregs and started a fresh pot. She poked around the room for breakfast ingredients to surprise him. She hoped wherever Rolf had gone, he would be back by the time she finished.

She shook her head at this twinge of domesticity. At home, a McDonald's drive-through was the most energy she expended to feed herself. It wasn't that she didn't enjoy food, especially Mrs. Kalmarsson's cooking. And she had the means. Her kitchen shelf at home was filled with recipes and cooking gadgets. But learning more than the simple basics of cooking to feed only herself had always seemed like a waste of valuable time that could be spent reading and writing.

After considering her limited skills, she settled on bacon and eggs, and hoped Rolf wouldn't get the idea this would become a normal occurrence. Copper pots and pans hung over the stone-topped kitchen island in an orderly fashion.

She smiled as she thought about her large collection of vintage cookbooks. Friends knew better than to make the assumption that her knowledge of food was synonymous with being a gourmet cook. It was the readers who reached that conclusion, and sent countless letters asking about the ethnic recipes presented in each book. Lea always replied, but only to suggest various authors who might answer their questions. To her, cookbooks were a tool that helped bring her *Adventures of Lisa* to life. Her teenage heroine roamed the globe solving mysteries. Recipes from the various countries were always part of the puzzle to be solved.

She pulled the bacon strips apart and placed them in a fry pan. The sizzling aroma filled the kitchen in minutes. Taking pleasure from the homey smells and sounds, it brought back a time when she enjoyed watching MorMor cook. No written recipes or measuring cups for her grandmother. It was a pinch of this, a handful of that.

"I miss those days with you, MorMor. I wish you were here to meet this fellow. I think you'd approve."

Rolf knew Lea was unaware he overheard her as he passed by the kitchen doorway. He quietly turned around to go back outside. If she wanted him to know her feelings, she would tell him, and besides, what could he say? He refused to assign a name to the sharp ache he felt whenever he looked at her, nor come to terms with the need to keep her close.

He didn't have any answers, at least none he would admit. After the mystery was solved concerning the diary and the death of her family, that would be the time to explore the direction of their relationship. The ringing phone changed his direction to the bedroom.

"Yes."

Along with other safety measures, Rolf had installed a secured telephone line when he built the cottage.

"Good work. The money will be transferred to your account." After listening to Stratton's background findings on Ulrik Orensson, he dialed another informant. Rolf trusted Stratton and his information just so far. He wanted to independently confirm the data with another source.

As he matched the two different reports he had been given on the phone, only Orensson's profile differed. Accounts of his physical description deviated. Probably nothing, he thought. Still, he wouldn't be satisfied until he knew more. He went back to the sheet profiling Per Knudsson, Inspector Youngmark, and the people at Kalmarsson Inn.

It had always been this determined attention to detail that kept Sundren Industry International highly successful and competitive. He did his homework and knew how to play the game. When Rolf sat across the table during a merger or buyout, he had already thoroughly researched and profiled the business, as well as the person he was negotiating with.

He ferreted out weaknesses that weren't apparent, both in the people he dealt with and the businesses they represented. Discovering unexpected losses in a glossy portfolio that someone tried to bury was not a rare occurrence. He had learned to measure words and not to underestimate the pull of ambition and desire in the most honest of men or women. He walked away from the bargaining table if the people or the package gave him doubts. This time, Rolf knew he was at a disadvantage.

Before Lea, he had never questioned the worth of his skills. But this was no merger, no takeover, and no game. He couldn't walk away and he couldn't lose, the stakes were too high.

Entering the kitchen, a look of surprise fell over his face as he saw the large breakfast waiting on the table. He watched her pour coffee into two mugs and spread jam on warm slices of toasted bread before untying one of Frieda Benton's aprons from around her waist.

As they sat down to breakfast, he admitted, "I underestimated you, Lea."

She looked happy and relaxed.

"You cooked, I'll do the dishes," he offered.

She watched Rolf, his arms immersed in soapy water, and wondered how long before he tired of this domestic play-acting, and her? How long before he wanted to return to his world and the glamorous women who inhabited it? She would never be able to compete.

"Do you have plans for today?" he asked, as he finished the dishes and put them away. The question was polite, however moot. He already knew the answer. She would be with him. He had no intention of leaving her alone, not after what he found on the beach.

Honing in on the use of "you" rather than "we," she guessed it was his manner of signaling he wanted to be alone. She might be disappointed, but she wasn't ready to admit that fact to him. It was easier to give him what he wanted, not the time for frank honesty.

"I would guess you have business to take care of and I don't want to be in your way. I'll walk back to the inn for some clean clothes and check to see if Reverend Sedgely arrived. Before I left home, we made plans to get together on Öland. He's staying at the inn. I'd like his opinion on the diary."

"Until we find out who broke into your room, don't you think it would be wise to limit access to the book to only those who have already seen it?"

"That's ridiculous! I've known the reverend for years."

"I have a telephone. You can call. If he's arrived, invite him here."

She looked at a clearly irritated Rolf. What made him so annoyed?

"What's wrong with you? I was only doing what you…" Looking up, she saw frustration and something more, fear. What was he keeping from her? Last night, they openly shared confidences. Daylight brought changes. The walls were back up.

"All right, where do you want to start?"

If he wondered why Lea easily deferred to his plans, he didn't comment.

"The runic language is obviously an important part of this mystery, and as luck would have it, one of the most famous runestones is nearby." He kept his tone light.

"Fine. Give me a minute to get ready."

He wanted her away from the cottage. If the intent of their watcher was to only search the beach house, Rolf would offer time and opportunity. While they were at the Karlevi stone, he would tell Lea about the drawing, and try again to explain what happened to her family.

Considering the history of their involvement with the diary, Rolf thought it likely the Stasi were closely monitoring their movements. It made sense that agents wouldn't rush to dispose of Lea as they had her grandmother and parents. This time, they would have to be more careful. The secret police had tried to gain the diary through murder and failed. As the last of her family, if something happened to Lea, the book might be lost to them.

He set the hidden security system, activating the camera to switch on if any of the silent alarms were breached. If someone were to visit while they were out, he would know.

Rolf had given a name to the treasure he thought was aboard the submarine. Last seen in the city of Königsberg near the end of WWII, it had long been the subject of legend, speculation, and countless modern-day treasure hunters. The city of departure, along with the piece of carved amber, gave him enough reason to believe that the boxes mentioned in the diary contained the fabled Amber Room stolen from the Russian summer palace.

And even though the inspector and Professor Orensson pleaded ignorance because the journal was incomplete, Rolf felt sure the two men had guessed the subject of the diary as well. He also considered it reasonable to assume while Orensson examined the drawing, he had found the rendering of Sandby. But did he find more?

Rolf knew the two men only had access to the journal for the hour Lea was present in the inspector's office. It wasn't enough time, even for someone as notably skilled in runes as the professor, to discover the subtle inconsistencies and sift through the multiple layers pointing to Karlevi. The difficulty of finding the initial set of runes would have taken Orensson the better part of their meeting.

Mulling over the information compiled by his sources, Rolf looked for reasons to search for the diary. Greed was a great motivator, but hate, revenge, and politics made willing partners. He was tempted to include Professor Orensson, but there wasn't enough information on the man to make rational inferences on what might be a motive. Rolf concentrated on three names.

Gunnar Johansson's hatred for the Russians was well documented. A carpenter by trade, he was lured to the Nazi movement by the money and steady work. Captured and taken prisoner by the Russians in 1945, Johansson suffered twenty years of abuse and torture in a Siberian gulag. After his release and time spent in a hospital trying to heal scars, both mental and physical, Gunnar came home a broken man. Once healthy with a quick body, the person who returned to Öland had a clumsy gait and fragile mind. The man had every reason to want revenge, but was he capable of attaining it?

Inspector Youngmark was someone not to be underrated. He had worked in intelligence before the death of his wife. The report claimed the inspector's honesty, ethics, and loyalty were never in question, but he took Hulda's loss extremely hard and his resulting instability was labeled a risk to security. The detective's retreat to Öland had not been by choice. Could a forced departure cause enough bitterness against the system to push him into collaboration with the enemy?

The clearest choice however, was Per Knudsson. Both contacts linked him directly to the Stasi organization. Remembering how sick and disoriented Lea had become the night of midsummer, Rolf guessed the bastard fed her drugs in an attempt to get the diary. And if he failed to gain the information before Rolf interrupted, Per might have chanced breaking into Lea's room to search for it. Rolf had to give Stratton's report to Lea. The longer he put off telling her what happened to her family, and the danger she was in, the more difficult it would be to tell her. He had no idea what Lea would do with the information, or what her feelings would be for withholding the knowledge from her.

20

ROLF'S COTTAGE, 1989

Getting ready to leave the cottage, Lea wanted more information on what they were after and where it was located.

"Rolf, what's the name of the stone?" She asked.

"What?" he replied.

"The runestone you're taking me to see, tell me more about it and how far away it is."

"The Karlevi Stone. It was raised around 1000 AD to celebrate Sibbe the Wise. It's only a few miles or so from here." Rolf knew the explanation was short, but at the moment, he was more concerned with scanning the area for unwelcome company than talking about fallen Danish chieftains. He didn't want any more surprises.

Rolf spotted the massive granite rune through the trees. On the open ground surrounding the monument, he relaxed somewhat.

"It's magnificent," Lea exclaimed when the stone came into view.

He laughed as Lea impulsively pulled his face down to give his cheek a quick kiss. Her skin smelled of soap, her clothes a fragrance of sweet wood smoke. It was hard to let her go.

Walking toward the runestone, she pictured a scene of battle-hardened warriors gathered to honor their fallen leader.

"I never cease to be amazed by the treasures that cover this island. At home, I've always enjoyed the historical sights. To look at a house, or handle an object that might be two hundred years old took my breath away." Lea gently ran her fingers over the ancient stone. "But here, to read someone's thoughts about a man who's been dead almost a millennium is unbelievable."

Before Rolf had a chance to comment or ask a question, she looked toward the expanse of water and continued.

"I know this sounds foolish, but in the nightmares I've had since my grandmother's death, I am always in water. There are frightened people. I hear their screams. I smell machine oil..."

"Lea, I might use a lot of adjectives to describe you, but foolish isn't among them. Are you talking about the people aboard the submarine?"

She was surprised by his interest. Lea had expected skepticism and disbelief, maybe because that's how she felt.

"Until I read the diary, it was a nameless nightmare. But now, yes, I think it is the people in the submarine. It sounds crazy, even to me. That's why I haven't said anything. But when Professor Orensson talked about the runic language, I couldn't ignore the connection any longer.

"Remember the rhyme I told you about? It was always the beginning of my nightmare, but I could never remember all the words after I woke up. When the professor talked about the ancient form of twenty-four symbols being reduced to sixteen during the Vikings era, the entire verse came back to me."

It can be seen where twenty-four meets sixteen
In an ancient place where scalds still speak
Of earth scarring battles and blood stains deep
Brave warriors lost and treasure taken
Separate the eagle's dance with the raven
The old gods speak tales of foreboding
Evil seeks the lines unbroken."

Rolf knew the words. They were the same she repeated while standing on the Kalmarsson Inn porch.

"You're not imagining things, Lea. This stone, Karlevi, is the oldest known rune found on Öland. The importance stems from the fact that it's the only example found of an original, complete skaldic verse recorded during the Viking Age. The bulk of runic material that survived comes from a later time and the messages are different. Even the runic script changed form again to accommodate Christianity. But the drawing in your journal doesn't show a scene depicting a medieval fortress church or castle. This picture reminds me of the earlier Viking era. It was common in those sagas to talk of eagles and ravens gorging on battlefield corpses."

Taking the diary, Rolf opened the book to the black-and-white drawing and repeated the first line of the rhyme. "It can be seen where twenty-four meets sixteen. Look at the four rune symbols in the drawing. The first two that you see originated from the ancient Germanic form of twenty-four symbols, while the other two are found in the later Viking era alphabet containing sixteen."

Rolf showed her everything he found earlier in the ink drawing, explaining why he thought the artist intended Karlevi as the actual link, rather than Sandby.

He could tell by her nods she was receptive to his logic. Rolf noticed her stiffen when he stated his skepticism about the inspector and Professor Orensson.

"I'm not sure I completely trust them, Lea. Age, profession, and homeland makes them very familiar with the events surrounding World War II. They would have known your diary almost certainly referred to the Amber Room. Why didn't they mention it?"

Lea didn't answer. She admitted not knowing much about the professor, but he was a good friend of the inspector and she had put her faith in the detective. Rolf's comment wasn't enough to diminish it.

"You seem to have a problem with everyone I know. You had a fight with Per. Now it's the inspector and Professor Orensson. Why leave out Mrs. Kalmarsson and Gunnar? Maybe they're after the diary as well."

Maybe they are, he thought.

"You were even suspicious of the reverend."

"I have a hard time trusting any of your acquaintances until we find out who broke into your room."

Rolf knew she had stopped listening. It might be wise to drop any more character assessments. He put the drawing down.

"Let's look at this another way. I think it's a good bet the rhyme is connected to the diary, possibly written on the missing page of the book. We need to learn more about it, understand how it was meant to be used. If you can focus on the book and your dream, maybe we can figure out when and where your parents got the journal and how you learned the rhyme," he suggested.

Grateful to be away from discussing personalities, Lea thought back to her years in Evanston.

"When your nightmares first began, is there anything unusual you remember, something that stands out in your mind?"

"I know the dreams started when I was fourteen. I always blamed them on what happened with Brad and the death of my grandmother. Until last night, I spent my life trying to forget those memories." She shook her head.

"Think of the time around your birthday. Were your parents at home?" he prompted.

"No. Mom and Dad were out of the country until the morning of my birthday. My friend Sara was off visiting her cousin, and was due home the same time as my parents. Her brother Jake was busy with a new girlfriend, and I was bored. I remember MorMor trying to keep me occupied. She kept me busy in the kitchen. We poked around Andersonville for one of her bargains, and then there was the auction." She hesitated. "The box from the auction house. About a week before my birthday, we went to an auction. My grandmother bought a box that originated here, in Öland. She wasn't going to unpack it until my parents returned from their trip, but we were both too excited to wait. The crate was packed tight and when she pulled off the cover, only the top layer was visible. There were pictures, baby clothes, just all kinds of memorabilia and knickknacks a family would have. But my favorite was a piece of gold jewelry, a ring. This ring."

Lea opened the locket, took out the small stylized gold ring of a bird's head and wings, and handed it to him.

"I was impatient to pull the ring out of the crate for a better look and didn't notice the piece of string attached. I only realized the other end of the strand was fastened to a book when I ripped a page loose. I felt so guilty. I gave the page to my grandmother and promised I would find which book was damaged and repair it. I remember her saying, 'Don't worry. We'll do it together,' but we never got the chance. After the funeral, I found the page caught in the sleeve of her nightgown. I was so angry at losing my grandmother, I tore the paper to shreds." She shook her head, trying to forget her sadness.

He put his arm around her. "Do you want to keep talking about this?"

"I need to finish."

He nodded. "What about the ring, Lea?"

"I couldn't wear it on my hand. Every time I looked, it reminded me of when I found her. I…" Lea fidgeted with the locket. "It was the last thing she gave me. I couldn't get rid of it. The locket was the perfect place to keep the ring."

Rolf held the delicate ring in the palm of his hand. He noticed the unusual cutout design and color of the band, the offset of the head, the intriguing markings that defined the wings. The eagle was a popular subject among Scandinavian artists. Maybe it was a well-made piece of jewelry, but it seemed to be an unfinished work. Something was missing.

"The carving of this band is remarkable." He handed the ring back. "Did you take anything beside the ring?"

She shook her head no.

"When was the last time you saw the box?"

"There was a bad storm that night, and even though I was embarrassed to admit it, I was afraid of thunder and lightning. My grandmother understood and never minded if I crawled into bed with her." Lea could almost see herself climbing onto the high tester bed, snuggling next to MorMor.

"The box was on her bedroom floor, I almost tripped over it. Books and papers were scattered over the bed. At the time I didn't think much about it, I was counting."

She smiled as Rolf furrowed his brows in a silent question.

"Didn't you ever use that trick as a kid? I always counted the time between the flashes and booms and divided by five. That way, I could figure out if the storm was getting closer or moving away. It helped take away some of the fear. Now that I think about it, I remember she was determined to solve something. What was it she said…'riddles,' she was trying to solve a riddle."

Lea focused on remembering every detail. "We really made a pair. I was counting in this ridiculous singsong voice and my grandmother was repeating words, probably trying to translate something from Swedish to English."

Or from German to English, Rolf thought. If Lea had fallen asleep while her grandmother translated the diary, and the woman continuously repeated the rhyme in an attempt to break the cipher, Lea could have absorbed the words without ever being aware.

After the attack by Bradley Farmer and her grandmother's death, the verse became the precursor to her bad dream; while the nightmare itself, with its visions and smells, seemed to mirror the account written in the diary; frightened people, panic, water. It all fit.

"When my grandmother died, my mother and father sorted through her things. I refused. I don't know what they did with the box from the auction. It might have been put in the attic, but more likely, my parents donated it to a charity. I never asked, and I never looked."

"I think the diary was in that box," Rolf said.

"That's a real stretch. It still makes more sense that my parents acquired the book when they were out of the country on one of their trips for the State Department. They always liked to shop the local markets."

"No, I don't think so. Everything took place around the time you brought the box home from the auction house. Remember, you said when you were attacked the night of your birthday your parents ran out of the house, but that your grandmother stayed inside. If a Stasi agent chose that time to look for the box, your grandmother might have caught the person. The agent would have killed her just as the Stasi later murdered your parents. Now you're the one in possession of the diary and the one in danger."

It took a moment for him to realize what he'd done.

"Oh God. Lea, I'm sorry!" The words from his throat were hoarse. "I had no intention of telling you this way."

She was in shock. Her family had been murdered. How did he know? Why hadn't he told her?

Rolf expected a blowup and was uneasy with her silence. "After your room was ransacked, I searched for any information that would tell me if the break-in was random or planned, if you were in danger. My contact unearthed an internal report. It's suspected the East German Secret Police were responsible for what happened to your parents, as well as your grandmother's death. But there was no mention of a diary."

She refused to acknowledge anything he said.

"I wanted to tell you earlier. I was trying to find the right time, the right words."

There was still no sound. He raised the level of his voice, as if decibels would compel her to speak.

"Don't you understand? The Stasi are a dangerous group, and any one of your friends on Öland could be involved. I couldn't let that information get out until I knew who could be trusted."

Nothing. He wanted to provoke an argument. Outbursts of anger he could accept and counter. He grabbed her arms and held tight, hoping for a reaction. She refused to fight and stood still, staring blankly into his face.

"I understand this is your affair, but I won't let you do this alone!" He tried to take on a softer tone as he loosened his grip and reached with one hand to touch her cheek.

"Please, talk to me!" Looking at her face, still empty of response, he finally dropped his hands.

Her sense of betrayal cut deep, but shock turned to fury. Lea refused to give him the satisfaction of admitting how much he hurt her. Remembering her loss of restraint during past arguments, she was grateful for the ability to speak in a controlled manner.

"Oh, I understand. You gathered information concerning the murder of my family and kept it to yourself. You assumed I couldn't handle the truth and needed a protector, someone to keep me safe from people you don't trust. Does that sum up your rationale, or was there something I missed?"

Rolf shook his head in denial, ready to break in and argue.

"No, don't interrupt. You wanted me to talk, let me finish!" Lea lifted her hands and shoved his chest to keep some distance between them.

"The question is why me? Two weeks ago you ignored me. Now you insist on interfering in my life. Why the sudden change? Could it be the diary? You refused me the discretion of handling a personal argument, and for all intent and purposes, blackmailed me to abandon my date and leave with you. Was that to make sure I would be away for the time it took your accomplice to search my room? I can understand your need for the romantic setting, and why you made love to me. You needed my cooperation. But why start an affair? I'm guessing it was your way to hold my loyalty, keep me under control and make sure I wouldn't confide in anyone else. Were you ever really interested in me, Rolf, or has it always been the Amber Room?"

Her fury was spent. When the sounds of pain crept into her voice, she stopped. She wouldn't give him the satisfaction.

"You're wrong! I don't give a damn about finding your treasure." Rolf thought Lea should be a politician. She took everything and spun it to fit her own interpretation. He had to make her understand.

"I didn't want you hurt." Rolf was thinking not only of the danger from whoever murdered her family, but also of Per and his mistreatment of her at the Midsummer festival. "You can be so gullible when it comes to people."

"I think you're absolutely right. And that naiveté stops here and now with you!" She could feel the heat creep up her neck to her cheeks. She felt ready to explode. "If you couldn't trust me enough to share information about my own family, why should I trust your judgment or explanations? You can't control everything and everyone simply to suit yourself. This was my family. I had a right to know from the beginning."

"Lea, I'm not trying to control you." How could he convince her? What words did she want him to say? "I only wanted to protect you. Is that so wrong?"

"Yes!"

"I couldn't take the chance. I won't apologize for that. You're certainly no match for the Stasi. You're like a porcelain doll, beautiful and easy to break."

He watched anger flash into her eyes at the analogy. Rolf had no more arguments to throw out. There was no getting around what he had to do.

"All right, you asked for a direct answer to your question, I'll give you one. I want you in my life." That should make her happy.

Lea concentrated on his last words. "Why?"

"After last night, you have to ask me that?"

"Because we're good in bed together, is that your reason? You want me to be a full-time mistress at your beck and call. I won't do it!"

Now his temper was over the edge. He'd given her every concession, and she wanted more.

"I won't say that's the whole story, but I admit the sex is one part I particularly enjoyed." He was developing feelings for her. Why couldn't he tell her? "And unless you're the best actress around, you feel the same about me."

"Yes, the sex is great, but without love, that's all it is. And it's not enough." She paused, hoping he would say something.

He was silent.

Seeing an automobile slow down, she recognized Gunnar Johansson, the inn gardener. She ran toward the vehicle, and when it came to a stop, got in. "Goodbye, Rolf."

21

ÖLAND, 1989

"Mr. Johansson, thanks for stopping. Are you going to the inn?" She noticed flowers and a bottle of liquor in the back.

Gunnar looked out the rear window at the man standing in the middle of the road, and then at his passenger. "I must finish my errand to see my sister, then we return." He shook his head. He thought she was such a nice woman, always taking time to admire his garden. He didn't like to see her so unhappy.

She settled into her seat. Lea could only think about her argument with Rolf. What right did he have to decide what was best for her? He investigated her family, then found out her parents and grandmother were murdered but not tell her?

In trying to explain his actions, Rolf had compared her to a porcelain doll. A resemblance he meant as a compliment, she took as an insult. It wasn't the first time a male looked at her small frame, wrongly assuming she was someone to be pampered and protected.

She had always taken the mistake in good humor. So why was it different with him? Why didn't she laugh at his analogy instead of being furious? Why did it matter so much he didn't see beyond the surface?

But it did matter, and it hurt. She had never cried, never run away, and never lost her temper because of a man. She had also never let her guard down before.

"What's so wonderful about being compared to a lifeless object, put in a glass case to be protected and admired? I'm a person, damn it, not a possession!"

Gunnar looked over at Lea, surprised at her outburst. But she wasn't talking to him. She was paying him no attention at all.

"How the hell would he like it if I had done that to him?" She smiled, thinking of Rolf's reaction if she had taken it upon herself to intrude in his life, put a cocoon around the president of Sundren International Industry, soothed and shielded him from worry or hurt.

"What would he say if I compared him to a favorite car that you took great care to polish, used frequently for enjoyment, and then put back in a locked garage for protection from the elements? Wouldn't he be insulted?

"What does he mean by 'I want you in my life'? He assumes, he commands. I want, I intend! He doesn't ask. It feels like a hostile takeover rather than the beginning of a relationship." After a few more minutes of venting her temper, she calmed enough for a spurt of conscience to trickle through. The man was wrong for not telling about her family. She felt deceived, though he was upfront in telling her not to expect a lasting commitment from their time together. He gave her the choice of entering into an affair with him or declining.

In the moment, she felt she had to run away. She had no doubt, after her performance, he would be glad to get away from her and return to the women who accepted him for himself.

To try and take her mind off Rolf, she concentrated on the beauty of the island as it flashed by the car window. Gunnar soon stopped and turned off the motor in front of a familiar house on the beach.

"Who lives here?" She asked.

"This was home to a fisherman and his wife. They are both gone now."

She got out of the car to take a closer look at the cottage.

"Can you tell me what happened to them?"

"The woman, Inga, was my only family, my baby sister. I had a sickness after the war," he clarified, "World War II. I spent much time in hospitals. When I finally returned to Öland, I found my sister was dead many years. The baby she carried, never born. The passing of time never took away the hurt for her husband, Ragnar. He sorrowed for more than thirty years…" The old man stopped a moment to compose himself. "One day, they discovered him," Gunnar peered through a window and pointed his finger up, "hanging." He moved away before continuing. "The villagers believe the ancient ones punished my family. My sister's husband stole from the dead, from a girl already claimed by the sea. To take away the evil after Ragnar's death, all belongings from the house were sent away." The old man shook his head. "There is nothing left, no pictures, no remembrance. But she is here, my sister. I come many times to talk. She waits for me in the ground behind the house."

Lea stayed behind when Gunnar walked to the back. She opened the door of the home. Glancing around, she recognized the room from the pictures she pulled from the auction box. Memories came flooding back of the night she and her grandmother had opened the wooden crate. She had been so excited about the articles she found and curious about the family who once owned them. Looking up at the wooden beam, it was sad to find the truth. She walked outside again toward the water.

Until Gunnar spoke of Ragnar and Inga, no one had recounted a specific legend or curse to her. Only veiled inferences were used to imply what might happen to those who ignored the sea's demand for respect and tribute.

Normally, Lea would be anxious to put Gunnar's account on paper, a great addition to her growing collection of folk myths. Instead, her thoughts were with a young girl and a story she knew all too well from her nightmares.

Gunnar's words were too close to the writings in the diary for her to believe it a coincidence. She walked out to the water. Even with tears blurring her vision, Lea could picture the beach in winter.

Dark skies, howling winds, and frigid water would have greeted anyone trying to flee the sinking submarine. She imagined the final hours of the young girl.

Lea could almost feel the fear and panic of those aboard the submarine as the water invaded. The screaming, the last pleading for life, and the quiet acceptance when hope for escape ended and knowledge of death became inevitable. How did the young girl get out?

Shivering, she backed away from the water. Once again, she felt the welcome heat of the summer sun on her arms as she walked to a nearby field of flowers. Stooping to pick a bouquet, Lea slowly worked to tie the stems into a semblance of the crown she received from Gunnar for midsummer.

Moving back to the water's edge, she threw the circle of flowers into the waves to honor a forgotten girl and those who met death with her.

Rolf had been right when he guessed the diary came from the auction box. Maybe he was right about other things as well. Looking around for Gunnar, she found him in a clearing at the back of the house placing a bouquet of roses on his sister's grave.

"Mr. Johansson, I have something for you. My grandmother bought a box from an auction in 1978. Along with other goods, there were photographs showing a man and woman standing in front of this house. While I don't have any of those pictures to give you, I do have this."

Lea opened her locket, took out the small, gold ring, and handed it to the old man. "This came from the box. It must have belonged to Inga. Please, take it."

Gunnar's eyes narrowed as he cast a speculative look at Lea before examining the fine quality of the gold band tinged with red. He knew exactly where it had come from, just as he had recognized the diary she showed him.

KÖNIGSBERG, 1945

When working in Königsberg, Gunnar received an order to build many crates of different size and shapes. A man and his daughter came every day to inspect the quality of his work. The man was very demanding, constantly measuring the dimensions and insisting on only the best wood. The girl, Liese, smiling and full of life, talked incessantly. Even after all these years, Gunnar couldn't forget her.

She was a happy child who loved to tease and chatter while he worked. She picked flowers for him and chased butterflies. Her father tried to scold the irrepressible child. "You are bothering the man. He cannot do his job." The young girl just laughed, kissed her father, and kept talking.

Gunnar enjoyed the child and looked forward to her visits. He remembered the ring she wore. It was unusual to see such an intricate ring on a young girl's hand. The father wore a similar band, only larger and more elaborate. Gunnar handed the ring back to Lea, struggling through his emotions to find the right words in English to explain.

ÖLAND 1989: GUNNAR'S MEMORIES 1945–1989

The pale face and frozen posture worried her. She reached out to touch his arm. "Are you all right?"

"Tack...thank you, miss. I cannot...It is not from Inga. It is cursed." He put the ring back in Lea's hand.

"But, Mr. Johansson..." Lea's voice trailed off as the old man shook his head.

"No! No more now. We leave!" The problems had started for Gunnar one night last year when a specter appeared from his past. He remembered nothing else until Lars Youngmark found him in the garden, his body shaking violently. Gunnar was terrified the madness had returned.

Days and nights spent without remembering where he was or what he did. Splitting his mind from his body, as a way to keep his sanity during imprisonment, became a curse he couldn't erase in freedom. The time spent in hospitals only taught him to keep it under control.

Lars had stayed with him until the old fears quieted. But the sighting of the ghost had triggered bad memories and they came more frequently. Even with the strong pills he used to collapse into sleep, Gunnar could not find the peace he craved.

Instead, he was forced to relive the years he spent in a land with deep green forests of birch and pine, a land that looked so much like his beautiful Sweden. But it was at the mouth of the River Amur, in a place many called Devil's Hell Hole. It was Siberia.

Tortured, given starvation rations, the men were slave laborers. The lucky had an early death. Some went insane, many committed suicide.

And then there were those like Gunnar, whose spirit died slowly, a day at a time. After Stalin's death in 1953, numerous prisoners were released from the camps, but not Gunnar. His skills with wood were always needed. They held him in that prison for twenty years. Afterward, there were the long years spent in hospitals.

After returning to Öland, the few times he was able to visit his brother-in-law, Ragnar talked only once about the monster and the child he found floating in the sea. He never mentioned Inga and Gunnar could never bring himself to ask. Ragnar's sorrow silenced his questions.

He listened to the stories told by villagers, but never confided to anyone his suspicion about Ragnar's sea serpent. After his time spent in prison, Gunnar was no longer sure he could separate imagination from reality. His fantasies of freedom had been his escape, his salvation. Now it was a constant torment.

After Ragnar's death, Gunnar was unable to claim any physical memory of his sister. The villagers made sure he was not around to interfere when the household belongings were removed and sent to the United States.

With the help of Inspector Youngmark and Sigrid, he had a few good years. He was losing the strength to fight the attacks that had begun plaguing him again. The doctors were sure to send him back to the hospitals. He couldn't stand being away from his home again.

He remembered the last time he saw young Liese. It was at the pier in Königsberg. Gunnar hid in a shed under the docks after escaping the Russians. He watched men, women, and children board a submarine. Gunnar was close enough to recognize father and daughter, and clearly saw the man they called Ulrik. He could hear the conversation about their destination of Öland. Before he could find a way to stow aboard the vessel, all three disappeared inside the U-boat and his chance was lost.

After years of staying in his garden rarely leaving the inn, during this Midsummer celebration, Gunnar saw the man from the submarine again. Even with age masking his features, he knew it was Ulrik. But unlike his sighting a year ago, this time he saw the man in daylight talking to Per Knudsson in the area of the town square. He had tried to clear his head, afraid he was losing control again. Then he realized this was no ghost, no shadow. Ulrik was mortal, a man of this earth.

Gunnar understood the scene he saw in 1945 was not a dream. The monster from Ragnar's story was the doomed submarine. The girl he remembered as Liese, and the corpse his brother-in-law found floating in the Baltic, were the same.

Ulrik had been on the submersible with the girl and her father. Yet, the villagers said the only human remains found were of a child. If Ulrik had survived the sinking ship and freezing water, and managed to come ashore for help, he would find only one building on the wide expanse of deserted beach, the house of Ragnar and Inga. Gunnar remembered his brother-in laws's story about finding the drowned body of Inga. Ulrik murdered his sister.

22

ÖLAND, 1989

The planned meeting at the Brewhouse tavern on Öland had taken its toll on Ulrik and the inspector. Ulrik had shown himself visibly shaken, but not surprised, when Lars bluntly questioned his integrity as an agent, and tersely offered the terms for protection set by the Swedish state.

A look of regret crossed Ulrik's face.

"I admit the masquerade has been difficult. There have been many time over the years I have been tempted to tell you the truth, Lars. I am glad it is over," Ulrik admitted.

"Do you fully understand what you have done? Because of your greed, countless agents were compromised and murdered. You put our country at risk by selling information."

"Your condemnation is not warranted, Lars. It was a job, a complicated job, nothing more. I had the needed skills. My conscience is clear. I have no guilt. What I care about is to spend my last years in comfort and safety."

The detective said nothing. Up to this point, a part of him had refused to believe the accusations from Swedish authorities that Ulrik was a communist agent. Hearing the words directly from the man's mouth left no doubt. His best friend, his mentor, a person he thought he knew, was a traitor. Ulrik offered no excuses and showed no shame for betraying his country and its people who trusted him with their national security. He didn't say he was sorry. He said he was guilty.

"I learned of the book and its importance while examining Nazi archives. I found a letter referring to an important paper, the *Hitler Document*, hidden in a diary cover and smuggled out of Russian-held Königsberg by submarine. I've spent years tracking that book. When you called with news of a diary, I couldn't believe my good fortune. My clients are excited about such a find. I'll have no problem finding a buyer if Swedish authorities decline my offer.

"I knew from your description it was the right one. Your mistake was leaving me alone with the journal. When you and the American woman left the office, it was all the time I needed to retrieve the paper from the inside front cover."

"Why should I believe you?" asked Lars.

"There is no point in lying. We both know the government will test the document for authenticity before giving me refuge. I know Swedish intelligence has grown more suspicious of my actions in recent years, but they had no direct evidence against me, until now. I underestimated them, or I've gotten a little sloppy in my old age. My only choice is to trade the paper for my safety. Only you are to act as my intermediary, Lars. The agency will keep its distance until suitable terms concerning my defection can be reached, or no deal! Of course, there are many other important bits of information the state will be interested in, but those are kept here." Ulrik tapped his head.

He pulled papers out of his briefcase and handed them to Lars. Reading the file, the detective understood why this document would be sought by governments and corporations.

Lars scanned multiple columns that noted numbered bank accounts. The accompanying inventory listed specific capital and in what currency it was held. Each record gave the town or city where the assets originated, who would receive the monies, and the purpose.

"I will leave the *Hitler Document* with you as a bond of good faith, Lars. Cut a small piece of the paper for the authorities to examine and test. I'm sure it will only take a day, two at the most, to confirm." Ulrik got up to leave the tavern. "I have every confidence in your skills to broker a fair exchange."

Terms had to be agreed upon by the detective and Swedish authorities to ensure Orensson's safety, and an ample amount of cash paid for the renegade spy's retirement. Lars understood that negotiations had to be short. Ulrik's life depended on getting the man into protective custody. Out of harm's way, Ulrik would give permission for Lars to release the paper. Maybe he would stay in Sweden, but it was more likely a larger, richer nation state would negotiate to bring the double agent to their shores.

On the way back to his office, Lars stopped at the cemetery with the intent to visit Hulda. Instead of going directly to her gravesite as usual, he walked in, sat down, and spoke to an empty church.

"Someone I've known for years, a man I thought I could trust and called friend, is a traitor. Why couldn't I see what he was doing? When I confronted him, there was no sorrow at what he had done, only relief because he was tired of running. A man with no morals, no honor, a user who cared nothing for the safety of a people and a way of life. He was concerned only about himself and what he could gain. I didn't see the truth. There is no punishment for what he's done, only reward. He will receive a good amount of money for the information and be protected for the rest of his life."

He left the quiet, dim church and walked into the sunshine toward Hulda's grave. Lars had no revelations, no answers, but the knot in his stomach seemed a little less painful than when he entered. For the first time, he had spoken his feelings aloud, even if only to the walls of an empty church.

KALMAR POLICE STATION, 1989

The inspector drove across the four-mile bridge to Kalmar. Normally, such an important paper would have been locked up in the station's safe, but Lars didn't want anyone retrieving the document before he was ready.

There were other ways to keep it secure. Many times the detective placed important papers among the countless stacks littering his desk. Interspersed into such a jumble, the document would virtually disappear. However, he decided against leaving Ulrik's papers in the open. There were too many people who had access to his office, and lately, one of his officers gave him an uncomfortable feeling. Looking around, a more suitable hiding place came to mind.

At his desk, Lars placed a call to military intelligence. "This is Inspector Youngmark from Kalmar. Please connect me with Agent Erick Swansson.

"Lars, you have news for me?"

"Ulrik is willing to defect with the *Hitler Document*. He has given me a list of his demands, which I will turn over to your office. I am to act as intermediary," he related. "Whatever instructions you give me, Erik, I will follow."

"I will get back to you, Lars, on how the exchange will take place, and who will be your contact to discuss Ulrik's terms of defection. Well done, Inspector."

Lars hung up the phone. He knew intelligence was anxious to get the paper, but events were moving too quickly to suit the detective. Ulrik had lied for over thirty years. Even under the present circumstances, Lars wasn't sure he was telling the truth. It would take more to convince him.

"Inspector." Lars looked up to see his aide open the door. "A suicide has been reported by the bartender of the Brewhouse."

BREWHOUSE TAVERN: ÖLAND, 1989

"I will leave immediately." The phone call had the detective hurrying back over the bridge. An acrid smell had brought the Öland barkeep from the main room to a small, windowless cellar beneath the building. The room had once been used for ice storage. Lars opened the door to an overwhelming odor of petrol. As his eyes adjusted to the oily haze, he saw a charred shape sprawled on the dirt floor.

The detective knelt by the figure searching for some sort of identification. Facial features were beyond recognition. Carefully, he pried open the mouth. No teeth. Still there was some soft gum tissue that remained. The man's saliva and swelling of the tongue must have given some protection. He felt around the body for a set of false teeth and found the melted blob of plastic.

"What would make someone do this?" He looked around the corpse for anything that would give him a clue. Catching the very edge of his vision was something white. Folded neatly in the corner of the cellar was a pair of cotton gloves.

Lars carefully rolled the body to examine the back. Unlike the front, the clothing was somewhat intact due to the damp soil of the floor. Reaching into the back pocket, he pulled out what was left of a cigarette box. The detective could make out enough of the print to conclude it was the British label Ulrik favored. He returned the body to its original position.

Once outside, he filled out the necessary crime scene reports and spoke to anyone who might have information. Lars had not seen the man, but learned from the bartender that Gunnar had been in the tavern earlier, and bought a bottle. Lars called a doctor to the scene to identify a possible cause of death. The detective met the man and walked him downstairs into the underground room.

"After you, Doctor. Before the body is moved to the morgue, I would like your visual opinion."

The man put down the bag he carried. "Outward appearance points to a suicide, Inspector. The position of the body, empty can of petrol, a glass jar with the odor of a known accelerant. All things that could be used for self-immolation."

"Thank you."

Once the man left the room, Lars took out his notebook. He knew the truth of the history professor's background. Other factors had to be considered.

Lars turned around when the heavy door creaked. "Who is there?" He got up to look outside and then slammed the door shut. The detective wanted to be sure he was alone before continuing his search. He needed to examine the body and scene again.

With protective gloves on, Lars found nothing sifting through the dirt until he stuck his fingers into the soil underneath the corpse. Pushed into the earth from the weight of the body was a metal pen. The moisture had saved the device from melting.

Holding the small writing mechanism in his hand, the detective recognized its true purpose. Agents used these innocuous instruments as a convenient method of execution. Pushing the top button released a pen point filled with a fast-acting poison. The effects are quick and lethal. Judging by the shape and configuration, he attributed the weapon as one issued to Stasi operatives. Carefully, he examined the skull. Around the area that once was an ear, he discovered a small hole. The suicide was staged. He bagged the metal object. If the murderer assumed the pen would melt from the heat, it was possible the weapon was handled without gloves. Maybe prints could be found.

The detective understood he would have to continue to rely on circumstantial evidence if the victim was Ulrik. Confirmation would be virtually impossible. Orensson had no information on file and looking at the condition of the corpse, if this person did have fingerprints, they were gone. The detective remembered Ulrik's determination for anonymity as they sat talking one night, years back.

"Lars, it's not as if I have a family to grieve over my remains. If I'm killed on enemy soil during a mission, I will make sure nothing can be traced to Swedish intelligence."

Lars tried to reason who might benefit from Ulrik's death and what was the motive? The man was a double agent. If the East

Germans realized he had been unmasked and planned to defect with the documents, the Stasi would act in quick order. Lars doubted murder was the original intent. Bringing the turncoat back to communist soil made more sense. Maybe the assassin bungled the assignment.

Per Knudsson had already been confirmed as an East German operative and several witnesses saw him talking to a man fitting Ulrik's description shortly before the body was discovered. Where was Per now? He called one of his officers in the Kalmar station.

"This is Youngmark. I want a bulletin sent out giving orders that Per Knudsson is to be detained for questioning. There is reason to believe he might be involved, or have knowledge of, a murder. Put together a small team to look around Knudsson's apartment on Öland." Lars knew the physical land area was too large to search for the operative, but someone could have knowledge of his location, and useful evidence might be found at his home.

After the body was removed to the morgue, the inspector left the ice cellar and walked around the main building to enter the outside section of the tavern. He looked at his watch. It had taken him over two hours to sift through the material in the cellar. It was almost time to meet Rolf Sundren.

The minister waited for a time after the detective left the tavern area before coming out from hiding. It was done. Ulrik was dead and who would care? No one grieved over a traitor. Everything was as it should be, and only minor problems remained.

At first, the reverend had been careful walking about town, not sure the reaction toward a stranger. Were people afraid a murderer was loose? Fear was in the air. In a group of pack animals, it showed in the frozen stance before chaotic flight. In the closely knit human community, it meant locked doors, empty sidewalks, and furtive looks toward anyone unfamiliar.

People sitting around the tavern's outdoor tables were already talking about the tragic event that took place in the cellar, but there was no evidence of apprehension. Gossip traveled quickly, and the watcher heard enough to be satisfied that the inspector was interpreting the clues satisfactorily.

It was unfortunate he was unable to stay in the area to witness the next episode, but the key to success was to move events along quickly. He could not allow the detective opportunity to think and mull over each occurrence, only time to react.

Rolf walked quickly toward the tavern where Inspector Youngmark would be waiting for their meeting. He had set suspicions aside and called to ask the man's help in finding Lea. He had recognized the driver who picked her up as Gunnar Johansson, but arriving at the inn, he saw no sign of Gunnar's car, the man, or Lea. And no one had answered the bell.

This was his fault. Lea's description of his controlling personality was accurate. Rolf had been afraid that if she was left to make her own decisions, she would have contacted someone like Per for help. What started as a jealous competition had changed to fear for her safety once he learned of the murders of her family and the true identity of Per as a Stasi agent. And if Rolf had repeated the entire story, including the petty reason of jealousy that initiated his deception, she would have walked away. As it turned out, he lost her anyway.

BREWHOUSE TAVERN

He entered the pub through the black ornamental iron gates. Used only during summer months, the area had a high whitewashed wall enclosing a large stone floor. Wooden beams supported an overhead framework massed with tangled vines. The only light came from various lanterns hung from the greenery. The combination of wall and thicket served to block the noise from Färjestaden's nearby market area while giving a feeling of intimacy to the outdoor tavern.

The place was crowded with tables and chairs in a random configuration. It forced patrons into a zigzag pattern to reach the bar or claim a seat. The place was almost empty except for the few who were eating a late lunch. Adjusting his eyes to the shade of the tavern, Rolf glanced around and saw the inspector stand up from a back table.

"Sundren, here." The detective kept his eyes on a man that had entered the tavern right before the American and appeared to be looking for someone. Something bothered him about the man. His gestures were stilted. Lars watched the man move closer to Sundren as he smiled and excitedly raised one hand in greeting to his companion sitting in the tavern rear. The man's other hand grasped a large bouquet of flowers, an intended present for his friend. But the man's suspicious body language reminded Lars of something from his past, something ingrained from his days of being an agent.

When he first arrived at the tavern, Lars made sure the back tables of the room were empty before he sat down. Had he made a mistake? Was there someone back there waiting for the smiling man and his gift? The detective watched the man move the flowers closer to Rolf Sundren. He had to decide quickly.

Walking toward the back, a glimpse of metal in the inspector's hand stopped Rolf in his tracks. He watched Lars raise his weapon, aim, and fire. Behind Rolf, a body fell to the ground. In his hurry, he had not seen or heard the other man.

The inspector leaned over to check for life before removing a dark wig, revealing Per Knudsson. It had not been his intent to kill the Stasi agent. Suppressing the urge to turn around, Lars had fired the gun. He intended only to disarm, but the man's sudden movement changed the bullet's projected path from a shoulder directly into the heart muscle. Death was immediate.

Lars took out a pair of gloves and unclenched the dead man's hand to see what it held. His suspicion had been correct. He carefully untangled the slim stick from the bouquet of flowers making sure to have no contact with the sharpened end. The back of the pub remained empty. It would have taken only a second of hesitancy for Per to murder the American. If Lars had turned around, he had no doubt Rolf Sundren would be dead.

The detective placed the assassination tool in a sealed bag. It would be sent away for toxicology. There were no weapons on the corpse. Hidden in a secret pocket under one arm, he found a cyanide capsule packet.

Curious or not, Lars didn't try to open the locked briefcase that stood next to the body. According to regulations, it would be turned over to Swedish authorities.

The detective shook his head. This was no accident or a case of mistaken identity. Why the American? Information had shown Sundren to be a successful businessman, nothing more. He hoped the careful search of Knudsson's apartment would unearth answers. He also wanted to check with the lab examining the murder weapon pulled from the tavern cellar. Would the fingerprints found on the weapon match Per Knudsson? The inspector sat back on his heels. Two people were dead. Would there be more?

23

BREWHOUSE TAVERN, 1989

The smell of blood mixed with the sweet fragrance of flowers. Rolf said nothing as the inspector did his job. The man had saved his life. He would never have backed away from an innocuous bunch of flowers. Without the detective's intervention, he would be the one lying motionless on the ground.

He looked at the face of the dead man. Rolf had been so obsessed keeping Lea safe from the Stasi, he never considered himself a target of the East German Police.

To calm the American's fears, Lars made a quick call to Kalmarsson Inn. Speaking in English, Lars wanted to make sure Rolf understood his words.

"Sigrid, is Miss Reardon there?"

"Ya. She is visiting with a friend from America, Reverend Sedgely. He arrived last night. Do you want words with her?"

"She is there with a Reverend Sedgely. Gunnar has also returned?"

"He is out tending the garden." Unsure why the inspector wanted information on their whereabouts, Sigrid went on to explain. "Gunnar visits his sister's gravesite every weekend after marketing chores. He said Lea needed a ride back to the inn after she left Rolf Sundren. He took Lea with him to Inga's grave, and then back here to the inn."

"Gunnar is out in the garden."

"I just told you this."

"Thank you, Sigrid."

As the innkeeper hung up the phone, she wondered what was behind the strange conversation.

Relieved at finding Lea safe, Rolf was ready to answer the detective's questions.

"Mr. Sundren, is there any reason why this man, Per Knudsson, would want to harm you?"

It was time to be blunt. The detective's reaction would decide how much information he revealed. Rolf disclosed the results of background checks, and his suspicions of Per, Gunnar Johansson, Ulrik Orensson, and the detective himself.

He talked in broad terms about the diary, relating only selected pieces of what he'd found, but was particularly candid when repeating his concerns about Lars and Ulrik, and their likely interest in the Amber Room.

Lars took no insult at what he heard. "Sundren, I understand your hesitancy to trust anyone."

That comment persuaded Rolf to continue the story. He told about the murder of Lea's family, the stalking last night, and her leaving with Gunnar today.

When he finished, the inspector opened his briefcase, pulled out three burgeoning envelopes stamped "Reardon," and set them down on the table in front of Rolf.

"I appreciate your candor. My office had no knowledge regarding the Reardon family's deaths as suspicious." Lars remembered Ulrik's statement about the Stasi's frustration in trying to recover the diary, but he had conveniently forgotten to mention any deaths.

"Mr. Sundren, the problem and Achilles heel of any agency that has the responsibility of national security is integrity. A nation trains its agents to expect loyalty and trust from their own, but it cannot afford those same sentiments toward another country. A friend today might be an enemy tomorrow. Many times critical information is never shared. But sometimes loyalty is misused, and trust is blind."

The inspector opened his files to discuss what he could with Rolf. Lars reviewed the facts they had in common and those that were different. He talked about Orensson's last visit.

He took Rolf to the underground ice house. The burned smell of flesh was strong.

"This is where I found the body," disclosed Lars. "The general size and frame of the corpse, which was approximately five-foot-six and slim, the false teeth, cotton gloves folded in the corner of the room, English cigarettes in the back pocket, all of these things convinced me to identify the remains as Ulrik.

"In life, Ulrik stood five-foot-seven, 150 pounds in American weight. He had gray-blond hair, blue eyes, and false teeth. He wore white cotton gloves to hide extensive scarring on his hands. Unfortunately, it might be impossible to ever know for sure this body is Ulrik. There is nothing to positively identify the man in any file. A good agent is like a mirror. Whatever reflection you expect is what you see."

After Lars revealed Ulrik's pose as a double agent, Rolf understood the detective's refusal to divulge more information, and appreciated what the inspector had confided. Knowing Ulrik was a double operative, the conflicting files received from his own sources could be explained. Something didn't fit, however, and he wanted time to think it through.

The two men went upstairs to the pub. "Gentlemen," the bartender set down plates and glasses. "Lunch and drinks are on the house."

"No, thank you," said Rolf. "But I will take some strong coffee." His stomach rebelled at the thought of anything else.

"Bring Mr. Sundren your special drink," insisted the inspector.

The pale yellow concoction of beer and milk surprisingly calmed Rolf's insides.

After lunch, the two men talked about the possibility of Gunnar's involvement.

"Your information about Gunnar's internment in the Russian gulag and his period spent in hospitals is accurate, but one thing you have missed. In your time here on the island, have you heard the story about the sea monster and the fisherman, Ragnar?"

"I heard mention of a sea monster while in one of the local taverns, but I admit not paying much attention. The ancient Viking mariner sagas interest me. However, I like to deal in the realities of what I can see and touch, not modern fables of UFOs, Big Foot, or sea serpents such as the Loch Ness variety."

The inspector smiled. "In December 1945, a sea monster was seen off the coast of Öland by a fisherman. The man found the body of a young girl floating near where the creature submerged. The fisherman took the valuables he found on the body, including an amber box. Robbing the dead brought the man misery. He discovered his wife's drowned remains a few days later. For over thirty years, Ragnar suffered the loss of his wife. He became a hermit, leaving the grounds where his family was buried only to take his fishing boat out to sea.

"The fisherman committed suicide in 1978. Believing the man cursed, people from the village took everything from his cottage and gave it to charity. The wife of Ragnar was Inga, sister of Gunnar Johansson. And since I also deal in 'realities,' Mr. Sundren, I would guess the monster was a submarine."

"A submarine!" Being close-minded, refusing to consider options he dismissed as not worth a second look, Rolf missed an important connection.

"Then the crate Lea's grandmother bought at auction was from Ragnar's house." He didn't remember her mentioning an amber box. "The diary from the submarine was probably in the box, which is how it came to be packed with the goods from the cottage," Rolf surmised.

"I believe that is what happened," the inspector agreed. "And even though the journal did not give a written account of destination, the dates coincide with the legend. I doubt Gunnar had any involvement in a Stasi operation, even with his family's link to the diary. Circumstances still point to Knudsson as responsible for the break-in, Ulrik's murder, and the attempt on your life, Mr. Sundren.

"The dead cannot harm Miss Reardon," the inspector said in reference to Per and Ulrik. "Still, until the investigation shows more conclusive information, no one will be eliminated. I sent some of my men to Knudsson's apartment to search for more evidence."

As the inspector received a phone call, Rolf rose to leave. Lars motioned him to sit down again.

"The team in Knudsson's apartment uncovered a hidden cache. They found Miss Reardon's camera with the film intact. The camera was sent to the lab for processing." Lars pulled off his glasses before continuing. "They also discovered graphic evidence linking Per to the murders of Miss Reardon's mother and father. I think we have our answers, Sundren. The dates and circumstances correspond. Ulrik's confession traced Stasi interest in the diary to 1978, which was also the date of the first death, Miss Reardon's grandmother. The search for the book continued until Ulrik succeeded in stealing the papers hidden in the diary's cover when he came to my office to examine the journal."

Lars looked at his watch. They had been talking for over two hours. "Come." An officer approached and handed a report to Lars. "Excuse me, Sundren." The detective quickly read the message and indicated the officer to leave. "The lab report states the camera had been tampered with, but they managed to save one frame of film." Lars handed a copy of the print to Rolf. "As you see, the picture clearly shows Per Knudsson pouring something into Ms. Reardon's glass during the Midsummer celebration. She needs to be informed of the situation." Lars shook his head. "I prefer not to speak of this over the telephone. I would like to set an appointment for tomorrow forenoon in my office in Kalmar for you and Miss Reardon. All of this information will come as a shock. It would be good to have a close friend standing with her."

Rolf did not inform the inspector that Lea might think of him as many things right now, but doubted friend was among them. It didn't matter. He would be there in the morning. Ulrik and Per's deaths should have put an end to any lingering worry over Lea. It had not. The pieces were all there, except he did not like the way they fit together. He had ignored a story told in every tavern on the island until the inspector pointed out the obvious link to the diary. Rolf knew from his own business that repeated second-guessing could cripple any decision process. Still, after what he missed, he would keep searching for any and all answers until he was satisfied.

"Inspector, I'd like to make sure of one detail before I leave. Did you or Professor Orensson find a rendering of Sandby churchyard hidden in the diary picture?"

"I saw no picture of Sandby, and Ulrik mentioned nothing while we were together. The only thing he was able to pull out of the pen and ink was the rune script, which he found immediately."

Rolf looked at the inspector with a quizzed expression.

"Orensson found the script fragments right away?"

"Yes, within the first few moments after opening the book. Ulrik was not only an expert in deciphering ancient languages, he was one of the most experienced men at the agency able to ferret out hidden messages and break codes. He learned from the best minds at Bletchley Park. After finding the symbols, Ulrik tried to interpret a meaning, but without more runes, he claimed the script was unreadable. You examined the drawing. Was that your opinion as well?" asked the inspector.

"As the writing stands now, I agree. It would be like stringing together letters of our alphabet without making any words. But it doesn't mean the symbols aren't important as a piece of the puzzle to locate the Amber Room."

The inspector nodded in agreement. "I did ask Ulrik if the Stasi thought the diary picture might be some type of map pointing out the location of the Amber Room. He insisted the Stasi was never interested in the journal's written content or anything hidden in the drawing. From their extensive search after World War II, East Germany concurred with the general view of other nations that the Amber Room either lay at the bottom of one of the many flooded mine shafts, or was destroyed in a bombing raid. In either case, unobtainable.

"The East Germans were after something more concrete, something the ministry was positive existed and knew where to find. Ulrik's mission was to steal the *Hitler Document* hidden inside of the diary cover."

"Did you believe him, Inspector?"

"Like you, I had decided the diary referred to the Amber Room, and yes, I believe Ulrik would have been tempted by the possibility of finding such a great treasure. I have also seen the paper in question and know the worth is considerable. The man I knew was a practical one, not someone to chase daydreams if another fortune was within reach."

Lars stopped speaking for a moment. With no comment from the American, he continued.

"Until Ulrik confessed before his death, Swedish intelligence was aware of the document's existence but not where it was hidden. That paper is now in my hands."

"Did Ulrik ever hold the diary pen and ink to the light to examine it?"

"Yes. That was the first thing he did when he opened the book, why do you ask?"

"I'm not sure yet. I hope to have some answers worked out by tomorrow morning."

"Mr. Sundren, if I need to reach you before the meeting in Kalmar, will you be at Karlmarsson Inn?"

It's where he wanted to be, but knew better. "No, you can reach me at my place."

As the two men went their separate ways, the detective found himself thinking about Sundren as he got in his car and traveled back to Kalmar and his office. The American had found reasons not to be satisfied with the investigation results, and was determined to find his own explanations. Lars thought he could be correct. The words the detective spoke earlier, "The man I knew," had come too easy.

Obviously, in spite of all the years spent together, he had not known Ulrik at all. It was a definite weakness for himself and the Swedish state, and one Orensson had surely used against them. Lars decided to recheck the evidence bags from the two death scenes.

It would be good to have an opinion from someone with no predisposed assumptions. The detective had been impressed with Sundren's ability to arrange a wide variety of seemingly unrelated facts into a logical pattern. He would be very interested in hearing his conclusions at the morning meeting. He would call Lea Reardon to set the Kalmar appointment as soon as he reached his office.

Rolf left the tavern for home. It was a long way, but walking allowed him to clear his mind. He considered the last pieces of information the inspector had given him. The Amber Room had never been a consideration for the Stasi. Their only interest in the diary was the secret paper concealed in the cover, a document that had been stolen by Orensson, but was now in the hands of Inspector Youngmark.

Two East German spies were dead. Everything fit together, no loose ends. It remained unsaid, but Rolf guessed Swedish intelligence would want to examine the diary before Lea took it home. The agency would want to make sure the book held no additional secrets.

Unless information was found proving the Amber Room wasn't at the bottom of a mine or destroyed by fire during the bombings, that part of the journal would be written off as nothing more than curiosity. Rolf should be satisfied, but he wasn't. Ulrik had not found Sandby churchyard in the rendering.

For someone that experienced in solving cryptic puzzles, it should have jumped right out when he first held the page to light. Yet, according to the inspector, it was the runes imbedded in the background that Orensson discovered immediately. That was the scenario Rolf couldn't accept.

Without any suspicion of what the drawing held, directly spotting and isolating the script from the multi-lined setting would have been impossible. It couldn't have happened that way, no matter what Orensson's level of skill.

A man of detail, the inspector would not have exaggerated the amount of time it took for Orensson to find the runes. Rolf needed to know how he did it.

24

ÖLAND, 1989

Rolf searched for answers while he walked to his house, but only one made sense. If he hadn't been told to the contrary, Rolf would assume that Orensson had access to the book before meeting Lea at the inspector's office. It was the only way Ulrik could have found the hidden runes with such ease.

That speculation brought another question. If Orensson did have the book earlier, why not remove the important paper? Why wait? Why would he still have interest in the diary? He ran through different schemes to try to understand the spy's intent. In the end, he found logic in only one objective—Ulrik's goal from the beginning was to find the Amber Room.

If Rolf was correct, the idea of a secret document hidden inside the journal cover was nothing more than an elaborately staged hoax created by Ulrik to mislead both the Stasi and Swedish intelligence. He began to lay out each detail of such a deception to see what worked and what didn't.

Hungry, he stopped for a snack. "Good day." He exchanged pleasantries with the young boy minding the counter of a small family-owned grocery. Choosing a bag of fresh strawberries and a carton of milk, he sat down at the small table outside the store.

Someone with Orensson's background knew exactly what type of information made governments salivate. He would be capable of authoring a credible forgery, or could find someone who was.

Cognizant of the inner workings of democratic and communist agencies, privy to classified information from both sides, he would avoid their strengths while using weaknesses to his advantage. In the thick of the Cold War, it wouldn't be difficult to set up hostile situations between the two powers playing to their fears. Such a situation would allow Orensson time to search for the treasure without worry of interference.

It was the reason why sophisticated communist espionage organizations had no success in obtaining the journal. He made sure they failed.

Only when ready would Ulrik allow the discovery of the forged papers. It made perfect sense that the less time the phony pages spent under intense scrutiny, the better, and it forced any who were after the *Hitler Document* to react quickly.

The different agencies would become turf conscious. Even those flying the same national flag would become reluctant to share information or expertise with one another.

If Ulrik did have access to the journal at one time, why would he have let the book out of his possession? Rolf found the answer surprisingly simple.

Having read the journal and deciphered the picture, Orensson knew the diary lacked a key part of the puzzle. Keeping the book would have gained him nothing. It was the missing piece he had to find.

He pushed for a solution to the next question. He was convinced the script played an important part in solving the puzzle. Thinking back to Lea's description of the meeting in Inspector Youngmark's office with Ulrik, he wondered why the man would chance revealing the important clue to Lea and the inspector?

For Ulrik to intentionally focus on the runes risked giving away his true intentions, yet that was just what he did. Rolf was stumped. There was an answer. He was missing it.

Finished eating, he got up from the table and threw away his trash.

As he continued through town, Rolf became oblivious to his surroundings. He didn't notice a smiling woman saying hello as he passed. He paid no attention to the man trying to sell him flowers from a pushcart. His mind sifted through the details.

If the Reardons knew an important document was in the diary, what was their reason for not turning it over to the State Department? If it was a traitor they were concerned about, they could have contacted the CIA with the information. Why try to broker the document themselves, unless they wanted the money it would bring; or worse yet, they were traitors.

Still, the circumstances were assumed. Everything Lea had told him about her mother and father, the kind of people they were, the ethics they professed, it was the opposite of the situation presented.

Unfortunately, Rolf guessed Inspector Youngmark would have argued those same points to defend the character of a man he had known for over thirty years, until the double agent was caught and confessed the truth. Yet there was an important difference. The detective had heard the admission of guilt directly from Ulrik.

Espionage is a dirty game. The possibility existed that someone had purposely shaded the situation to point guilt at Mr. and Mrs. Reardon. It was very convenient the people who were most involved with the journal and could answer questions or defend their actions were all dead, but one. It was the reason Ulrik had sought her out and chanced revealing the disguised runes. The solution had to be with Lea!

Since access to the diary was no longer an issue, there was something else, something not in the journal. What did Lea have to make her indispensable? The answer was sudden. "The rhyme," he said aloud. Only she knew the rhyme.

Rolf had already told her he thought the verse could be the missing page from the diary because the stanza meshed so well with the journal drawing. Now he was sure.

She admitted not remembering the rhyme in its entirety until returning to the inn after Ulrik jogged her memory by pointing out the concealed script. It was also the apparent reason her parents had been kidnapped. What if Mr. and Mrs. Reardon had known nothing of the verse?

Rolf stopped, looked around, and realized he had walked a mile out of his way. Turning back toward the beach cottage, he continued fitting pieces of the puzzle together.

Right after her grandmother's death, Lea found the scrap of torn page in the woman's nightgown and ripped it up. The rhyme must have been written on the paper she destroyed.

Thinking about the time element of when her parents arrived home and the death of her grandmother, Rolf bet that initially Mr. and Mrs. Reardon had no knowledge of the rhyme. Even with the book in their possession, when did they take the time to examine the diary, translate the verse, and understand the diary's worth? From what Lea said, she never talked about the rhyme with her parents, never thinking it important. To her, the words weren't something from real life, only the trigger that set off her nightmare.

Rolf still couldn't understand why Mrs. Reardon left the journal specifically for Lea, with no explanation. What did make sense was that it took the Reardon's deaths for Ulrik to finally focus on Lea.

His reasoning of Ulrik's intentions sounded plausible, except how would the spy have found out any information in the first place? "It had to think of only one way. It had to be someone with close ties to the family. Someone who knew about her nightmares gave Ulrik the information!"

The man and woman walking in front of Rolf turned around to stare at the American.

"Are you talking to us?" They asked in unison.

"What? No..." He had no time to engage in conversation with the friendly couple. He needed to get home. Rolf ran the last half mile.

Reaching his door and disconnecting the alarms, he hurried to dial the phone on his secure line.

"This is Rolf Sundren. Put me through to CIA Agent Chico, immediately."

"I'm sorry, sir, Agent Chico is not available at the moment," replied the secretary.

"I don't care what you've been told to say, I want to speak to him, now! Put me through."

Unfortunately, barking at the secretary, who told him the wait to reach the intended agent would take at least a half hour, only got a phone slammed in his ear. Rolf curbed his impatience, swallowed his pride, and dialed again.

"This is Rolf Sundren again. I apologize for my outburst. Please have Agent Chico call me at his earliest convenience. Let him know it's extremely important. Thank you."

He had a love-hate relationship with the Central Intelligence Agency. It rankled the CIA that he used paid sources to gain intelligence, in many cases the same contacts used by the agency. On the other hand, after the debacle of losing a sensitive bundle of information, the agency sought his talents.

They accepted his expertise in designing intricate security systems, but not his conclusion as to the cause of the breach.

Although the agency insisted it was a rare occurrence, Rolf bet it was far from being an anomaly. He released his information, hoping the agency would focus on the man, but realized that like Inspector Youngmark and Swedish intelligence, the CIA was a closed system that tended to look outside for blame, overlooking or minimizing indiscretion among their own.

Rolf purposely gave nothing in writing, only voicing his opinion and recommendations to the small group of agents who worked closely with him during the investigation.

By temporarily keeping the issue out of the spotlight and away from the media, the agency would have a better chance to limit the damage and solve the problem in-house before the story became public. Immediately showcasing the CIA's vulnerabilities put additional risk on the lives of countless field operatives and chanced leaking the names under suspicion.

Rolf held no illusions. He was a businessman, an outsider to the system. He suspected it was for that reason the CIA chose to submit his conclusions ad nauseam to a gaggle of committees for consensus, losing whatever time edge he gave them.

It was a lesson political science students were taught, and the reason many governments and CEOs found it time and cost effective to do business with dictators, rather than democrats. Like the autonomy of a single business owner, dealing with one person with the power to make decisions for an entire country was far easier than persuading numerous committees to accept your ideas.

Still, the CIA had been grateful for Rolf's discretion. He hoped grateful enough to push his one friendly contact inside the agency to help him now. The knowledge that Ulrik Orensson was a double agent had narrowed his channels.

Considering Orensson's area of operation around the Baltic and the artifact in question, Rolf had decided to concentrate on gaining information from the files of the KGB rather than continuing his focus on the Stasi.

If the Kremlin had quietly pursued the stolen treasure, he doubted that the suspicious Soviets would trust anyone from the German Stasi to front the search for the Amber Room.

That meant Ulrik took orders from Moscow, not East Berlin, and the answers he wanted could only come from a highly placed Soviet operative loyal to the CIA.

Whatever scheme Ulrik had put in place, it appeared to be unfolding to design, even after his death. For Rolf, it meant that someone was still out there, someone who knew all the details but managed to stay in the background—someone unnamed, unrecognized, and waiting.

If he was correct about Orensson's plan, everything was coming to a head. Rolf dragged his fingers through his hair. The unease he felt earlier increased. The paper had been recovered from the diary cover and Ulrik had pointed out the runes to spark Lea's memory of the rhyme. Whatever the next step, he was certain it would happen soon.

He kept thinking of Lea. He didn't like the idea of waiting until tomorrow to see her, but interrupting her visit with the reverend would provoke another argument. Rolf felt a needling discomfort about the visiting cleric. However, to be fair, men of the cloth generally had that effect on him. Was it the man making him uncomfortable or what he represented? Lea had already made clear what she thought of his opinions, what she called his mandates.

"I'm not one of your employees who have to jump at your commands in order to get a paycheck," she had said.

He tried to check his frustration at this continuous game of catch-up, of hoping to react in time. It had been a long time since he had no control over a situation and he didn't like it. He felt the same numbing anxiety that filled his childhood, a little boy with no power, and no say over who walked in and out of his life.

Now it occurred to him why Lea felt betrayed when he had taken the choice of a decision away from her, and that like his father, Rolf was afraid of anything he couldn't manipulate.

After his wife left, if Erik Sundren couldn't bend someone to his will, he took it upon himself to destroy the person. Business associates, employees, friends, mistresses, his own son—there were no exceptions. Is that what he had done to Lea?

Rolf couldn't wait for his meeting with the inspector the next day. He needed to reach him now with his speculation that Ulrik Orensson had a partner in the United States, someone who knew the family and had knowledge of Lea's nightmares.

29

KALMARSSON INN, 1989

The phone rang in the inn kitchen, but no one was in the house to pick it up. Mrs. Kalmarsson hummed a Swedish song as she busied herself setting the outdoor table for afternoon coffee.

"Let me help, Mrs. Kalmarsson," offered Lea

"No, no, you do enough. I never had a guest make beds before." Sigrid patted the young woman's hand. "Sit, sit. Enjoy your company." The innkeeper shooed Lea toward Reverend Sedgely.

"Reverend, did you know this young lady made Swedish pancakes?" Sigrid bragged. "There are a few left for you to try. Cold pancakes sprinkled with sugar are a treat my guests love."

"Hello, Reverend. I'm glad you decided to stay on Öland." Lea smiled a greeting as she joined the man under the sheltered arbor. "It seems I've been relegated to a comfortable chair with instructions to relax and enjoy." She sighed and the smile disappeared. "Mrs. Kalmarsson reminds me so much of my grandmother."

"I never met your grandmother, but I've certainly heard about her wonderful cooking." He smiled and patted his generous stomach with exaggeration. "Does this mean you've been taking lessons from Sigrid, and might need a poor minister and his wife to test your culinary skills? You know," he whispered conspiratorially, "Susan and the kitchen stove don't meet very often."

"You better hope Mrs. Sedgely doesn't hear that remark," she laughed.

It was easy to understand why people from the church were attracted to such a magnetic personality. He exuded strength of character, a person to confide in. He was popular with men and women equally. His empathy and sense of humor were the tools he used to put everyone at ease.

She was a teenager when the new assistant pastor joined the church. He was a gregarious man of generous proportion, with a mane of silver hair, full beard, and warm brown eyes with a twinkle that glasses couldn't hide. Reverend James Sedgely was an imposing figure, a man who wore his age well, and a charmer.

Lea had never really taken the opportunity to know the minister on a one-to-one basis. Except for her "service summer," when the pastor taught beginning German to her and a few other teens from the church, their conversations were few. While her family invited the reverend and his wife to their home many times for dinner, she followed her mother's example of distant congeniality and respect due a churchman. Right now, though, it felt good to laugh again. In such a relaxed setting, she cautiously let her guard down.

"How is everyone? Are the Farmers enjoying their first trip to Europe?" Lea wondered what caused the reverend's sudden unhappy look at the mention of his wife's sister, Brenda, and her husband, Ben. Then she decided a trip that included Brenda Farmer as a traveling companion would challenge the patience of anyone.

While James exchanged news and polite comments with Lea, his mind wandered to his jacket pocket, and the syringe filled with the neurotoxin he had gotten from Knudsson. It hadn't taken much of the poison to get rid of his brother-in-law. The women were stronger. He had calculated the dose carefully to make sure their deaths fit the timeline he set.

"I am very concerned about Benjamin. He's complained the trip is too much for him. I've tried to help by letting him remain at the hotel and rest while I accompanied the ladies on the local tourist excursions." The reverend shook his head.

"I have to admit that I'm starting to wonder about his bad stomach. He was well enough to drive me to the ferry. In fact he ate a large breakfast. Sometimes he seems like two different men. I think it's possible that much of his problem is mental, rather than physical.

"I'm sorry. I shouldn't be talking about Benjamin like this. It's uncharitable. The man does the best he can." The minister smiled. "I just hope that in my absence, Susan and Brenda will leave the poor fellow alone.

"Between you and me," he said, drawing closer to Lea's ear, as if the women might somehow be listening, "a man's got to draw the line somewhere. I just hope the ladies get their fill of bargain hunting before I return so I won't get pulled along on their next shopping junket."

She was openly chuckling at the reverend's story of lost luggage and strange escapades, when he abruptly changed the subject. "Let's talk about you, Lea. How are you enjoying your time in Sweden?"

She tried to start her explanation with the diary and her parents, but seeing sympathy in his eyes, Lea decided to talk about Rolf, then stopped as tears threatened.

"Whatever's wrong, Lea? It might be better to talk about it. Something or someone is making you very unhappy." He reached over to gently take her hand.

"I'm so confused. It's Rolf Sundren, a man I met here on Öland. I…we…" Lea's hands covered her mouth unconsciously and she stopped talking again. She liked the minister and appreciated all his support, but there was something inside that cringed at the thought of disclosing such personal intimacies.

James Sedgely leaned forward in the garden chair waiting for her to continue. Misunderstanding the young woman's unwillingness to share her relationship with Rolf Sundren, the minister attributed her lack of speech as an inability to speak about sexual matters after the attempted rape by Bradley Farmer.

"If there's anything I can help you with." Compassion was evident in his eyes. "Though I do understand if you're unable to discuss such matters with me. Maybe it would be easier if you talked about this to Mrs. Sedgely. I realize we have no children, but Susan thinks of you as a daughter."

Smiling at the thought, Lea knew she would never discuss her relationship with the reverend's wife. As much as she liked Susan, the one time she attended a church coffee, it was obvious by the woman's stiff posture and terse remarks that she was uncomfortable with the idea of sex.

"Spiritual relations and friendship," Susan had voiced, "not physical relations, are what's important in a marriage." After her experience with Bradley, she had readily agreed with Susan's ideas, but not now, not after knowing Rolf.

Maybe age played a part. She remembered the couple being in their late fifties when they wed ten years earlier. Lea imagined what her feelings toward Rolf would be at that age. Somehow she couldn't conceive wanting him any less.

"Thank you, Reverend. I appreciate your concern. It's something I'd rather keep to myself."

"All right. But as an old friend, may I give my observations at what I've seen and heard so far?"

"Of course."

"Then let me say what I think is good about your association with this Rolf Sundren. It tells me you're finally ready to accept the untimely death of your parents and go on with life. And that's how it should be.

"I know how difficult these past months have been for you, and frankly, Mrs. Sedgely and I have been worried. This is a healthy beginning for you."

She tried to smile, but tears were close.

"If your friendship with this man is not meant to be, there'll be another to take his place." He gently squeezed her hand. "Right now, when you're so far away from family and friends, my advice would be to keep this man at a distance until you understand the best course to take."

James got up from his chair to see if Sigrid had returned from the kitchen. Still he lowered his voice. "You know, Lea, when you bury yourself in a problem, it's very difficult to step back and look at the issue with an open mind. Believe it or not, the answers you want will come."

Guilt sat heavy with her. The minister's offhanded reference to her parents' death was a sharp reminder of what the focus of her thoughts should be.

"You've already helped me. What's important right now is finding the Amber Room and the people responsible for destroying my family, not solving my problems with Rolf."

"The Amber Room…destroying your family? What are you talking about?"

"Everything is ready. Come, come while coffee is hot," Sigrid called.

"I have a lot to tell you," Lea said, looking toward Mrs. Kalmarsson. "Later, when we're alone."

James nodded in agreement, as the innkeeper walked over to prod her guests to eat and drink.

"You are a gracious hostess, Sigrid. I will certainly enjoy my stay here." The reverend said a thank-you prayer before politely seating both women.

"Mrs. Kalmarsson you've outdone yourself." Lea said, smiling.

A large basket filled with warm rolls, fresh honey butter, and jams sat next to a plate stacked with little pancakes. The table, with its hand-woven linen cloth and large vase of garden flowers, was set with sterling silver and fine china.

"How lovely." Lea held up a tissue-thin cup and saucer, admiring their delicate sprinkling of violets.

"A gift from my Ernst on the day of our wedding."

It was nice that such beautiful things were used and enjoyed, not simply considered objects of art to be viewed through a glass case. It reminded her of childhood, her grandmother, and Sunday afternoon tea parties.

Like Mrs. Karlmarsson, MorMor didn't believe in plastic plates, paper napkins, or store-bought baked goods. Even tea parties with a child brought out the good dishes, cloth napkins, and homemade breads or cookies. Afterward, grandmother and granddaughter planned their next adventure as they washed and dried the fragile china. Today, those dishes were packed away in a cardboard box.

The talk was lively around the table. The reverend's coaxing brought out many of the innkeeper's best stories, as well as involuntary blushes at being made the center of attention. That didn't surprise Lea.

She remembered when the popular bachelor chose Susan to be his wife. The entire church had attended the marriage ceremony. Through generous donations, the congregation supported the assistant pastor's strong determination to continue his fight to win pagan souls in foreign lands. The months he was away doing missionary work, Susan dutifully remained behind spending her time involved in local church work.

Finally, the minister pushed back his chair. "Now, young lady, if it wouldn't be too much trouble, I'd enjoy a personal tour around this wonderful island to see some of the places you've spoken about."

Lea reached for her sweater and purse. She had seen Rolf's car and ignored it. "Do you mind if I use your car, Mrs. Kalmarsson? I'd like to take Reverend James around and show him the old castle, some runestones, maybe Eketorp. Just a little taste of what I think makes Öland special."

"The car is yours to use." Sigrid nodded her approval as she looked at the distinguished older man. It would do Lea good to get away with a friend and not think about Rolf Sundren. "Mr. Johansson has the keys."

Reverend James stopped in front of the innkeeper and held out his hand in a gesture of thanks. "Sigrid, *tack så mycket* for your hospitality."

"*Var så god, var så god.* You are always welcome here."

As he gave his Swedish "thank you" with a warm shake of hands, Lea enjoyed the innkeeper's blush. She wished it had been Inspector Youngmark who put the color in Mrs. Kalmarsson's cheeks.

Sigrid had confided to Lea the night of the Midsummer Dance that she and Lars had known one another since childhood. The two remained friends, even as both married and went on to different lives.

When Lars returned to Öland after the loss of his wife, Sigrid had tried to include him in the various activities around Färjestaden.

"I invite the man to dinner, but he always makes excuses not to come." Sigrid made sure Lea understood the thoughtfulness of the detective. "He calls on my birthday and visits on holidays. That is the limit of his attentiveness."

Lea wondered if after a marriage of many years, the inspector wanted to be left alone. Maybe he was content to live with his memories. She hoped that wasn't the case.

She had discovered how destructive it was to shut yourself off from everyone and keep pain locked inside. Lea hoped Inspector Youngmark would find the means to tuck the past away in his heart, and learn to celebrate and enjoy life in the present. She thought about her own family and Rolf. Funny, she couldn't follow her own advice.

Walking to the back gardens with the minister, she saw Gunnar bent over clipping roses. "Mr. Johansson, I'd like you to meet a friend from the United States, Pastor James Sedgely."

"Lea, Lea," Sigrid called.

"Excuse me for a moment. Mrs. Kalmarsson wants me for something." Lea left to find the innkeeper.

The gardener stood up to shake hands with the reverend.

"It's a pleasure, Mr. Johansson, to meet someone who has such a way with flowers. How wonderful to see these colorful gifts from God tended by such caring hands."

Lea returned with a sack of cookies and put them in the car. Ready to go, she saw the two men deep in conversation and decided not to disturb them. She left them alone to discuss gardening techniques, or whatever two elderly gentlemen found in common.

When Lea noticed they were finished, she took the keys and walked back to the car. Opening the door, a ball of yellow fur streaked off the front seat. Knocked off balance, the contents of her purse dumped on the ground.

Sigrid rushed to help pick everything up. "Bad cat. The cookies are my Gerda's favorite. I always keep a few to give her. This time, she is too greedy. I will get more for your trip."

Lea laughed as she picked up the empty paper bag and spied Gerda sitting in the garden, washing the crumbs from her face and whiskers with her tongue. It took only a minute for Sigrid to return with a fresh batch.

Once on their way, the minister commented again about the talents of Gunnar and his beautiful garden.

"Reverend, you have no idea what a remarkable man Mr. Johansson is. He knows every inch of Öland and the stories he tells about the island aren't found in any guidebook."

"While you're playing tourist guide, tell me more about Gunnar and some of the other people you've met on the island."

Lea smiled at the minister. He would not push her into any explanations concerning her family until she was ready. She appreciated his patience. "I think my connection to Mr. Johansson is the most curious. When he picked me up today, he was driving to visit the grave of his sister, Inga."

As she passed by the castle ruins of Borgholm, the windmills of the alvar, and the stone houses of the Broddesta fishing village,

Lea talked about the different personalities she had met on Öland. Turning off the main road, she headed toward the water, and the cottage of the fisherman Ragnar, and his wife, Inga. She stopped the car in the front of the house.

"You met the gardener, Gunnar Johansson. He was related to the couple who lived here, Ragnar and Inga. In 1945, Ragnar was fishing in the Baltic when he saw a sea monster. After the creature disappeared, he found a young girl, drowned, clutching an amber box. My grandmother was born on this island. In 1978, she bought a crate from a Chicago auction that originated here. The photographs I took out of the box were of this house. After Mom died, I found a package in the bookcase. Inside was a diary from World War II written in German." Lea handed the book to the minister.

"Rolf Sundren thought the journal came from the auction box, but that it possibly originated from one of the submarines trying to escape the Russian invasion at the end of the war. He speculated if you considered the submarine's port of departure, Königsberg, the diary might hold clues to a stolen masterpiece, possibly the Amber Room.

"Another opinion came from Professor Ulrik Orensson, a teacher of Swedish history. The professor agreed with Rolf that the journal likely came from a submarine. He said, considering the time period, the clues in the diary pointed to one of the many artworks stolen by the Nazis and never found. Because the diary was incomplete, a specific work or its location could not be established."

26

ÖLAND, 1989

The two walked to the back of the cottage and Lea pointed out Ragnar and Inga's grave markers to the minister. "I need to be able to sort through all of this, and I would appreciate your opinion, Reverend."

"Well, I can certainly understand your confusion. This whole episode is difficult to grasp." He looked out over the water and shook his head in sadness.

"The suffering those souls on the submarine must have endured. What a horrible accident. After coming so far, almost reaching safety and the young girl you spoke of. It's hard for me to think of a child at the bottom of sea."

She said nothing, her emotions allowing only a nod in agreement.

The minister took a few moments to page through the diary and then handed the book back.

"Let me make sure I understand this correctly. You are telling me an East German espionage group murdered your entire family for the sole reason of gaining this diary, and if Rolf Sundren is correct, to find the Amber Room."

"Yes." Lea nodded her head in agreement.

"In my opinion, it sounds like a bad spy novel."

"I wish that was the case. Unfortunately, it's all too real. I don't know why, or to what extent my family was involved in trying to find the treasure, nor what they intended to do with it. And right now it doesn't matter. What I do know is that, because of an object stolen over forty years ago, I've lost people I love. I'm not going to let the bastards who murdered my family get their hands on it!"

He ignored her profanity. "Lea, I admit the lure to treasure hunters would be obvious, if it is the fabled Amber Room at stake. My initial thought would be to start at the beginning, take emotions out of the mix, and be realistic. I would make sure the diary is authentic before I continued with the search."

She couldn't believe her ears. "You think my parents were murdered for a fake? Where's your outrage at what happened to them, Reverend James? These were people from your congregation, friends you've known for years. You've sat at our dinner table. How can you be practical and unemotional after what happened to my family?"

Seeing the incredulous look on her face, the minister continued, "I'm sorry to be so direct. But my sympathy won't bring your family back. The best way I can help is by being practical and unemotional. That will allow me to think with a clear head. Now, let's get back to the question."

"Which is?" Her cold tone was not lost on him.

"Were your parents murdered for a fake?" He held up his hands when she started to speak. "It's the only word I can use, and I have good reasons to ask the question." James took the book again, arms extended to see the picture more clearly. "Forgot my reading glasses," he muttered, shaking his head. "They're in the automobile. I need to get them if I'm going to make any sense of this rendering. We can continue sightseeing another day." As the two turned around to walk back to the car, James continued with his thinking.

"You believe your grandmother found the diary in a box from the auction. If that is true, I would guess the diary to be genuine. However, if your parents acquired the journal during their travels, it could easily be a fraud."

She opened her mouth to argue, but James held up his hand again. "Wait. Let me explain. Didn't your mother and father spend a lot of time in those areas of Europe where much of this story took place?"

"Yes."

"I know the Baltic region to some extent from my travels for the church, and have seen firsthand the extreme poverty of the population. I'm also aware of the significant small-scale industry that puts out quality forgeries. Anything that might attract the gullible public—paintings, ancient books, scrolls, furniture, all created and sold to help the people sustain themselves.

"Buyers are so excited at the thought of getting a good price for a work by a renowned artist, they don't always check the provenance of a piece. Or maybe, they're afraid if they examine the object too closely, they might find out its stolen. In any case, the result is the same.

"Unfortunately, I'd place the diary in that category. The temptation would be undeniable for someone who knew the story of the Amber Room to create such a work. It could be sold for a good sum of money.

"Except for those few aging men and women from World War II who served in the area around Königsberg, the Amber Room treasure is mainly unknown by the general American public of today. A forged document wouldn't be expected. The sad tale of the drowned girl gives the book a plausible background and historical accuracy. I would guess the story is well known throughout the entire Baltic region, not just on Öland. Superstitions, like the story of Ragnar, which are based on a kernel of truth but change and evolve with every telling, are notorious for spreading far and wide."

Reverend James turned to look her straight in the eye. "You know the reality of what I'm saying. Your books are filled with myths and legends from different cultures.

"Still, the question remains…was someone clever enough to put it all together in the form of a diary and sell it to your parents, or is it the genuine article?"

She shook her head. "I can accept someone like myself being fooled. But it seems unlikely people in the field, experts such as Professor Orensson, would be taken in by a fraud. And what about the Stasi? Why would they murder my grandmother and parents for a fake?

She stopped and opened to the picture before walking again. "Whoever drew this rendering created a complicated series of puzzles that first had to be uncovered, and then interpreted. We've started finding a few of the answers. Would a fake demand that much detail?"

Lea spoke of the runes hidden in the background that Professor Orensson had found, and held the picture to the light as Rolf had done, showing the minister the lines that depicted Sandby churchyard.

She explained the theories as she understood them, articulating Rolf's method of carefully stripping away the forms to reveal Karlevi, and repeated the reasons which caused him to choose Karlevi over Sandby.

"Then, there's the rhyme and my nightmare."

"Rhyme? Nightmare?" he questioned.

"Do you remember the overnight you and Mrs. Sedgely had for our teen group?

"The party you gave us to celebrate the end of our 'service summer.'"

"Oh, yes. Certainly, I remember. A fine group of young people helping in God's service. I…" The minister stopped talking for a moment to search his thoughts. "You had a bad dream in the middle of the night. I found you sitting up, unable to sleep, in tears, upset about dead people and something to do with numbers."

"Yes, that's right. You have a good memory."

"You wouldn't let me take you home. Refused to talk about your nightmare, and against my better judgment, made me promise to say nothing to your parents." He rubbed her arm gently. "After I agreed, you and I spent the rest of the night drinking hot chocolate and playing chess."

"I know you wanted to tell Mom and Dad. But it was such a bad time for my family, and I figured hearing about my nightmares would have made things worse.

"Anyway, those words and the nightmare started with the death of my grandmother and never went away. I thought if I could recall the complete verse, it would make the dreams stop. But I could never remember anything more than the first few lines after I woke up. Until now."

"What happened to change things?"

"When I was at the inspector's office…"

"Why were you at the inspector's office? Did something happen?"

"My room at the inn was searched. Everything was thrown around."

"Lea, why didn't you tell me about this? Are you okay?"

"I'm fine, Reverend. I wasn't in the room. And the only thing missing was my camera."

James looked at her, his features showing he wasn't convinced.

"We'll talk about this later. Maybe I could have a word with the man who is investigating your case, Inspector Youngmark. I'd like to make sure the police department is following up." The two continued to the car.

"When I was in the inspector's office, Professor Orensson talked about the history of the runic alphabet and how it changed from twenty-four symbols to sixteen. As he was explaining the script found in the diary, the complete verse suddenly came to me." Lea repeated the entire poem for the pastor.

She pointed to the ripped area from the book. "I think Rolf's theory is correct. The rhyme was written on the page torn from here." She stopped walking and looked out over the water. "I'm still not sure how I learned the rhyme. There are so many holes in my memory. I…" She shook her head. That was enough talking about the past for the moment.

"If you look at the complexity of the puzzle, and the connections between the picture and the rhyme, I think there's evidence to consider the journal genuine."

James Sedgely took the diary and paged through one more time before handing it back. "Your points are well taken. It is definitely worth a closer look. And this time, when I have my glasses."

"I'm glad you agree." She put the diary in her purse.

"A better understanding of the rhyme might be a good place to begin. Take each line and try to find a meaning. What do you think?"

"You and Rolf think alike. If you don't mind, I'm going to skip the rest of the sightseeing and go back to the inn." The expression she saw on the minister's face made it clear she was not fooling him.

"You know, my earlier talk about avoiding Rolf Sundren was only a suggestion. You don't have to follow my advice concerning your lifestyle or find excuses to leave me." His tone was more hurt than annoyed.

"Here they are." Back at the car, he picked his glasses off the dashboard and started to climb into the passenger seat for the trip to town. He stopped and shook his head. "I'm forgetting what it's like to be young. Even at this age, I remember my feelings the first time I saw Susan. Why don't you go ahead without me?" He smiled. "I understand."

The minister bent to pick a lone flower and pointed to the profusion of wildflowers in the field beyond Ragnar's cottage. "I do my best thinking when surrounded by nature's solitude, and I want to have some ideas about the journal and rhyme when the three of us get together. Besides, I need to check and see how Benjamin is doing. I'll see you back at the inn."

He moved closer for a goodbye hug, but the only arms Lea wanted around her right now were Rolf's. Moving behind the steering wheel, she left the minister with a wave.

As he watched the car take the rutted path away from the beach, Reverend James Sedgely looked down at the flower he still held in his hand and crushed the petals. Lea's departure gave him needed time alone. As for Rolf Sundren, it seemed the man had demonstrated himself entirely too astute.

27

ÖLAND, 1989

I t wasn't often James underestimated the extent of a problem. Rolf Sundren's discovery of Karlevi in the diary picture, and his insight to the importance of the rhyme, underscored the threat the American had posed to the success of his plan. But *had* was the operative word.

The minister looked at his watch to decide how long he had to complete his task before the young woman returned to the inn. He doubted she would find much information. Sundren's body should have already been moved to the morgue, and at the moment, thoughts on an exact cause of death would be few. Thanks to Per's choice of poison, there should be no telling clues.

When forensics made their final determination, the sudden loss of life would likely be attributed to a heart attack, until, or if, the toxin was found and analyzed. In any case, the cause didn't matter, only that the man was finally out of the way.

James wondered how the young Stasi had fared. Did the inspector kill the agent, or was it suicide that ended his life. "Don't get overly impatient," he counseled himself. "You'll find out soon enough."

Hurrying through the fields, he took every shortcut to reach the inn. Tiring from the fast pace and the heavy girth around his middle, James looked beyond some grazing cows and saw a pond with a grove of shade trees surrounding it. It was enough distance away from the milking barn to give him some privacy. He sat for a few moments of rest. Then looking at his watch, he knew it was time to get moving. Spotting the inn grounds, James stopped for the time it took to straighten his clothes. He had to look presentable. He looked to make sure no one was around. He found Gunnar sitting on a bench in the shade. The minister spoke in Swedish so the gardener would understand his words. "You asked me some questions earlier. I thought we could talk." Pulling out his handkerchief to wipe his face, a ring fell from his pocket.

Gunnar stared at the band and then at the reverend.

"I know this ring. Where did you get it?"

"Do you have a drink of water, Gunnar?"

"In the shed," he replied.

The two men walked toward the far back corner of the garden. Once inside, Gunnar pulled out a bucket and ladle for the minister and took the whiskey bottle for himself. He pointed to a chair for the minister, while he sat on a wooden box. Gunnar waited for the clergyman to speak.

"When I arrived in Kalmar three days ago, I took a room for the night at a local inn. At dinner, a man noticed my religious collar and joined me at the table. This was a man in pain. Not physical pain, you understand, but the kind only a tormented soul can bring. The years hadn't been kind to him. Time couldn't take away or ease the suffering he felt at the horrendous act he committed. He told me a story of a U-boat that had escaped Germany during the last days of the war. And he talked about a pretty young woman. It weighed heavy on his mind because he insisted her death wasn't intentional."

Gunnar listened and said nothing.

"Close to the coast of Öland, the sub became crippled and quickly began to fill with water. The man was near a hatch. He managed to grab a child and both escaped. Unfortunately, the girl died almost immediately from the cold water. There were no others. He was the only survivor.

"When the man reached shore, he saw light from a cottage. Needing dry clothes and fresh water, he climbed through a window. There was never any harm intended toward the woman. He made that very clear to me. Unfortunately, she saw him and screamed."

James paused to make sure the gardener understood the obvious. There was no reason to dwell on distasteful details.

"He was truly sorry for the tragedy of her death and wanted forgiveness. When he finished his story, the man handed me this ring and asked me to take it. The band symbolized all the grief and sorrow of his past. He wanted no part of it."

Gunnar couldn't get the words out. After all these years, to finally know what happened to his baby sister was overwhelming and emotional. How frightened Inga must have felt. And then to be dumped in the water like a scrap of garbage to be torn apart by the fish. It was too painful to comprehend. Did she feel pain? Dirt streaked across the gardeners face as he wiped away tears with the back of his hand.

"I don't believe his story. How could a man who tried to save one life take another? What you call a tragedy, I call murder," said Gunnar.

Frustrated by the injustice, Gunnar lashed out at the minister. "Some of this shame rests on your shoulders, Reverend. Why do you keep this monster's secret?"

"I can understand why you hold such hatred, Gunnar. But as a minister, I could not in good conscience turn this person over to the police or tell others of his sins. War always demands the worst from men. Unconscionable acts are committed by all sides. You saw the cruelty inflicted by the Nazis. But did the atrocities end when the liberators arrived? Did defenseless women and children deserve pain and death any more than Inga and the young girl from the submarine? The retribution must stop somewhere, Gunnar! World War II is history. Now it is left for the scholars to choose who is a hero or villain. Besides, the person responsible is dead. When I was in town, I heard that his body was found earlier today."

The gardener reached for a single glass, poured a bit of whiskey into the bottom, and handed it to James.

The reverend raised his glass in salute. "To Inga." When he finished, he slipped the empty glass in his pocket.

Gunnar nodded. "To Inga." Gunnar tipped the bottle and drank. The liquor was soothing and warm in his throat and encouraged him to talk.

"As a young man, war meant nothing to me. Politics wouldn't fill my belly. Inga tried to persuade me not to leave Öland in 1939, but a chance to work in Germany was hard to pass. The Nazis offered good money and appreciated my skills with wood. I was convinced that the events in Poland were not my affair. By the time I realized my mistake, it was too late."

The minister shook his head in sympathy, and moved closer to Gunnar.

"Near the end of the war, I was working in Königsberg and received an order to make some boxes. I was never given the name of the man who arrived to oversee my work. This person wore the ring you have. Every time he came to my shop, the man brought his daughter, a child he called, Liese. Always a pen in her hand, writing in a book, she was." Gunnar took one last swig and replaced the cork in the bottle.

"The final time I saw the two, it was early morning at the pier. The Russians had already burned my shop and were looking for me. Hiding under the dock, I saw and heard everything as a man they called Ulrik climbed into the submarine with Liese and her father. I heard them say their destination was Öland. That was the last time I saw anyone from the U-boat until…Wait, I get ahead of myself.

"Only once did my brother-in-law talk about my sister Inga, the monster, and the girl he pulled from the water. It was right after my release from the hospital. From Ragnar's words, I knew the child was Liese, but after so many years, it was hard to keep my thoughts straight. My mind confused easily. After a while,

I wasn't sure what I remembered. Sometimes it was real, other days, it seemed more a dream. Until a year ago…spring." Gunnar rubbed a hand over his eyes to clear them.

"Early morning, near Ragnar's house, I saw a ghost. Fog lay heavy on the beach, but it thinned enough near the house so I could make out the form and face of the specter."

Gunnar lifted the bottle in his hand. "I had a flask of whiskey and I admit to taking a few sips. Sigrid doesn't allow me alcohol at the inn. But I know what I saw. The thing was as close to me as you are right now, dressed in black, it was. I crouched low next to Inga's gravestone, but it paid me no attention. Moved right past and vanished into the water.

"I couldn't rid the sight from my brain. I feared going to sleep at night, even during the day I suffered spells. The ghost triggered memories buried from the war…from the years I spent in the gulag…the hospitals. I thought I was going crazy." He reached for the bottle again, pulled the cork, and downed the liquid to the bottom.

"And now, during Midsummer, I saw the creature again. This time there was no mist or alcohol to cloud my vision. It was not a dead man, but a living Ulrik. Even with the years passed, I knew him." Gunnar tried to wipe the sweat from his face with his sleeve.

"I knew him. I stayed back, not wanting him to see me. He walked away from the celebration toward a cluster of trees. I followed and saw him meet with a man I recognized from town, Per Knudsson. I saw you speak to Per Knudsson early this morning. I thought you might know Ulrik Orensson as well."

"So that's how you connected me to Ulrik."

Gunnar nodded.

"How about some tobacco, Gunnar?" James took a cigarette pack and matches from his front jacket pocket."

Gunnar put down the bottle, eager for the smoke. He enjoyed the mildness of American cigarettes, but the cost was too high to afford them on a regular basis. Gunnar clumsily pulled a smoke free from the pack. It was the distraction the minister needed. James pulled out a gun, put his hand over Gunnar's, and forced the man to point the weapon at his own belly. Without hesitation or words, James pressed his fingers against the trigger.

The minister took a last look at the figure sprawled on the dirt floor. Odd that Gunnar had known the girl and her father, and that he had been at the pier to see the group leave in the submarine bound for Öland. Strange that he was Inga's brother. Still all those events were coincidence, nothing more.

James didn't accept the idea of fate or predestination. Unlike fools who thought the Amber Room and journal were cursed, he believed any outcome could be explained and controlled. His successful elimination of Gunnar underscored the correctness of his view.

He had to act quickly. The gunshot was loud and might attract attention. Still, he could not become careless.

He picked up the Chesterfield cigarette Gunnar had dropped and stuck it in his pocket. It was too obvious to leave behind.

Taking a rag from the shelf, he carefully picked up the pack of cigarettes and placed them in the shed corner. The edge of the Chesterfield box was visible.

Everything was in place. He found a suitable branch and crudely dug out several deep marks inside the shed.

James made his way from the garden, through fields, to the pond he had stopped at earlier. He wet his handkerchief and removed the blood from his face. He cleaned his hair and beard. The soiled clothes were another matter. The spurting of stomach matter had soaked through to his undergarments. It was too large of an area not to cause questions.

After rubbing his clothes with dirt, he picked up a sharp stick to mimic an attack. Making two long, deep gashes on his arm, James inhaled. He smeared his own blood over the shirt and pants.

Looking around the secluded grove, he decided to stay for a period and work on deciphering the rhyme. It wouldn't be smart to be close to the inn when the gardener's body was discovered. The scratches hurt, but nothing could take away his overall feeling of success.

When found by the inspector, the cigarettes would incriminate Benjamin Farmer. With a suspicion that he might find a use for them, James took the numerous packs of Chesterfield cigarettes from his dead brother-in-law, and made sure Benjamin's prints were on them. It was unfortunate the whiskey glass wouldn't show Ben's prints as well. He took the glass from his pocket and heaved it far out into the water.

Benjamin Farmer's sudden disappearance, a pack of the man's tobacco found at Gunnar's death scene, and the cigarettes he had scattered at other places, would center the inspector's attention on the missing Farmer long enough for James to get off the island.

His plan was on schedule. Now it was time to get to work. He mulled over the lines of the verse which Lea had remembered.

He already knew from the hidden picture in the diary that the first two lines of the rhyme referred to Karlevi. Starting with the third line of the verse, he repeated it slowly, letting the words roll off his tongue. "Of earth scarring battles and blood stains deep." Battles and blood were a common theme in Viking prose. Was it just a reiteration of Viking lore or a runic symbol?

Earth could represent the color black and blood might equal red. It was possible many runestones of the Younger Futhark were colored to make the sixteen-symbol alphabet easier to understand. Was this what the line meant?

James had wondered how using the text on the Karlevi Stone would point the way to the Amber Room. He examined the monument many times, trying to figure out where the treasure was hidden. If there was a way to change the story by using color on the different symbols, it was possible the stone could reveal the hiding place of the treasure. But he had found nothing in the diary that referred to color. No, it had to be something else. The fourth line, "Brave warriors lost and treasures taken," he took to denote the stripping of the Amber Room by the Nazis.

> Separate the eagle's dance with the raven
> Old Gods speak tales of foreboding
> Evil seeks the lines unbroken.

This part of the rhyme he had yet to understand. Eagles and ravens were pictured in the diary, but the birds were a common theme.

It was likely Lea either left out lines of the verse, or changed some words. He had no doubt that when the rhyme was correct, it would decipher the code. Once he was certain the woman's expertise was no longer needed, she would join her family in death. He glanced at his watch again. It was time to carefully make his way back to the inn. There he would find a spot where he would remain concealed but could hear and observe. He wasn't sure what his next step would be, but he was ready.

28

KALMARSSON INN, 1989

Back at the inn, Sigrid stopped washing dishes when she heard the phone. Wiping her hands carefully before turning down the radio, she answered on the third ring.

"Kalmarsson Inn. Sigrid speaking." The anxiety she heard in the woman's voice as she told her story was alarming.

"This is Susan Sedgely. My sister's husband, Ben Farmer, is missing. He never returned to the hotel after taking Reverend James to the ferry. My sister and I returned to the room after shopping and he wasn't there. That was days ago. No one has seen him," she told the innkeeper. "His clothes, papers, everything is missing. He left a note, but it is personal."

"I understand. Is there something I can do, Mrs....? Yes. I will give the message to your husband when he returns and tell him to return to the hotel, immediately. Goodbye."

Sigrid opened a kitchen drawer to pull out a pad and pencil. The reverend was to contact his wife and make arrangements to return to Denmark. She had enjoyed the comical stories about the mishaps with the reverend's traveling companions, Mr. and Mrs. Farmer, but now Mr. Farmer was gone.

Four days earlier, the sisters had gone out shopping to Copenhagen, and it was late evening before they arrived back at their rooms. Brenda found it strange that her husband had not returned from his early morning drive to take Reverend James to the Helsingor ferry docks, a trip only a short distance from their hotel.

The room held no clues to his disappearance until the women opened a closet door. The large dressing area that earlier held all of Benjamin's clothes and personal papers was empty. An envelope taped to the wooden clothes pole was the only thing left. Without a remark to Susan, Brenda crumpled up the paper, tossed it into the wastebasket, and walked out of the room. Susan retrieved the printed note and read Ben's words of betrayal.

The women arrived the next morning at the ferry docks to find the car abandoned in the parking lot. The sisters asked for information, but no one remembered seeing the man. Brenda Farmer was in a state of shock. Susan waited another two days before contacting the inn on Öland. She hoped Ben would come to his senses and call or return. He had not.

Both women had become ill. Brenda, the stronger of the two, could still function. For Susan, the nausea was overwhelming and it was becoming difficult to think straight. Bizarre visions crowded her thoughts.

"Brenda, I feel sick." Susan ran to the toilet.

"Susan, show some backbone. It's only the pickled fish we had for lunch. I'm feeling nauseous myself. This is Ben's fault! The man thinks only of himself." Brenda sat down on the couch and stayed very still. If she didn't move, her stomach might not cramp. "He'll be back," she said assuredly. He couldn't get along without her.

Sigrid thought about the phone call from Susan Sedgely. From the words she inferred, Sigrid could easily guess the content of the note and understand the grief. Marital infidelity was common around the world.

She had been without her man for a long time. And even though it was death that took Ernst rather than another woman, it didn't heal the ache or memory of what it was like to reach over in the night, only to remember the one you loved was no longer sleeping next to you.

Sigrid just put her hands back in the water when the phone rang again. This time without bothering for a dishtowel, she picked up the receiver.

"Kalmarsson Inn. Sigrid speaking." Her words took the tone of irritation at being interrupted again. It took a moment for the news to register. "Lars's friend, Professor Orensson, and Per Knudsson dead. How could such a thing happen?"

Sigrid hung up the phone and decided to walk out to the garden to tell Gunnar the news. Then she would call Lars to make sure he was safe. The dishes could wait.

"Gunnar…Gunnar!" She called. He didn't answer. She returned to the house to check his room. It was the man's habit never to leave the inn without telling her or writing a note on the kitchen chalk board. She was worried.

This last year had been difficult for him. Sigrid was aware of the many pills he consumed trying to gain a measure of rest. The sleeping potions had become ineffective. Last evening, plagued with night spells, she heard him roaming the house during the late hours.

She had tried to get through to Lars. She would try again after her chores.

KALMAR POLICE STATION, 1989

The inspector put down his pen, incapable of concentrating on office work. He had sifted through the evidence bags a second time, but Sundren's words still rang in his ears. What did he know about Ulrik Orensson? There could be no more assumptions. Obviously, he had been shielded from the real person. Lars had worked at the man's side for many years. Was it possible for Ulrik to disguise every facet of his personality? The detective didn't think so. The trick was to search for memories revealing the man's true character, elemental traits that would be difficult to mask.

At that point, Lars decided to open the briefcase found with Per. He knew from past training that it should be handled only by Swedish security, and he was a man averse to breaking rules. Ulrik would have known that. It was time to do the unexpected.

The inspector took the suitcase across from headquarters to a shielded building used for police training. If the thing was going to blow, he didn't want anyone else hurt.

Hands sweating, he carefully unsnapped the lock. The case opened smoothly. Taking only the contents, he walked back to his office. He would leave examination of the leather shell to the lab.

He picked up the phone. "I will take only emergency calls," he said to the secretary. Spreading the contents of the case across his desk, Lars separated out and opened a small zippered case. A syringe and a small bottle of fluid fit snugly inside. He guessed it was the same mixture Per had tried to use on Rolf Sundren. Taking no chances, he placed the small case on a blue dot inside the station safe. He found one of his officers. "No one is to open the safe without a direct order from me." If the case was moved, he would know.

Looking at the pile of papers from the briefcase, Lars noticed a message addressed to Per from Stasi headquarters. He put on gloves to protect the papers from contamination. Picking up the document to read, he realized it was two sheets. An extra page had accidentally been torn from the pad.

He pulled the papers apart, and for the moment set aside the letter and concentrated on the empty page. Shaving off some lead from his pencil, he scattered the carbon across the paper. The settled dust exposed indentations left from a previous correspondence.

Taking the sheet, Lars left his office and walked upstairs to the lab desk. He liked the head man and trusted the preciseness of his work. "Try to bring out the text on this paper. Whatever you find, contact me directly, Lindberg."

Returning to his office, Lars sat at his desk and picked up the letter addressed to Per. The formal order informed the young agent that he was being pulled from Öland. A new set of identity papers would be provided when he reached Berlin. Per Knudsson's signature was at the bottom showing his acceptance. A second piece of correspondence from Stasi headquarters was more interesting.

"Connect with East German submarine immediately after assassinations of Rolf Sundren and Ulrik Orensson." The coordinates to reach the sub were included in the letter.

Apparently, Ulrik's death was not due to the mistake of an inexperienced agent, as Lars first thought. The Stasi meant to eliminate both men. Something bothered him about the directive, but he put it to the back of his mind for the moment. He would re-read the paper later. He was interested in the document stuffed inside a brown wrapper. After scanning the sheet, he knew this would prove to be the prize.

The *Hitler Document*, that Swedish intelligence had been so anxious to acquire, was worthless. The bargaining tool Ulrik had intended to trade for his immunity was a fake.

Lars dug out the sheet Ulrik left in his care and compared it to the one he took out of the envelope. The forgery was masterfully done. Only now, by looking at what must have been the practice sheet, did the inspector see the deception and recognize the author.

Ulrik was a perfectionist. When they had worked together, the sheets he remembered the man using when breaking codes for counterintelligence were arranged in a precise order. The sequence never varied for any reason. It was a superstitious quirk, and a characteristic that a rational-obsessed Ulrik would never admit. The practice sheet he pulled from Per's briefcase was organized in that exact same pattern. The detective doubted anyone, except himself, would have recognized Ulrik's handiwork.

Using a magnifying glass, the inspector closely examined the papers Ulrik left with him. He had no doubt that the papers and stamp used were the genuine article from Nazi–era Germany. The small piece Lars was directed to give Swedish intelligence for testing would have proved the validity of the document. Without the practice sheet, no one, including himself, would have suspected the *Hitler Document* was a fake.

"Inspector," the officer stuck his head in the door. "Mrs. Kalmarsson is on the phone. Will you take her call?"

"Urgent?" he asked.

The officer shook his head no.

"Please. Only emergency calls!"

Lars looked again at the practice sheet. What was the point? While the phony *Hitler Document* would have brought a great deal of money and notoriety for Ulrik, with his extensive knowledge of Stasi operations, Swedish intelligence would have still sought his defection and paid handsomely.

More interestingly, if this practice sheet was the only piece of evidence disclosing the masterful counterfeit, a careful Ulrik would have destroyed it. Why didn't he?

He would let that question sit, and instead try to find the reason the East German secret police wanted Ulrik dead.

While he understood why the Stasi might want to take a meddling Rolf Sundren out of the picture, assassinating Ulrik was not a practical step.

Since the counterfeit paper was found in Per's briefcase, it was possible the younger agent found a way to recognize the forgery and reported the reproduction to Stasi headquarters. Personally taking Ulrik's phony papers to Berlin after completing his assassination orders would certainly create a triumphant entrance for Per and generate a multitude of opportunities for the young Stasi agent. If that was the case, whatever plan Ulrik originally had for the fake document was compromised. However, eliminating Ulrik would have been a foolish waste of a valuable resource, and the Stasi were not fools.

If those in Berlin knew the document was phony, it made more sense to let the deception play out. The fallout from such a ploy would be enormous. Swedish intelligence would have bought a worthless paper implicating innocent people and corporations as Nazi collaborators.

The East Germans would expose the debacle by revealing the forger's practice sheet, but only after the damage was done. The credibility of any Western country, spy agency, or military organization that had jumped to support the original document would have been severely damaged. A media field day, and a communist press agent's dream.

What if the East Germans were not aware the document was false and discovered Orensson's traitorous plan to defect?

Both Lars and Ulrik knew the outcome if Orensson's plan was exposed by the Stasi before he was safely in the protective custody of the West. It was the reason Lars couldn't understand why Ulrik took such little precaution for his own safety even after voicing fears of capture. And to be lured into a trap by a young Stasi—it didn't fit. The price exacted against a renegade double agent was well-documented.

There were reasons why killing a turncoat outright was a solution only if the target was unable to be snagged and brought back. Rather, it was preferred to make the renegade a vivid lesson in dissuasion.

The custom of gaining information and discouraging independent actions might be more refined and private than the staged spectacles of days past, but it existed. The art of devising agony and torment for the mind and body of an enemy is a common practice, including those nations considered enlightened and civilized.

He did not like the way either analogy played, and suspected the East Germans had not initiated the orders of execution. It seemed this time the Stasi was not his prime suspect.

The knock on the door interrupted his concentration. "Yes, what is it? I told you not to disturb me."

"Inspector, the lab informed me your results on the paper are ready."

He waited until Peter left before he hurried upstairs to get the papers and bring them to his office. Whatever method Lindberg used, it didn't take much time to expose the hidden text on the paper. He separated the two pieces of correspondence. Lars blacked out all reference to Per's travel orders to better understand what else had been written. What he found was a short memo identifying ten names, locations, and a contact person, Ivanavich. Many from the group appeared to be British or American, but it was hard to judge nationality. One name on the paper was familiar, Agent Arnesson, from Vasterbotten County. He had worked with the agent years ago. The man had supported him and was non-judgmental when Lars was forced to leave Swedish intelligence.

The detective had to find out why these men were listed. However, before contacting intelligence, he wanted to pinpoint the organization responsible for the assassination orders targeting Ulrik and Rolf Sundren.

Going over the various groups associated with the Stasi, one name hadn't been eliminated. There would have been little for Ulrik to fear from the East German organization, if he had backing from the powerful group who worked hand-in-hand with the Stasi, the KGB. It made sense that Orensson was fronting a search for the Amber Room on behalf of the Soviets. The Kremlin would have positioned him in Berlin as the most logical place to mount a search for the treasure.

What if Ulrik had gone one step farther and decided to double-cross the Soviets to gain the Amber Room for himself?

After obtaining his protection and generous benefits from the West, Ulrik would find the practice sheet showing the document hidden inside the diary cover to be a fake. The authenticity of the book hiding the phony paper would become suspect as well, effectively ending any interest in the diary. Orensson would be left alone to find and claim the treasure.

A dangerous game, but one that fit Ulrik's ego much better than the old man image he presented to Lars earlier.

But someone beat the spymaster at his own game. Whoever wrote the order for Per to exterminate the two men made sure the briefcase would be recovered. This person knew the truth of Orensson's intentions and had double-crossed the spy. Logically, the person entrusted with Ulrik's plans would have been considered expendable. Ulrik would never allow anyone to remain alive with knowledge that the diary contained factual clues to the treasure. Who had made sure Ulrik failed?

29

KALMAR POLICE STATION, 1989

The inspector went upstairs to find an empty office. Recently, he had felt uneasy using his own space for important calls. Someone was watching him and likely listening to his conversations. He put in a call to Swedish authorities to report some minor details. It was an excuse to ask questions but not answer any.

Lars did not want to turn over the document Ulrik had left with him. Not yet. He also decided to withhold the existence of Per's briefcase and its contents.

Still, he needed to pry some information from the Swedish authorities.

"Agent Swansson, Inspector Youngmark from Kalmar." He greeted his one friendly contact. "I want to report that Stasi operative Per Knudsson carried a briefcase. It will be turned over to your office." At the end of his report, Lars quickly turned the conversation to common interests within the trade, and spoke about Agent Arnesson.

"I would appreciate anything you can tell me. It's been too long since I've heard from him."

"Hold the wire, Inspector."

Lars clearly heard the shuffle of papers and the slamming of a door. It took a few moments before Swansson picked up the phone again.

"You understand. This is not to be repeated. Arnesson was part of a covert group that has been captured. There's information the men were taken to Kaliningrad, but my guess is they'll end up at Lubyanka prison. There had been a trade-off in the works, but I was just informed today it has been put on hold. I'm sorry.

"Inspector, since I have you on the line, is there a reason we have not received the sample of paper to be tested from the *Hitler Document?*" A click signaled the conversation had ended. Lars returned to his office downstairs.

His young aide opened the door a crack.

"Lea Reardon is on line one. She said it was important."

Nodding, he picked up the phone. "Miss Reardon."

"Inspector, Gunnar Johansson…he's dead." She had a hard time saying the word. "Mrs. Kalmarsson found him."

"Say no more, I will be right there." The detective picked up the papers from Per's briefcase, selecting the ones he wanted to take. He put them together with documents he removed from his secret place and stuffed them into his brown satchel. Everything else he returned to the hidden space under the floor board.

Today the inspector's feeling that his office was compromised became physical proof. After going upstairs to the lab, papers on his desk had been shuffled about. The officers knew not to touch anything in his office. Most people thought he had no idea what documents were on his desktop. They were wrong.

The detective had a good idea who was keeping him under observation, but not what organization he represented. The man could be from any covert agency—Swedish intelligence, Stasi, KGB, CIA, or others. Lars checked the safe often to see if Per's syringe and vial were missing. No different than trying to catch a fish. He would keep letting out line, tease, and play the intruder until he figured how best to use him. Deciding to leave the dog behind, he called his secretary.

"Notify off duty officers they are to report to Kalmarsson Inn. I will meet them there."

KALMARSSON INN, 1989

The inspector and his aide arrived at the inn and went directly to the shed to examine the body and death scene.

"It appears to be a suicide, Inspector," Peter voiced his opinion. "An empty liquor bottle to give him courage." He pointed to the empty container.

"Maybe," Lars answered. His own knowledge of the man's escalating troubles was backed by Sigrid's confirmation of sleepless nights, increased drug use, and a mounting fear of returning to psychiatric hospitals. The motive for taking his own life was there. But looking closely, Lars saw other evidence.

"Gouges in the packed dirt floor. And here," the detective indicated Gunnar's arm. "Finger-sized bruises are spread across the body's wrist area. That gives reason to think there might have been a struggle. Someone of strength could have grabbed his hand, forcing the weapon to fire into his stomach. The main question remains. Did Gunnar Johansson take his own life, or was he murdered?"

Among the gardening tools, Lars picked up a small, white box trimmed in red. The Chesterfield box was easy to identify. If he was lucky, there would be prints. He placed the cigarette pack into an evidence bag. He would keep it with him until he found someone he could trust to take it to the lab. Lars was concerned the evidence might be compromised if he left it with Peter.

"Inspector Youngmark?" the man inquired entering the shed.

"Yes." Lars stood up to look at the two men from the morgue dressed in protective suits and gloves. "I will fill out the necessary forms when I return to Kalmar. If the pathologist notices anything unusual, he can reach me at my office or here at the inn." Lars watched the men cover Gunnar with a sheet, and lift him onto the stretcher. "Take the body around the far side of the inn." He didn't want Gunnar's remains carried past Sigrid and Miss Reardon. After the van left, Lars walked quickly to the inn. He was ready to talk to Sigrid and Lea Reardon.

Seeing the inspector leave the garden shed, Lea left Sigrid sitting in a chair on the patio and went in the house to make coffee.

"Sigrid. It is necessary to ask you questions." Lars took out his notebook and pencil.

The innkeeper said nothing, but nodded her head in acceptance.

"Has Gunnar's drinking increased recently?"

"Yes," she answered softly.

"Has his personality changed in any way? Has his speaking, or body actions become erratic?"

"Gunnar has had a difficult time sleeping since he came from the hospitals, but lately it has become much worse. You know what I am saying, Lars. You have seen him roam the gardens in the middle of the night. He talks to people who are not real." Tears started to fall down Sigrid's cheeks.

"Come, come, Sigrid." Lars put down the paper, and placed his arm around his old friend for a moment. "Has Gunnar met with anyone new, someone you are not familiar with?" He began his notes again.

"The last person who spoke with Gunnar was Sedgely, Lea Reardon's friend from the United States. He just arrived. He has the room next to Lea. That reminds me, the minister's wife, Mrs. Susan Sedgely, called from their hotel in Denmark. She asked if I had seen her brother-in-law, Benjamin Farmer. He is missing, Lars. I told the lady when the Reverend returned to the inn, I would have him contact her. Please make sure he gets the message if you speak with him first."

"I will do that." After questioning Sigrid, the detective left the woman drinking coffee. He was grateful for the fresh pot Lea made and hoped it would have a calming effect on his friend. It had been an awkward situation.

He had always known Sigrid to be a sturdy, independent woman. Like others of their generation, she had survived war and adversity. She had accepted the death of her husband in a stoic manner, and went on to build a handsome business asking for no man's help.

However, during the questioning, when it had become increasingly difficult for Sigrid to answer and tears had formed, Lars had stepped out of his role as detective in a sign of sympathetic camaraderie.

That moment of social intimacy disturbed and confused the detective He hoped his blunder wouldn't compromise their years of friendship. Aware the accurate recalling of the event would become confused and blurred if too much time elapsed, he had had no choice but to continue.

In addition to Sigrid's information about the gardener, she had repeated the message concerning the absent Benjamin Farmer. He stopped in the kitchen to make a phone call to Denmark. Lars needed a description of Brenda Farmer's husband.

"Between fifty and sixty." Brenda stated. "He didn't celebrate birthdays. He's skinny, graying blond hair, blue eyes, and he wears false teeth. The military would know blood type. He wasn't much of a husband. He was always in the hospital for one thing or another. He's a chain-smoker. Always a Chesterfield in his mouth. The man might as well roll up dollar bills and burn them."

Mrs. Farmer, do I have your permission to check your husband's medical records?"

"Why?" she asked, her voice tinged with suspicion. "He was sick because he drank and smoked. Isn't that enough for you?"

The testiness in her voice wasn't lost on Lars.

"Your husband is missing. My department needs background information from every source if we are going to locate him."

"Fine. Yes. Wait...what did you say? Who are you?" she mumbled.

"I will keep you informed. Goodbye." The woman didn't seem alert.

Lars addressed his officers. "I want residents questioned within a two-mile radius. Describe Benjamin Farmer." He handed out sheets with Farmer's information. "It is possible someone has seen this person." He had two mysteries that split his concentration and the resources of his office. He had to find out if they were connected. He needed an answer soon.

Lea walked back and forth on the inn porch, unable to sit. After leaving the reverend, she had driven back to the inn on the slim hope Rolf might have left her a message. The scream from Mrs. Kalmarsson had her racing to the garden shed. She had helped the older woman back to the house, called the inspector's office, and sat with Sigrid until the detective arrived.

There had been no words of conversation between the two women while waiting for the police. Sigrid's meeting with Inspector Youngmark was kept private. Lea went back to the kitchen. It was the only room downstairs the police didn't occupy.

She wondered how long it would take before the detective wanted her story. She looked out to see the man hurrying toward the house. She waited a few minutes to make sure the inspector didn't need her, and went back outside to check on Sigrid.

"Is there anything I can do for you, Mrs. Kalmarsson?" Lea asked.

"*No tack.* Thank you. Gunnar, he was unhappy, yes, but this—I never expect him to…" Tears fell down her cheeks.

Lea understood Sigrid's grief, but sensed words of sympathy were not what the woman needed.

"Mr. Johansson grew such beautiful flowers, and I know he made the lovely table in my room. Tell me more about him."

"Gunnar was a wonderful craftsman when he was younger. He could make anything with his hands, but he was especially gifted with wood. When he left to work for the Nazi party, I told him it was a mistake. Gunnar wanted to make money. The Third Reich offered high wages. After the war, he was hunted and caught by the Russians. He was imprisoned for a decade in a Siberian gulag and spent years recuperating in hospitals. Gunnar's broken body never healed completely. His mind never recovered. He had good years here at the inn. Lately, problems from the war came back."

Once the innkeeper started, time passed quickly as tears were mixed with smiles and laughter.

The inspector finally returned with a number of papers.

"Sigrid, I would like you to read these before you sign them. It is the conversation we had about Gunnar." Lars placed the sheets in front of the innkeeper, and stood by in case she had questions.

"Inspector. Take my chair." Lea excused herself and got up.

She headed for the kitchen to search for something to drink other than coffee. Lea felt a furry body rub against her legs. Bending down, she gave the cat a quick pat before opening the refrigerator. Gerda had other ideas, and remained directly in her path, making any step impossible without tripping.

"What is it, girl? What do you want?"

"She must be hungry," Lars answered.

She hadn't realized the inspector had entered the house again. As soon as he opened the cupboard door, Gerda started meowing excitedly, circling the man's feet.

Murmuring soft words to calm the impatient animal, the detective took out a box of cat food, poured some in a bowl, and set it on the floor behind the cook stove.

"You little manipulator." Lea laughed. Gerda sniffed her food bowl and left the kitchen with a flick of her tail.

The kitchen phone rang.

"Youngmark," the detective answered.

She wondered if he wanted privacy, but Lars didn't motion Lea to leave the kitchen or try to disguise his conversation. His quick answer in Swedish made it hard to recognize anything but a man's name. Why was he interested in Benjamin Farmer?

Lars saw the curiosity on the young woman's face turn to recognition when he spoke Farmer's name. It told him she knew the man, but how well?

The detective remained uncertain of the extent, if any, of the involvement the man had in Gunnar's death. The report from Agent Swansson of Swedish intelligence informed Lars information on the missing Illinois man was almost nonexistent.

"Data concerning Farmer has been pulled or erased. We have nothing to fill out his profile. There are no pictures of the man in his home. His son, Bradley Farmer, takes up the wall space. Fingerprints were taken from the hotel in Denmark, specifically from Benjamin's toothbrush. The Americans located a set of prints from the military that were overlooked. They are a match, Lars. That is our one lucky break, and the only exact information we have on the man. A file of his prints will be sent to your Kalmar office," stated Agent Swansson.

"In addition, Swedish intelligence has decided to examine other possibilities," Swansson continued. "The circumstances surrounding Farmer's disappearance and the lack of information are suspicious. If he is connected to any US investigative agency, a direct link hasn't been located at this time. The next step will be to search federal databases after Chicago agents make sure the Outfit is not involved."

"The Outfit?" Lars frowned, not recognizing the name.

"Better known as the Chicago Mob. It is possible Farmer testified against a crime boss, was given a new identity, and put in the Witness Protection Program. We will get answers when the Americans, either the CIA or FBI, are able to narrow the hunt by searching through their records, and can untangle fact from fiction. Such are the problems of a large US bureaucracy, eh, Youngmark. People get lost. I will contact you when there is more. Goodbye."

He was grateful for the information from Agent Swansson and listened politely to his opinion, but disagreed the problem was specific to the United States.

The inspector thought about what he knew. Instead of pulling events together, the information culled from the various agencies added confusion. Even the "proof" unearthed in Per's apartment might have been altered or placed there on purpose to misdirect. Could Ben Farmer be Stasi or KGB?

"Sir." Peter entered the kitchen. "A dairyman has news for you."

"Send him in." He had sent officers out for information on Benjamin Farmer and any activity on the nearby beach. This man was the first to respond.

"Inspector Youngmark." The large-boned farmer shook the detectives hand in greeting. "A few hours back, I was out bringing my cows in for milking, and I saw a man pass by my barn. He matched the description from your officers. I did not recognize the man as local."

Daylight would soon be gone. It was logical for the man to stay hidden until darkness allowed his escape, most likely by water.

Would the person stay close to Färjestaden, waiting for a chance to cross Kalmar Sound to the Swedish mainland, or would he travel east across the island and slip a boat into the Baltic? There were numerous areas a vessel could be concealed and launched without causing notice.

Rather than contact more agencies, his normal procedure when he once worked such cases for the government, Lars decided to redirect his focus to Lea Reardon.

The woman personally knew Benjamin Farmer, but unlike a family member, was not close enough to harbor biases "for" or "against" the man based solely on familial ties. From past conversations, the detective knew that if he could get the young woman to talk, her information would be candid and without exaggeration.

30

KALMARSSON INN, 1989

"Please join me at the table." Looking at his watch, he realized how much time had passed since he requested the young woman to stay in the room.

"I apologize for making you wait. It was unavoidable." He got straight to the point. "How well do you know the Farmers?"

"They've been neighbors and acquaintances for years." She answered without hesitation. "Their house is not far down the street from my parents' home in Evanston."

It didn't escape the detective that "friend" wasn't included in her description.

"My concern is Mr. Farmer. The man has been missing for days under unusual circumstances. There is reason to believe he might have knowledge of Gunnar's death. I have already talked to his wife and checked with US investigative units reviewing his background."

Though she had heard the inspector refer to Benjamin Farmer on the telephone, it still came as a shock to think he had anything to do with Gunnar.

"I don't understand. I thought Mr. Johansson's death was a suicide." She stopped when the inspector shook his head.

"No such thing has been determined."

"Reverend Sedgely is Benjamin Farmer's brother-in-law. I'm sure he would be able to give you more information."

"When you left the reverend, did he say he was returning directly to the inn?"

"Actually, I thought he'd be here already. He might have made some stops. We planned on meeting later."

"Just you and the reverend?"

"What? Oh…no. The three of us."

"The three of you?"

"Rolf, myself, and the reverend…to try and pull more information from the diary. I'm sorry. It's hard to think straight after what happened."

"I understand. Take your time. I will talk to the reverend, but your thoughts are also important to me."

As usual, Inspector Youngmark was a complete professional. She heard no sentiment in his voice as he asked questions about Benjamin and the reverend. Even when she spoke of Gunnar, his manner seemed neutral, unchanged. Then she saw his face.

It took only a brief second after mentioning the gardener for his features to harden again, but the man's sorrow was evident.

The inspector did not link Gunnar's death to the diary, nor mention the murders of her parents and grandmother. Yet, it was likely he knew the circumstances of their deaths.

The detective didn't fabricate a story to comfort her on the injustices dealt her family, nor did he link her parent's proof of innocence to any help she might give. He didn't try to steer or pressure.

"What is it you want to know about Mr. Farmer?"

"Just whatever memories you have of the family." He reached into his jacket pocket.

She waited until he put on his glasses and took out his pad and pencil before beginning a history of what she remembered about Benjamin Farmer, his wife, and son.

It was still difficult to talk about the night of her fourteenth birthday, but the story had to be included. It soon became obvious the bulk of her personal knowledge concerning Mr. Farmer came from others.

"His business took him out of town a lot. My memories of him are from when I was a kid and most is what I heard from other people."

"What was said?"

"Just that he was very unhappy with his wife, drank a lot, and used his business to stay away from home."

The refusal to meet his eyes accompanied by the short, terse summary gave away her discomfort. The young woman didn't like to repeat gossip.

"Is there anything you personally can recall about the man?"

The kitchen phone interrupted. "Yes, Youngmark. Hold the line for a moment." He turned to Lea. "Will you excuse me, this is a private call. Please, do not go far."

He put the phone back to his ear. "What do you have, Lindberg? Results on the print analysis. Two...a thumbprint identified positively as yes, and what? The other print...thank you. Goodbye."

Fingerprints the lab had been able to lift from the cigarette pack belonged to two different men. One was identified as Gunnar's. The other was compared against the set of prints of Benjamin Farmer that Lars had received from the hotel in Denmark. It was judged a match.

Who was Benjamin Farmer? A spy for the US government, a communist agent, a husband running away from his wife, a protected witness, or none of the above? The answers didn't matter quite so much now. He would find the man, then establish who he was.

He left the kitchen in search of Lea. He no longer needed her to complete the interview. The identification of the prints on the cigarette pack made her background information unnecessary. Still, the prickle at the back of his neck wouldn't go away. He would finish. He found her looking out a window, over the garden.

J.L. GUSTAFSON

"Miss Reardon." The inspector pointed to a chair in a room off the inn's kitchen. He shut the door to have more privacy. "Please, sit down and continue."

"The few times I talked to Mr. Farmer, he seemed like a nice enough man. I do remember one thing. He was a klutz."

"Klutz? What is this?"

"He was a clumsy individual. Tripped over his own feet when he drank, people said. They laughed about it behind his back, but I never thought it was funny. I noticed bruises, black and blue spots, cuts, and I sympathized with the man because there were times I had similar marks."

"Go on," he prompted.

"I was the one who tripped up steps, bumped my head on a locker, skinned my knees. You get the idea."

Her face took on the appearance of the embarrassed adolescent she remembered. It was only after taking martial arts lessons that she had learned to move her body with the rhythm and grace of an athlete.

"Was Benjamin Farmer there the night you were attacked?"

"No. I remember my parents saying he was in the hospital. They talked only to Mrs. Farmer." She thought back to her earlier conversation with the minister. "Even today, the reverend said Mr. Farmer missed most of their trip because he was sick, a bad stomach."

"Can you tell me the hospitals in your area?" His head was down, his pencil moving quickly over the page. She had given him a date and names. He appreciated the woman's straightforwardness, especially considering the personal nature of the material she revealed.

Lars had heard enough and decided to stop the conversation. There might be a record of the man as a patient and the detective was anxious to check.

He put away his glasses then took both her hands in his. "Thank you, Miss Reardon."

An officer appeared at the door.

"Yes, come." Lars got up to confer with the man before returning to Lea.

"Someone has telephoned the inn trying to reach you, but the officer knew not to interrupt our conversation or give any information." He smiled at the young woman. "I won't go into a translation of the words he told my officer." The detective looked at his watch. "But I can assure you a very irritated Rolf Sundren will be here shortly."

Returning the detective's smile with one of her own, she was anxious to change clothes before Rolf arrived.

"I'll be in my room, Inspector." Running up the stairs, Lea reached the door and used her key. Her mind was busy thinking how much she missed Rolf. Suddenly, a hand snaked around and covered her mouth, silencing any scream. When the door slammed shut, the hand dropped away. She turned and saw Reverend Sedgely.

31

KALMARSSON INN, 1989

Lea didn't think to ask the minister how he got into her room. She looked at his torn, blood-stained clothes. "What happened?"

Sweaty complexion, shaking hands, she worried he was going into shock. "I'll get the inspector. You should be in a hospital." She started to open the door.

"No, no!" Roughly grabbing her arm, the minister pulled her hand away from the knob and closed the door. "I'm okay, just short of breath from running." He rubbed his hand over the bloody marks. "The wounds aren't deep. It gave him pleasure to pull his knife over my chest just to see my reaction."

"Who did this to you?"

He shook his head. "I still can't believe it. It was Benjamin!"

"Mr. Farmer?"

James nodded his head in confirmation.

"I'll get you some water." As she filled a pitcher with cold water at the bathroom sink, Lea automatically looked into the mirror and observed the minister wiping his glasses, carefully combing his hair and beard into place. An odd gesture under the circumstances, but maybe it was the man's way to calm his nerves.

"Here." She poured him a glass of water, leaving the pitcher. "I thought this might help." She handed James a wet towel.

As she turned around to dry her hands, Lea noticed he moved the chain lock into place across the door.

Motioning her to sit on the bed, Reverend James took the chair farthest from the window. He didn't touch the water and put the wet cloth aside. Flexing his arms to express strain, he got up from the chair to move around the room.

"After he tied me up and decided I was no longer a threat, Ben talked about his plans." James shook his head. "He was so detached, Lea, so cold. I couldn't believe it was Benjamin." He stopped behind the curtains to look out the window.

"And you were right. It is all about your diary and the Amber Room. Ben admitted working for the Stasi." He sat in the chair again. Fingers drummed nervously against the arm rest.

"There's a group of them, you know—Per Knudsson, Ulrik Orensson, Inspector Youngmark, even Sigrid—all Stasi agents. Ben told me how they've tracked you since your arrival on the island and manipulated your actions to gain access to the book."

She listened to the minister, saying nothing, until he mentioned the inspector and the innkeeper. "Not Inspector Youngmark and Mrs. Kalmarsson! I don't believe it!"

"Why not?" He got up quickly from the chair and stood in front of her. "Just because the detective and Sigrid act like good, caring people doesn't mean they are. You've known them a month. You've known me since you were a young girl.

Do you always give your trust and allegiance so casually? They're very good at what they do and their job was to gain your friendship and confidence. It's obvious to me they've succeeded." Hurt was evident in his voice.

"They're all working together to secure the Amber Room for East Germany." There was no need to be intentionally cruel. He wouldn't tell her Rolf Sundren was dead. Not yet.

"It was Sigrid who killed Gunnar when he found out the truth. The murder of your mom and dad," his voice softened again, "that was Per Knudsson and Ulrik Orensson."

"Oh, God!"

"Benjamin told me the men injected a lethal drug into your parents to mask any appearance of a crime, and to make sure their deaths were labeled accidental."

Reason replaced emotion. "I can't believe this!" Lea got up to find a tissue to wipe her eyes. "The man is crazy! "You talk about me trusting Inspector Youngmark and Mrs. Kalmarsson. What about you? You're taking the word of a mad man. If Ulrik and the inspector are Stasi agents, why didn't they steal the diary when they had the chance?"

He answered her passionate outburst with a soft reply. "They didn't need to. They had enough time to examine the diary. It's the missing piece they're after. And you have it."

"The rhyme!"

"Exactly." James watched her switch from utter surety to deflation. He forced her head to his shoulder so he could comfort her.

"I know it's hard to accept all of this. That was my reaction at first."

Lea pulled away from his arms. She needed space.

Sitting down in a chair, he continued. "Benjamin took pride in reciting every intricate detail of the plot. He wanted me to appreciate his cleverness and skill of planning. Not because I was his brother-in-law. It wasn't personal. I was just a receptive audience he could play to." The reverend got up and paced the floor.

"I encouraged his bragging, stroked his ego, humored him, anything to keep him talking. My hands were tied." James rubbed his wrists. "I needed time to work the rope loose for a chance to escape and get help.

"Up until that point, I thought he suffered a nervous breakdown. I didn't take a word he said seriously, or that he would hurt me. Then he talked about the night of your birthday and…I changed my mind." Relishing her color-drained face, James let his last words linger a bit before continuing.

"Remember, I arrived in Evanston not long after you were attacked. I don't think it was a secret from anyone in the congregation that Brenda took every opportunity to push her version of what happened, hoping to gain my allegiance. But no one," he lowered his volume, and slowly, purposely, enunciated each word, "no one was aware your mother and father came to me for counseling on the matter."

Lea was sure she misunderstood him. "My parents came to you?"

"Does that surprise you?" The minister walked back to Lea. "Your mom and dad were so worried about you. It was obvious to them how much stress you were under, yet you refused to talk about it." He looked directly into her eyes. "The bitterness you held inside was very apparent."

"I didn't think they knew how I felt." She lowered her head, staring at the floor.

"But they did." James put his finger under her chin and gently forced her head up so she had to look at him. "And it hurt them. It hurt you wouldn't confide in your own parents. Your mother and father told me the entire story of what happened that night. They hoped I could find a way to reach you. Benjamin had no idea I talked to your parents. Like everyone else, he assumed I learned what happened from Brenda's gossip. He was anxious to tell me his version along with the truth of his background. That meek, sickly exterior was all a sham." The minister shook his head.

"Remember how often Ben was out of town? It wasn't because he was a salesman making a living for his family." James paused. "The man was a mercenary, a murderer, a paid assassin. It was the reason the Stasi contacted him.

"The East Germans didn't learn of the diary until 1978, after the book had already left Sweden. By the time the Stasi traced it to the United States and contracted for Benjamin's services, it was too late. Your grandmother had the box."

"Ben only found out the buyer was your grandmother after stealing the purchaser's list. He stayed close to your house for a week, watching, waiting for an opportunity to search for the diary. The night you were attacked gave him the chance."

Out of the corner of his eye, James noticed her stiffen when he mentioned the word attack.

"Farmer knew no one would suspect he was in the neighborhood. Brenda had already given him the perfect alibi. She told everyone he was in the hospital, another one of his many 'accidents.' However, it was the complete serendipity of the situation that gave Farmer his greatest pleasure. How he was inspired to mimic your screaming after you lost your voice and called out to Jake O'Brien for help. In effect, saving you from being raped by his own son.

"Of course, it wasn't you he considered important. The attack was the perfect diversion to get your family out of the house. The more people that became involved outside, the better. Since your mother and father told me the same basic story, including the part about your voice loss and your insistence that you never called Jake, I realized Benjamin couldn't have known such details unless he was there that night. That's when I knew he wasn't suffering from delusions, but was the murderer he claimed to be. When your parents rushed outside, Ben had his opportunity. Unfortunately, your grandmother got in his way." He slowed his speech for that one sentence, making sure his voice showed the proper respect for the dead.

"The time it took him to take care of your grandmother forced Benjamin to abandon his search for the diary. The Stasi was determined to claim the journal and ordered Farmer to stay in the area until he had the book. Benjamin handled the American sector while Ulrik Orensson was in charge of the overall operation.

"Years of failure made the East Germans impatient. Pressure steadily increased for results. Your parents must have become suspicious that someone close to them was after the diary. But they didn't know the identity of the person, or who to trust.

"At that point in Ben's story, the rope around my wrists had loosened enough for me to slip it off. I grabbed a rock and knocked him unconscious." James stopped as he looked down at his hands. When he began again, his speech was slow, as if trying to find the right words. "I'm ashamed to admit it crossed my mind to kill the man. I picked up his knife, but I couldn't." He sank back heavily into the chair looking at Lea. "That's everything I know." He had learned through his preaching experience that trying to judge a response before the end of a sermon divided his concentration. The momentum suffered. He focused to gauge her full reaction to his words.

He delighted in the anger written on Lea's face. It was a feeling he intended to escalate into a range of emotions that would effectively dull any rational thought. Off balance, she would be easier to persuade, more willing to follow directions without a barrage of questions.

James had considered medication, but decided not to chance a reaction. When talking about the rhyme, her mind had to be clear. It was time to get moving before the inspector or that nosy innkeeper came to the door.

Her phone rang, ending the silence.

"Be very careful what you say." James stood in front of her as she answered.

"Yes."

"Inspector Youngmark speaking. Sandwiches have been put together. Will you come down, or do you want a tray brought to your room?"

"Neither. I'm not feeling well. I'm going to rest for a while. Please don't call or send anyone up." She hung up the phone.

James shook his head in approval. "Well done." He moved again to look out the window overlooking the garden. "We have to leave now. Once Farmer regains consciousness, this is the first place he'll come."

With his back to her, Lea allowed her face to reflect the fury she felt. You deceitful, murdering bastard. She felt hot, and her jaw hurt from clenching teeth together. She saw his fear and heard his distress, but the reverend's passionate expressions were only on the surface. Everything about the man was a lie.

Why hadn't she noticed the layers in his personality before? That kind of suspicion was reserved for strangers, boyfriends, or those acquaintances she knew to be cautious around, not a man of God, a position she was taught to respect.

His performance had given her time to swallow her fears and emotions and focus on what to do. Her only edge was that the minister didn't suspect she knew the truth. Her only option was to beat him at his own game.

Was he working alone? Since he was so anxious to get her out of the inn, she guessed no one downstairs was involved. The only reason she was alive was that he needed something from her.

Lea would take a page from the man's own book of lies. Act the way he expected, follow his plans until she could find a way to alert someone, or escape. Lea wondered if Inspector Youngmark understood her cryptic telephone message. The detective knew she was anxious for Rolf to arrive. Did her insistence of no visitors throw up red flags, or wasn't it enough to clue the detective she was in trouble?

At first she had been skeptical about the reverend's accusations that were based solely on one man's hallucinations. After he recounted Benjamin Farmer's story of the attack, she became a believer.

If he had stopped there, she would have followed any instructions he gave her. However, the man had wanted to be more convincing, show her more evidence. The minister had no way of knowing that by using her parents to prove the truth of his story, he accomplished the opposite.

She had wanted the incident over. It had been unnerving to see the guilt on her mother's face, her father's sadness after she jerked out of his arms when he tried to hug her.

Lea knew that had she claimed an unknown person helped her, it would have kept the door of uncertainty open. Who was it? Why hadn't they come forward? Her mother and father didn't need more questions. The death of her grandmother was enough trauma for the family. That chapter of their lives needed to be closed.

For that reason, she had never told her parents about her voice loss. She never told Sara or Jake; she told no one. There was only one person, beside herself, who knew what really happened.

After all these years, she knew the identity of the person who called Jake O'Brien that night, the person Lea once considered a hero, the one who helped save her from being raped. It wasn't Benjamin Farmer who hid outside her house that night. Reverend James Sedgely was the murderer. She considered that he might have had an accomplice. If there was someone working with the minister, she had to find out.

"Hurry Lea! We have to leave before the inspector and Benjamin come looking for us. In order to buy some time, I think you need to write a note."

He took a piece of paper from the desk and handed it to her. "Let's see…'Inspector, don't worry about me, I'll stay close to the inn. After what happened, I need to be alone for a while. Lea.'" He took the paper from her hand and propped it on the table.

"Okay, time to go." James was annoyed at her slow movements. "Come on! Don't you understand? These people will murder anyone who meddles with their plan to get the Amber Room. Once they discover you know the truth of who they are, there won't be any more niceties. You'll be taken to Berlin." Fear showed in his eyes. "The atrocities committed on women during interrogation are well known."

He could have saved his theatrics. She wasn't listening. Lea didn't argue, and she followed his instructions to write the note. Adrenaline pumped through her body as she searched for ways to get away from the minister. Not here, she decided. Any direct confrontations at the inn would be too risky.

She concluded Inspector Youngmark had not understood her phone message, and without knowing the danger, the detective wouldn't stand a chance against Sedgely. She didn't want to risk Mrs. Kalmarsson or the inspector getting hurt. And it would only be a matter of time before Rolf knocked on her door. Two choices came to mind. Figure a way to get the minister to abandon her when he left the island, or find out where he intended to take her and leave the information. Either way, she had to act fast.

Getting up quickly, she purposely caught her foot in the rug, landing hard on the floor. Pain crossed her face as she got to her feet and tried to take a few steps.

"My ankle!" She again stepped gingerly on her foot before sinking back down in pain. "I must have broken something." The real tears in her eyes were a bonus. "Go without me. I'll only slow you down. I'll hide. Wait until you bring back help."

"No! I won't leave you behind. We're only going as far as Karlevi. You'll make it."

First idea shot down, but now she knew he was headed to the runestone. She had to find a way to let Rolf and the inspector know where she was going. "There's tape in the bathroom. I can wrap my ankle for support."

Deciding not to wait for his answer, she limped toward the bathroom. As she passed the dresser, she scooped up the money laying on top. By leaving the door open, she hoped to calm any suspicions. Still James came to check on her.

"Hurry."

While he watched, she got out the tape, gingerly took off her sock and started wrapping. After a minute, she cocked her ear to one side. "Is that Mrs. Kalmarsson calling me?"

James left her alone to unlock the door and peek into the hallway, she hurriedly moved the coins into place and held her breath. If Rolf noticed her arrangement, he would know her destination.

"There's no one. Are you ready?" He looked out the window and saw two police officers in front of the inn. The other one was likely still in back. He would gamble there was no change and take Lea the same way he used to get in. They would avoid the kitchen, go down the back stairs, and out. The tall foliage from the cutting garden would allow them to get away from the inn, unseen. It would be more difficult because of Lea, but the officers concentrated on the distance.

"Ready." Slow in getting up, she leaned heavily on the minister.

32

KALMARSSON INN, 1989

L ars still sat in the kitchen of Kalmarsson Inn with a phone to his ear. During his interview with Lea Reardon, the detective received information that Benjamin Farmer had been in a hospital the night of her fourteenth birthday. She had given him a list of Chicago-area hospitals.

He had received Mrs. Farmer's permission to view her husband's medical records, but the woman neglected to name the hospital. After reaching the third hospital on the list, Lars got the information he was looking for.

"Chicago Central Hospital. Mrs. Lucas of administration speaking. I understand, Inspector Youngmark, that you want information concerning one of our patients. After I secure approval, I will call back."

"I will stay on the telephone line and wait." Lars gave the needed information to reach Brenda Farmer. He hoped the woman would remember their conversation. He was troubled by her slurred words.

"Inspector, I have the data you requested. A man by the name of Benjamin Farmer had been a patient at our hospital during the night in question. Because of the circumstances, the hospital has agreed to send a copy of the hospital chart."

Lars was lucky Brenda Farmer had understood Mrs. Lucas' questions. He called the hotel in Denmark and asked for the manager.

"This is Inspector Youngmark from Kalmar, Sweden. I want you to check immediately on Mrs. Brenda Farmer and Mrs. Susan Sedgely. I have reason to believe one or both women are ill. A physician needs to be called."

"I will have one of my staff check on the ladies right away, Inspector. If needed, a doctor will be contacted." He hung up the phone.

Lars had held the side of his face to try and protect it from the rub of the receiver. He looked around the inn kitchen, to see if there was anything cool he could use to soothe his skin. The area around his ear had become irritated from the constant use of the telephone. He ran water in the sink, wet a dishtowel, and pressed the cold to his ear. The ringing phone had him quickly drying his face.

"This is Youngmark." Lars's office secretary was on the line to relay a message he had received at the Kalmar station. "Yes, read it to me."

"You received a call from Chicago Central Hospital. 'Due to a hospital renovation. Chart information is scattered in boxes. There is an emergency room doctor who kept his own files and was working during that period.'"

"What? Yes, give me his name. I will put the call through from Kalmarsson Inn.

This is Inspector Youngmark from Kalmar Sweden. I understand you have a Dr. Gerbari on staff. Is he in the "house" now?" Lars used the common term medical professionals used to denote a hospital.

"I will connect you, Inspector."

"Dr. Gerbari." After giving his official name and title, Lars explained the problem. "I understand you keep personal logs that go back to 1978." Lars gave him the date Benjamin Farmer was brought into the emergency room. "Will you search and give me whatever information you have from that date."

"My notes are in front of me, Inspector. It won't take long to find what you want.

"The night Benjamin Farmer was admitted, I was a young resident working the ER."

Lars wrote his notes in quick shorthand learned from his years of police work.

"A police car found the patient slumped beside a roadway and rushed him to Chicago Central. I was the attending resident. It became apparent to me that the patient's injuries had nothing to do with alcohol or drugs. In addition to obvious contusions, severe internal bleeding caused the man to be rushed into surgery. I took an interest in the case after witnessing his wife's lack of concern. Brenda Farmer had come into the emergency room insisting her husband's injuries were caused from his drinking, nothing more. Once she signed the necessary papers, the woman left for home without bothering to see her husband. X-rays showed evidence of past multiple bone breaks. Unless his work or hobbies explained such body abuse, there had to be another cause. After my shift was over, I located the file showing Farmer's prior stays. My suspicion was that Benjamin Farmer was a victim of domestic abuse. I wrote this observation on the chart and I added an alert to my superiors.

"When he regained consciousness, Benjamin was asked questions about his home life. He refused to answer. The hospital called the police. I had to go into the police department and make a formal statement. Brenda Farmer was in the interrogation room next to mine. The rooms had thin walls. It was easy to hear what she said. Brenda Farmer admitted to the detective that she 'hit her husband, but only when there was just cause.' That's an exact quote. I will never forget her words. I was called into Mr. Farmer's hospital room when the police asked if he would file battery charges against his wife. He refused. I would suspect the police dropped the case. I never saw the man as a patient again. That's everything I have, Inspector. I hope it helps you."

The doctor's words didn't surprise the inspector. It was not universally accepted that in some cases of domestic abuse, the victim was a man. Male pride and the incongruous idea that a man could be abused by any woman made the idea laughable. It made sense that Benjamin Farmer used his supposed bouts with alcohol as an excuse for his bruises, effectively hiding the truth.

Lars wrote his notes and decided he had been at the inn long enough. It was time to return to his office. Before he could walk out of the kitchen, the phone rang again. A superior from Swedish authorities was on the line.

"Inspector Youngmark. It has been reported that you cancelled off-time for police officers. My office has no knowledge of this. You have not filled out the required papers for such an operation.

"You are to concentrate on finding Benjamin Farmer. No more trying to broaden the case. No more suppositions or deviations. It is time to narrow and focus."

"Sir, I do have some information." He gave a short profile of Farmer gleaned from Dr. Gerbari and how it might relate to his case. The man listened, although he wasn't interested in speculation. His answer to Lars was terse.

"I expect your report along with any evidence collected at the scene to be brought here immediately!" Already exasperated from the detective's lack of substantive material, the agent voiced his irritation about the direction of the case. "Some in this department might judge your reluctance, this insistence to continue gathering reams of information, as unnecessary plodding—an inability to make a decision under emergency conditions. Your job as a competent leader is in question. This is not the first time. If it happens again, your career in law enforcement will be over."

Lars didn't answer as he hung up the phone. He knew exactly what the man meant. The month following Hulda's death, Lars remembered his loss of will to make the simplest judgments and an increasing dependency on Ulrik to care for himself and his daughter. Fear became overwhelming. Neither the doctor's visits nor Ulrik's homeopathic brew could relieve the anxiety or calm the dread.

Now he knew that the special drink Ulrik insisted Lars consume to calm his nerves after his wife's death was likely the cause of his exacerbated fears and depression. However, at the time, the detective did not defend himself nor fault the conclusions that ended with his resignation. He simply did what Ulrik told him was best.

Today, in 1989, the inspector would not allow outside pressure to change his opinion or manner of investigation. Based on the background data he received from Dr. Gerbari and Lea's observations, there was enough concern to keep the detective looking.

While Lars agreed with his superior that the detective's information could not absolve Benjamin Farmer of involvement in Gunnar's death, or being a member of the Stasi, it was added confirmation of Lea's account of the man being in the hospital the night her grandmother was murdered. And for the first time, the spotlight was transferred to another.

The timely arrival of Reverend Sedgely in Evanston, and his continued association with the Reardon family, put him in the right places at the right time. And now his presence on Scandinavian soil coincided with the deaths of Ulrik and Gunnar. The inspector wanted to find the minister.

Lars needed to return to Kalmar. He walked out to tell Sigrid.

"I have to return to my office, Sigrid. I will be gone for a time, but I will leave an officer behind.

It had been hours. He found her still sitting at the garden table. This was a woman who rarely sat still for five minutes. It worried him. His thoughts were interrupted as Rolf Sundren rushed up.

"Where's Lea?" Rolf blurted out.

"In her room." The inspector decided it would be better to talk about murder after the two spent a few moments alone.

His legs couldn't move fast enough. The door to her room was ajar and opened with a wide swing when he knocked. "Lea?"

No response.

Rolf entered the empty room. Where was she? He picked up the room phone and called down to the inspector. "She's not here."

"I will be right up." The detective looked at his watch. It had been about fifteen minutes since he called the woman's room and asked if she wanted any food. Trying to relay instructions to an aide while talking to Lea on the phone, he hadn't given her remarks enough attention.

39

KALMARSSON INN, 1989

Rolf looked around her room. Lea's camera was on the dresser. The bed was made but rumpled, as if someone had sat there. Her suitcase was tucked under the bed. He opened the wardrobe to assure himself her clothes were still there. The typewriter was on the desk, extra paper nearby. Her purse, with the diary inside, sat on the table. Everything was as it should be. Other than a half-full pitcher next to a glass of water, nothing seemed out of place.

Walking into the bathroom, he rummaged through the wastebasket pulling the remains of a package that once held a wide roll of tape. A few metal clips to keep the stretch tape secured were scattered on the bathroom sink. A wet washcloth hung over the towel bar. He looked, but there was no blood.

Hearing someone in the outer room, he turned to see Inspector Youngmark moving around. Ready to join the detective, his vision lowered to the small shelf above the sink. Rolf had noticed the coins before, and assumed Lea emptied her pockets, as he did, before getting into the shower. Then he looked again. There was something about the placement. She had the coins in two piles. He would let it go for the moment.

"Inspector, could she have gone off with the minister?" Rolf asked the question as he walked out of the bathroom.

"The minister is registered at the inn. He has the room next door, but it is empty of anything personal. Sigrid informed me that the two had coffee earlier and then went sightseeing. Miss Reardon came back alone. The minister has not returned."

Lars shook his head. "Why would she leave if she knew you were coming?"

As long as she's not with Sedgely, Rolf thought. "I'm probably the reason. We had an argument."

The detective didn't disagree, but that wasn't the impression she gave. The young woman seemed happy and anxious to see Rolf.

Lars bent down to retrieve a paper on the floor.

Rolf read the short note with relief. "She's out taking a walk." He re-read part of the note for Lars. "'After what happened, I need some time alone.' The paper must have blown off the table when I opened the door."

"Why are your men around, Inspector? Lea said 'After what happened…What does she mean by that? What's going on?"

Lars went straight to the point. "Gunnar Johansson is dead. Murdered, I believe."." He repeated Sigrid and Lea's role in finding the gardener's body and calling his office. He explained about the scraped earth, and the cigarette pack with fingerprints from Gunnar and Benjamin Farmer.

"Benjamin Farmer." Where had he heard that name? "Related to Bradley Farmer?"

"His father, and Reverend Sedgely's brother-in-law. Miss Reardon never talked about this man to you?"

"No."

The detective repeated what he knew about the group's trip to Denmark and the sudden absence of Farmer. He told about his own search for information on the man from various sources, including the hospital. "The physical evidence appears to put Benjamin Farmer at the scene, but…"

"But?" Rolf prodded.

"It does not prove the man committed murder. Dr. Gerbari gave a new face to this person. Two different people. The alcoholic husband and absent father the neighbors saw, or a battered and abused victim. Who is the real Benjamin Farmer?"

Rolf nodded and walked over to look out the window.

"It's interesting that the only evidence you have of someone in the shed, other than Lea and Sigrid, is Farmer's cigarette pack. And from what you said, it didn't take much to find it. If it wasn't Farmer, do you think someone staged it to frame him?"

The inspector said nothing.

"The timing, know-how, planning to pull off something like that would be…" Rolf stopped speaking when the phone on the desk interrupted.

Lars answered. "Hold the line." He signaled the call was for Rolf.

Before handing him the phone, the inspector took out his knife and removed the mouthpiece to examine it before giving it back to Rolf.

"Hello. Yes, this is Rolf Sundren. What about the name?"

"Sundren. This is Agent Chico, CIA. Nothing was found on the man to warrant searching at a deeper level."

"Yeah. Okay. Thanks for checking." He replaced the receiver before turning to the inspector and motioning to go out to the hallway. "What made you suspicious of the phone?"

"I found a listening device hooked to my office telephone. Old habits are hard to break. Every day I check. Today, caution was rewarded. To my knowledge, the rest of my office is clean. I believe as long as that one device remains viable, no others will be planted. I wanted to make sure nothing was put in the inn."

"Who did it?"

"I have my suspicions. However, to be on the safe side, Sigrid keeps a small office up here. It might be better to talk there." They walked down to the office and shut the door.

"Now, what were you saying about a name?"

"Someone from the CIA passed a name I gave them to an operative working inside the KGB," Rolf said.

The inspector raised his eyebrows in question.

"They were returning a favor. The information I wanted could only come from an agent embedded in the upper ranks of the organization." Rolf shook his head. "The name James Sedgely got no reaction." Frustrated, Rolf banged his fist on the table. "I know someone's still out there! With both Ulrik and Per dead, I looked for someone closer to Lea's home, another member to the group. Probably Ulrik's partner."

"His partner," the inspector shook his head.

Rolf remembered the detective's assurances when the two went over the files at the tavern. "Look, Inspector, I never discounted your opinion of Ulrik's cryptography skills or expertise on runes. However, in your office, the first thing he should have found when shining a light to the diary picture was a depiction of Sandby churchyard. Yet, you said Ulrik went straight to the rune fragments. That's what I couldn't accept."

Rolf walked down the hall to Lea's room and took the diary from her purse. Back in the small office with Lars, he opened it to the picture. "Even the best couldn't have found these runes during the short period of time spent in your office. There was only one way it could have been done. Ulrik had to have access to the diary much earlier. I think he got it from his partner, Reverend Sedgely."

Lars was interested in his reasoning. "If Ulrik had the diary, why not remove the paper hidden in the cover?"

Rolf answered easily. "Because the document was a phony, a dangled prize to make sure Swedish intelligence offered Ulrik immunity. But more important, a way to keep attention focused on gaining the paper, and away from the diary. I'm betting Ulrik has been after the Amber Room from the beginning, and not for the German Stasi.

"I don't believe Russia has ever given up searching for the Amber Room, and as for the Soviets trusting anyone from the Stasi to hunt for their treasure, that's laughable. Orensson might

---

have worked for East Germany, but I'm betting his orders came from the KGB."

"Sundren. How do you connect Ulrik to the reverend rather than Benjamin Farmer?"

"After what happened on Lea's fourteenth birthday, her parents would have never confided in the Farmers. It has to be Sedgely. He arrived in Evanston shortly after the grandmother was murdered. I doubt that was a coincidence. And a minister—the perfect cover to gain personal information.

"It took time, patience, and smarts. That tells me the minister is a professional. If not KGB or Stasi, I would guess one of the elite US coverts—maybe a rogue FBI or CIA agent. Mr. and Mrs. Reardon must have said nothing before they were murdered, or the pair wouldn't have gone after Lea. The book from the auction house, the one Lea tore a page from, it had to be the diary. Her grandmother took—"

"Wait, Sundren. She tore a page?" Lars asked.

"The day Lea and her grandmother brought the box home from the auction house, Lea told me she accidentally ripped out a page from one of the books packed in the crate. She had been anxious to try on a ring she found in the box. Her grandmother promised it to her as a birthday present, but she didn't realize it was attached to a book buried at the bottom of the crate until she tried to pull out the ring. The page ripped as well."

"I don't remember Miss Reardon wearing a ring or talking about one."

"It's in the locket she wears around her neck. The ring is a small band made to look like an eagle with outstretched wings. It has a lot of open work, much of it covered in red enamel."

Lars tried to picture the ring in his mind. It had to be the one Ragnar took from the dead girl. "Can you draw this ring?"

"I can come close." He grabbed a pad of paper from the small desk and found a red pen in the drawer. "Her grandmother took the page for safekeeping until they could find the damaged book and repair it. That night, Lea slept with her grandmother and remembered the woman talking in rhyme."

"Rhyme?"

"I think her grandmother searched through the crate and located the diary. After piecing together the torn paper, she became curious about the content of the journal and intent on deciphering the verse. If she read the words aloud, constantly repeating the account of the escape as well as the rhyme, both could have become ingrained in Lea's memory as she slept. After the grandmother's death, the story of the escape and the rhyme turned into her nightmare. You've examined the journal, Inspector, but this is what was on the missing page." Rolfe repeated the rhyme.

> In an ancient place where scalds still speak
> Of earth scarring battles and blood stains deep
> Brave warriors lost and treasure taken
> Separate the eagle's dance with the raven
> Old Gods speak tales of foreboding
> Evil seeks the lines unbroken.

Lars was particularly interested in one line from the verse. "Do..." Hearing footsteps outside Sigrid's upstairs office, the inspector opened the door of the small room and stepped into the hall. "Yes?"

"Sir, you are wanted downstairs," said one of his officers. Lars got up and walked down.

While the detective was gone, Rolf sat at the desk. Carefully, he traced the open feathered lines he remembered made up the band, and used the pen to recreate the red overlay. Underneath the drawing, he wrote the poem.

"Inspector, that was fast," Rolf commented as the detective walked back into the room.

"I was just informed my laboratory found Benjamin Farmer's prints on the weapon used to murder Ulrik. Once that information is given to Swedish authorities, my guess is Farmer will be labeled KGB."

"I agree it's a logical assumption." Rolf played devil's advocate. "If Ulrik was a KGB agent, and if the Soviets realized he had double-crossed them to go after the Amber Room himself, they would have sent an assassin to eliminate him. It's possible that person was Benjamin Farmer. He fits the criteria.

"A seasoned operator would have an elaborate cover created over many years. Farmer's weak personality, sales job away from home, a shrewish wife, and constant hospital stays would give him time to search out targets and eliminate them without people noticing his absence. All of the man's background information is missing. You have nothing from the military. There's not even a picture of him. All you found was one set of fingerprints. While it's noted in hospital records and Lea's memory that Benjamin Farmer was in the hospital the night of her attack and grandmother's death, if Farmer was an experienced agent, the man was capable of slipping out of his room, killing Lea's grandmother, and returning to his bed before the hospital staff noticed he was missing."

"Twenty-four hours ago, Sundren, I would have agreed with that scenario. Without question, I would have accepted the logic of the situation and the fingerprint results from the lab. Not now. The agencies are being manipulated." Lars shook his head. "Is there more to your story?"

"Right after her grandmother's death, Lea found the page with the rhyme tucked into the woman's nightgown and ripped it up. She wanted no reminder of the box and its contents. The ring was different. It was the last present from her grandmother. She couldn't get rid of it. She put it in her locket.

Rolf continued. "I think Ulrik risked talking about the runes in your office because he was desperate. The rest of her family was gone. The clue had to be with her. Ulrik hoped something he said would trigger a specific memory and it worked. Up until that day, she had only been able to remember the first two lines of the verse.

"As a double agent, Orensson had the ability to play Swedish intelligence against the Stasi, and now we know, the KGB as well. It effectively kept the agencies off balance and off his back. It gave him time to look for the treasure and create this elaborate plot with the reverend's help.

"As far as I'm concerned, Inspector, this new information claiming Benjamin Farmer is a communist agent changes nothing. I think the man was framed. As for Per, I'm not sure how he fits. In any case, like Orensson, death took him out of the picture. And Gunnar, why was he killed? His brother-in-law found the girl with the diary. Maybe he had information about the Amber Room or saw something he shouldn't. We might never know the reason.

"That leaves the two of us, Lea, the reverend's wife, and his sister-in-law as loose ends."

"It's a given he'll find a way to get rid of us and Ms. Reardon. As for the sisters, I'm not sure if they're in on his plan to gain the Amber Room, or just convenient trappings for the reverend's cover. Either way, I doubt he'll let them live. No complications, no liabilities. I have already notified the hotel in Denmark to check on the women."

The detective pulled two papers from his briefcase and handed one to the American. "This is the *Hitler Document*, the paper Ulrik used to gain protection from Swedish intelligence. It's a list showing what neutral countries and corporations collaborated with the Nazis. The document is a phony. You were right about that. I found the proof when I opened Per's case and found Ulrik's practice sheet.

"Only the two of us know about this." He handed Rolf the practice sheet used to perfect the *Hitler Document*.

"Compare them, Sundren. Look at the mastery. I admit he fooled me. Only after I found the practice sheet with these characters," Lars pointed out the written lines in the margin, "did I realize it was fake and penned by Ulrik.

"But why leave a paper that proves the document false and points the finger to himself? It made no sense until I realized there is no one alive today who would recognize Ulrik's method in breaking a code, no one, except me. Anyone else would see only a forgery.

"Ulrik still needed me to broker his deal with the authorities or he would never have taken such a chance. He was certain I would not open Per's briefcase because of my training, and he almost proved to be right. But you, Sundren, you questioned everything I said and did, you made me think.

"As you figured out, when the practice sheet was found, it would prove the document hidden inside the diary cover was a phony. The book would also be declared a fake. That would stop the interest of any nation in finding the diary, and leave Ulrik all the time he needed to solve the puzzle and locate the Amber Room," Lars said.

"The reverend is a very clever man," Rolf admitted. "It seems Ulrik took all the chances, while the minister stayed unnoticed in the background. Sedgely knew something of the rhyme because Lea told me he was present during one of her nightmares when she spoke some of the words. I don't think the minister knew the value of the rhyme then, and probably reported the incident to Ulrik."

"I agree, Sundren. The reverend must have discovered Ulrik's plan to defect, realized he was tricked, and was forced to surface. Sedgely figured Ulrik would get rid of him like he did the others. To prevent his own death, he acted first and killed Ulrik. The minister leaves evidence at each crime scene pointing to his brother-in-law as the murderer. Farmer is blamed for Ulrik's death and Gunnar's murder as well. With Ulrik and Per gone, Reverend Sedgely takes over the plan to find the Amber Room. The question remains—did Miss Reardon tell the minister the complete verse during their afternoon visit together?"

34

KALMARSSON INN, 1989

L ars finally looked down at the picture Rolf had drawn for him. "When Ragnar stole from the dead girl, there was rumor of a ring. Has anyone seen Miss Reardon's ring except you?"

"Before this morning, Lea said she never took the ring out of the locket. When I saw it, she was explaining about the night she slept with her grandmother. Neither of us connected the ring to the diary."

Taking out a pen from his jacket pocket, Lars drew what he could remember of a gold ring shaped like a raven.

"The ring was very unusual. Even after all these years, I remember. The wings stood out from the band with individual feathers crafted of black enamel. The eyes were red stones. This is the ring Ulrik showed me years ago." Lars handed the paper to Rolf.

"With such severe damage to his hands, I questioned why he even had a ring. Ulrik said it was an inheritance from a friend and he kept it for the memories."

Taking a pair of scissors from the bathroom shelf, Rolf carefully cut out the renderings of both rings. Placing them together, it appeared some of the open areas between the feathers fit together, forming a distinct pattern of lines. "Look at the marks on the wings, Inspector."

Lars picked up the sheet with the verse and read.

> Separate the eagle's dance with the raven
> Old gods speak of tales foreboding
> Evil seeks the lines unbroken.

Rolf looked at the drawings again. "If we had the actual rings to fit together, the marks could refer to specific runes on Karlevi. The red and black color would be the way to transform the stone into a treasure map. Think of the line from the rhyme: 'Earth scarring battles and blood stains deep.' Black earth, red blood."

"How would you do it, Sundren?"

"Since the Viking alphabet of sixteen symbols is more simplified than the earlier form of twenty-four, one solution for reading the script was to use color. Some of the most common pigments used were red oxide and black soot. If it were me, I might color odd words red, even words in black. Better yet, the subject in one color, the verb in another."

The inspector went to the phone. "Connect me to the station. Hello. Yes. I want an officer to return to Ulrik's rental cottage on Öland and look for a ring. Check the sink trap for papers. Call me with the report." Lars hung up the phone. "I am short on men and time. A man will search. If a ring is there, he will find it."

Lars ripped off the sheets of paper showing the poem and rendering of both rings. The two men walked back to Lea's room. Lars placed the sheets in the stove. Remembering Ulrik's mistake, he took the pad, lit a match to it, and added it to the other papers.

"How long did you say Lea's been out walking, Inspector?" Rolf asked.

Looking at his watch. "Half an hour," he replied.

Rolf nodded his head. As much as he was worried and wanted to haul her back where he could keep a close eye on her, it was better to give her the time she needed. With the police around, he had to trust she was safe."

Peter knocked on the door forcefully. "Sir, Mrs. Kalmarsson is unwilling to sign the witness documents. Will you come down?"

Lars walked downstairs out to the garden patio to see the innkeeper. "Sigrid, I…"

Lars expected her to ask questions or argue. She did neither. Every bit of feistiness had disappeared. It was difficult seeing his old friend like this.

"Have you read the report of your interview?

She nodded her head.

"Are the words correct, should any changes be made?"

"It is fine."

Lars offered a pen. Sigrid signed the papers and placed them on the table.

Walking into the main room of the inn, Lars opened the guest book. A skeleton of an idea had formed. Fleshing out the plan would be his next step.

"Tell Peter I want him." Lars asked the officer to fetch his aide. While the man was gone, the detective called the Kalmar Station from his mobile phone.

"I want you to go into my office. Right near the front of my desk, you will find a loose floor board. Leave it slightly ajar."

Lars hung up the phone as his aide approached. He handed the man an envelope. "Peter, take this information and give it to one of the officers. It is to go back to the station and be put in the safe." Lars had given an account of the contents found in the shed and surrounding grounds, and included the report linking everything to Benjamin Farmer.

The detective walked back upstairs and motioned Rolf from Lea's room back into Sigrid's office. He spoke softly. "I think there is a way to stop the minister and save a few lives in the balance, but I need your help." He explained about the ten captured agents.

"One of the papers from Per's briefcase had indentations from another message. The lab managed to pull out the writing. The Soviets have ten Western agents. There had been a trade in place, but it was cancelled. I have an idea how to get the agents out, and catch Reverend Sedgely."

"I'm in! What do you need?" Rolf asked.

"Before you agree, let me finish. There will only be the two of us. Ask what questions you must now, but you will need to follow my instructions without hesitation or deviation. Swedish intelligence, the CIA, not even my officers will know our plans."

"Done. I repeat. What do you need from me?"

Lars nodded, and reached under the desk in Sigrid's office to pull down his battered case. Rolf looked at the unmarked leather satchel the inspector had carried with him everywhere he went. "A Christmas present. I have many useless papers. This is a good place to keep them." He set the satchel aside, opened his old briefcase, and pulled out Ulrik's practice sheet. "When Ulrik broke a code, he would list the principle parts of the deciphered text in the left margin to use as a reference." Lars pointed to the meaningless phrases.

"His method never varied. With your background and knowledge in security, if you use Ulrik's practice sheet as a guide, I think you can manage a basic version of his signature code. I need to send a message to the KGB."

"You have a lot of confidence in my skills, Inspector."

The detective turned to leave and never heard the comment. He was already walking downstairs to retrieve his mobile phone. If the American was successful, he would need a secure phone line.

It was complicated, but Rolf understood enough of Ulrik's code to enable the detective to craft a simple letter to the Soviets. The names of the ten captured agents, along with Edvard Ivanavich, the coordinator and contact for the prisoner exchange project, were printed on Rolf's letter. Lars knew from intelligence that the agents were being held in a coastal city waiting transfer to Lubyanka prison, the KGB headquarters in Moscow. He had to act fast while the prisoners were together. He didn't know the reason the deal fell apart or what was offered originally for the ten men, but Lars was determined to make it work.

After an introduction to Ivanavich and volunteering his *vitae* to enable the KGB to verify his credentials, the inspector would suggest a new trade—the reverend in exchange for the captured agents delivered alive.

To prove this was not a bluff, Lars would include the communiqué from Per's briefcase, purportedly from Stasi headquarters, ordering Per to assassinate Ulrik and Rolf Sundren. And to make the transaction irresistible, he added the unsigned letter a cautious Ulrik hand-printed to Swedish intelligence outlining what he had to trade: a full accounting of those neutral nations, corporations, and others who covertly supported Hitler. The payment for this information beside money was unconditional Western protection.

The inspector placed the information in the packet and added the message Rolf had just written.

Lars chose one of his last two officers to make the drop. "Take this to the Kalmar food store in the market area. At the back of the building, locate a row of five flower pots and put this envelope under the third. Pull off a flower head, and place it directly in front of the pot."

"Yes, sir."

The inspector folded the envelope in thirds before handing it to his officer.

"Do it quickly. When you have finished, return to the Kalmar Station and call me." Turning to Rolf, he explained, "One of Ulrik's communiqués contained the drop point and signal he used to alert his handler. We will see if they are interested in a trade."

"Am I missing something? You don't have Sedgely in custody."

"Karlevi continues to be the draw. I think if we keep watch on the rune, it is the place we will find him."

"You must like to play poker, Inspector."

Lars hurried down from Sigrid's office to the inn parlor. Rolf started to follow, looked at his watch, and stopped. She had been gone too long. He was going to look for Lea.

As Rolf returned the scissors to the bathroom shelf in Lea's room, his eyes turned again to the two piles of change. When he emptied his pockets, he threw the change into one heap. She used American money and divided it into two piles. He stared at the money.

"Inspector," he shouted. Running down the stairs, he found the detective sitting at a table writing notes on the case.

"Upstairs, in the bathroom," he insisted.

Lars got up to follow, purposely leaving his deliberations concerning a signature behind.

Rolf pointed to the change. "She's not out walking, the note's a phony. She used the money to tell us where she's being taken. Lea knew her room would be searched. This is the message she wanted us to find."

Lars looked at the arrangement, but not knowing the values of American money, he didn't understand the significance. "Explain what you see."

"On one side, two dimes and four pennies While on the other, a dime, nickel, and penny. She's mimicking the first line of the rhyme. 'It can be seen where twenty-four meets sixteen.' You were right, Inspector! Sedgely is headed toward the rune. And if he's taking Lea with him, he doesn't know about the rings—yet. What about the KGB? When Sedgely realizes he's trapped, he'll use her as a shield or try for a tradeoff. We can't deal with the Soviets now. Better it's just us. Call your man. Stop him before he places the note."

Lars looked at his watch and calculated the time to drive over the bridge to Kalmar.

"Too late."

"Then we'd better call Swedish intelligence and the CIA."

Lars shook his head. "If any Western organization is informed, we will have no involvement. And the CIA will likely welcome the reverend with open arms. Reverend James Sedgely outsmarted KGB and Stasi agents to crack the greatest mystery left from World War II. Under the CIA's protection, the reverend will find the Amber Room and leave the Soviet empire with nothing. We need the KGB."

Rolf nodded. He knew the inspector was right.

The ringing phone interrupted. Lars hurried to answer. "Yes, what is it?

"Inspector, someone has been at Ulrik's rental in town. The room was taken apart and emptied. No personal property was found."

"Was anything found in the sink drain?"

"Yes, sir, a roll of bundled paper," stated the man. "I left the bundle untouched as you instructed. There was also a Chesterfield cigarette on the ground by the back door. I brought it to the lab. And, Inspector, the station just received a call from Denmark. Susan Sedgely and Brenda Farmer were found dead in their hotel room."

"Make sure I get a pathology report. Contact Orensson's rental landlord. No one is to enter the house until I am able to check it. That includes him." The detective hung up the phone and turned to Sundren.

"The women are dead. And someone has been in Ulrik's rental cottage. His possessions are gone, the rooms in chaos. Even the wallpaper was ripped down. But the officer did find a Chesterfield cigarette," Lars said. "The reverend continues to make sure Benjamin Farmer is blamed."

Rolf looked up. "We don't know if Susan and Brenda were part of the minister's plan, or just got in his way. Knowing Lea, she'll do everything in her power to slow him down, but we have to move quickly. If Sedgely does have Ulrik's ring, there's a chance he'll discover the matching band in her locket and find the connection."

Picking up his mobile phone, the inspector went to the inn room he used when he spent nights watching Gunnar. He grabbed his coat and threw it on the bed. He pulled out a large trunk standing in the corner and opened up a false bottom with a key kept on his neck chain. Inside was a number of weapons paired with corresponding ammunition rounds. Lars chose a pistol and put it in his shoulder holster. He fit a smaller piece around his ankle. He took the Nazi *Hitler Document* and folded it into his shirt pocket. Ulrik's practice sheet was another matter. Lars could not be caught with that paper. It was the only proof the *Hitler Document* was undeniably fake.

For his plan to work, the Soviets had to believe the paper was genuine. His satchel would be left out. He re-taped his briefcase to the underside of the desk. He wasn't concerned if his case was discovered. The documents he put inside were important, but still a red herring. The practice paper was another matter. He needed a safe place to hide it. He also carried the diary.

He hurried downstairs to the kitchen. Making sure no one was around, Lars grabbed a copper pot, placed the practice sheet and diary inside, put the lid on, and placed it back on the shelf. He called over the last of his men.

"Officer Jurgen, I will be gone for a time. You are to stay here with Sigrid. If there is a reply to my message, call me on my mobile. Where is Peter?"

"I haven't seen him, sir."

The detective understood his plan countered his superior's dictate to concentrate on finding Benjamin Farmer. However, there would be no accusations of misconduct charged against his officers. The men were following Lars's direct orders. If anything went wrong, only he would be held accountable.

35

ÖLAND, 1989

After traveling a short distance from the inn, Lea insisted on resting. "I can't go any farther." James looked around for a safe place and decided to return to the area around the milking barn. This time, however, he wasn't comfortable staying long. While the inspector's methodical regimen gave plenty of leeway, he didn't want to waste a minute. And there were still more answers to coax from Lea. "It's time to move."

Getting up from the ground, Lea made her hobbling more pronounced. "Reverend, I can't." She sank back down.

James narrowed his eyes. He couldn't judge the swelling of her ankle through the thickness of the bandage. It was still a distance to the rune, too early to arouse her suspicions. Even if he pushed her, it would take several hours to reach Karlevi. If he rendered her unconscious, he would be forced to carry the woman.

Looking around, James tried to see how far the barn was from the house. It was possible the dairyman lived a distance away and rented the barn.

"It's only a few more miles to Karlevi." James looked up into the sky. "It'll be dark soon. Almost impossible for anyone to track us after that." He patted her hand. "Come on, honey. Get up. You'll make it."

She listened to the feigned sympathy oozing from the man, but heard his exasperation beneath. It was time to find out how much room she had to maneuver. "I can't go any farther right now."

"All right, but only a little longer." Grabbing her arms, he pulled her up to a standing position.

"I'm going back a mile or so to make sure no one is following. I'll erase any tracks we've made and when I return, we'll continue to Karlevi."

James looked around the barn and frowned. "It's not safe for you here." He pointed with his finger. "Down the hill, behind that copse of trees, I see a pond. It will give better cover. Rest while I'm gone." James hurried off to backtrack the distance.

She had a reprieve to figure out if she should try to get away from the reverend and head back to the inn, or go to the pond and wait. Her ankle really was swollen. Except for the blanket of trees at the bottom of the hill, there was little camouflage to conceal herself from Sedgely. Without the cover of night, it wouldn't take him long to find her. If she tried to outrun the minister, the pretense would be over.

Even with age and weight, Lea didn't want to underestimate him. She tested her ankle by stretching and twisting. Damn. It really hurt. The ankle would definitely slow her down. Her martial arts training might help, but she could only manage one quick move. Lea had no delusions that she could overpower a skilled communist agent. Getting up, she started for the pond.

Hopefully by stalling, Rolf and the inspector would arrive at Karlevi first. But she had no assurance her clue was understood. The letter she was forced to write might be all they found.

The two men stood outside of Kalmarsson Inn.

"Rolf, there is a pickax, shovel, and paint tarp in the back shed."

"I'll get them."

Lars walked over to Sigrid.

"Lea is missing. I believe she was forced to go with Reverend Sedgely. The girl is in danger, Sigrid. Do not tell anyone about this. Officer Jurgen will stay at the inn with you."

"Lars. She…"

"We will find her, Sigrid." Lars took her hands in his. "Remember, say nothing. Please go into the house."

"Ready." Rolf stood with the gear.

Lars nodded. From the inn, the runestone was a little over three miles away. The detective decided to take the most direct route. He expected the minister to use less-traveled paths and stop often to check for signs of being followed. Lars needed to arrive at the rune first. The unknown question—what would Lea do?

She had been clever enough to leave a clue showing her destination. The detective hoped Rolf was correct and the woman would find ways to delay her trek to the rune.

The vibrating inside his jacket indicated a phone call. Lars signaled Sundren to stop.

"Yes?" he answered.

"This is Jurgen. The drop is completed, Inspector."

"When Peter returns to the inn, have him report back to Kalmar. He is to take the notes I left downstairs by the registration desk."

Continue to pass all calls for me through the mobile." He disconnected the call.

The two men started moving toward the rune again.

By using Ulrik's code, the inspector underlined his claim of intimate knowledge of the man. When the Soviets contacted Lars, he would push his story, explaining why Ulrik recruited Sedgely, and how the minister managed to double-cross Orensson, causing the spy's death. Lars only hoped the KGB was as meticulous examining documents as he remembered. The proof he wanted them to find depended on their thoroughness.

Lars's summation would be short and to the point. Reverend James Sedgely managed to outthink their best agents, playing them for fools. Ulrik, the Stasi, even the KGB, fell for his tricks. Finding the Amber Room for the Soviet Union was never a consideration for the reverend. It was only the bait to gain the help and protection of Ulrik and the KGB. The minister would depart with the prized *Hitler Document*, probably to the United States, and be under the shelter of the CIA before Soviet operatives were even aware of the man's involvement. It was an ending he knew would incite the communists.

One thought nagged him—what information did the Soviets have on Lea Reardon? Lars surmised Ulrik would have told them very little about the woman and nothing of her importance to the Amber Room. That was how it had to stay. Her life depended on it.

Once the KGB agreed to the deal, he would send broad coordinates. When all was in place, he would be specific. Lars calculated the time it would take to transfer the agents from the Russian coast to Öland. He wasn't sure if the KGB would use air or sea transport. Either way, he figured their arrival time as shortly after dark.

Close to Karlevi, the rumble inside his jacket indicated another call. Lars motioned Rolf to stop.

"Yes."

"Ivanavich speaking. So, Youngmark, you want to deal. It is an interesting proposition."

"The trade will benefit us both, Ivanavich." Looking at his watch, Lars realized how quickly the man had answered his message. The heavily accented voice was calm, determined to underplay his situation.

"The ten agents in return for the minister. After the switch, what you do with the reverend is not my concern. You are aware I have not contacted Swedish or American agencies. Once the minister communicates with them, it will be over. All I ask is for you to listen."

Lars repeated his practiced story to the communist and waited.

"Hold!" The line became muffled, indicating he covered the mouthpiece. "How do I know you will have the murderer?" The voice was clear again.

Lars didn't argue with Ivanavich's word choice nor did he answer the Soviet's question. He gave broad coordinates to the actual site. "Contact me when you are there and I will give you the exact location."

"The men you want are far into Siberia, Youngmark. It will take many hours to reach those coordinates."

Lars knew better. It would be a long game of cat and mouse with high stakes. "I will expect to hear from you before dark." He replaced the mobile phone inside his jacket.

"What about Lea? You didn't mention her safety."

"If I talk about her, give any reason to think she has importance, they will take her. We must concentrate on what Ivanavich expects. I doubt he trusts I am giving him the correct location. My guess is he will travel up and down the Swedish coast looking for Sedgely himself. When he is ready, I will hear from him."

Ivanavich looked through reports on the ten men once again. It was interesting this Inspector Youngmark contacted him. There had been talks between the CIA and the KGB for the release of the agents. Yet the detective mentioned nothing of the previous arrangement. The handoff had been cancelled at the last minute after negotiations broke down. Ivanavich blamed his supervisor for the problem.

As a senior agent, Ivanavich had helped prepare the Soviet part of the trade and all was still in place. It angered him to see his hard work dismissed. He would meet with this detective and follow the original plan. His superior would not be informed. If it came out as intended, he would be decorated and rewarded for his success. He would not think of the alternative.

KARLEVI RUNESTONE, ÖLAND

Approaching Karlevi, the detective stopped. "Search north of the rune for anyone approaching. I will take south. Don't be long."

Finding nothing to cause alarm, Lars returned first and selected a spot he could adapt for cover halfway between the runestone and the water. Beside concealment, the site offered a view of Karlevi and the surrounding plain. Scanning west, he noticed there was a break through the tree line, and beyond, Kalmar Sound.

Taking the tools the American had carried, the detective dug a trench deep enough to hold himself and Sundren. Lars ripped his handkerchief in two, wrapping one half around his left hand to lessen the abrasion on his blistered palm. Every bone and muscle had been pushed to the limit. It didn't matter.

Never a fan of Machiavelli's *The Prince*, Lars decided in this case, the end did justify the means. The detective finished shoveling out the hole when Rolf ran back.

"Someone's coming," he whispered.

"About time!"

Hurriedly erasing their footprints, both men jumped into the hole and crouched low. The detective pulled the brown tarp overhead to camouflage their position.

The murmur of voices was evident but muted by the thick tarp. The sounds rose and fell with unpredictability. The few bits of language Lars managed to catch were unmistakably Russian. With daylight almost gone, the boatmen used a light to scour the ground looking for movement. Once they moved on, the detective lifted the cloth.

The phone vibrated a half hour later. It was time to give the exact position. Ivanavich had argued, but Lars refused to give the directions until he spoke directly to several of the agents, confirmed their identity, and was assured they were on the transport.

Looking at his watch, the detective wondered how long before the reverend and Lea arrived.

"Just a bit more. Take it easy. Don't trip again!" James said. It had taken too long to reach the runestone, the sky darkening during the slow walk. She had been clumsy, stumbling and tripping over the ground. He rubbed his arm. It was sore from her hand clutching at him. Finally, they were there.

"What are you doing?" she wondered why the minister had stopped to gather a load of loose sticks and brambles as they approached the rune.

"Stand still and be quiet!" It was doubtful that anyone was waiting for him to walk onto the open plain. Still, he wanted to be cautious.

James piled some of the brush next to Lea. When he was satisfied with the height, he returned for the rest and made a second mound. Taking twine from his pocket, he wrapped the cord around the two shapes to hold everything in place. Standing away, he looked at his artistry. With scant illumination from the heavens, anyone searching would be fooled by his creations. He would take Lea, retreat far enough from the runestone to be safe, and watch to see if anyone approached the mounds.

36

Karlevi Runestone

The waiting was impossible and the quiet deafening. Lars had turned off his phone after giving the KGB their last position. With the destination revealed, Lars knew the Soviet could easily switch the captured agents with KGB operatives. However, Ivanavich was smart enough to understand Lars would expect such an obvious ploy, and have planned for it. No, it wouldn't be that easy. The inspector expected subterfuge, but in what form?

Talking between the two men was kept at a minimum. There was too much chance of being overheard. Legs pulled under him, Rolf tried to ignore the tight conditions and concentrated on searching every inch of the area with binoculars. Lea and the minister should have been there by this time. The thought that Sedgely might have already killed her ate at his insides.

Rolf wanted to protect her. He had called her naïve, yet she saw through the reverend's disguise. The woman thought clearly under pressure. The clue left behind using money to point out her destination was brilliant. She had managed to slow down the minister, which had given the inspector and himself time to reach Karlevi first. It was harder to judge what she could do physically.

Rolf stopped himself from going over every detail. He had to stay focused, be methodical, make sure nothing moved or changed since the last time he scanned the area.

A slight movement caused him to turn his head. Parallel to the runestone, there was just enough light to make out two shapes that hadn't been there minutes earlier. He touched the detective's sleeve.

"Inspector, over there. It's Sedgely and Lea." Rolf motioned him to look through the lenses.

Before taking the binoculars, Lars pulled the tarp over their heads. Looking where Rolf pointed, the detective was unable to see clearly.

"I see a size difference of the shapes. It could be them." Lars hoped it was Lea and the reverend. It had been impossible to create a definitive plan on how to capture the minister, there were too many unknowns. Their actions would depend on the situation. He thought he saw shadowy figures behind the reverend, but it was hard to tell.

Rolf aimed the binoculars north of the rune once more. Why hadn't Sedgely started toward the stone? He tried again to adjust his tall frame to fit the constricted space. His legs had gone numb. If he didn't stretch, walking would be a problem, let alone moving with any agility. There it was again. He didn't imagine the movement.

"Men behind the minister…Something's wrong. They're in trouble!"

"Shhhh!" The detective put a hand on the younger man's arm to quiet him. If Rolf made a move too soon, Lea would be dead before he reached her.

As he motioned Rolf for the glasses, loud voices and gunshots erupted. "What the hell?"

The detective turned around trying to find the origin, but bright lights from the water flooded the plain, blinding him for a moment.

"CIA. Stand down! You're surrounded. Put your weapons on the ground and come forward." The command was given in English, Russian, and German.

A small group emerged from the tree line with hands in the air. Rolf and Lars had front row seats to the action and crouched low to listen. The conversations were loud and easy to understand.

"Is this all of them?"

"We're not sure. These men are without papers, but their equipment is either KGB or Stasi issue."

"Good work. Jones, Mackie, make these hooligans talk. I wanna know if they've got buddies nearby. The rest of you search for any who got away."

Lars froze when he heard the narrative.

The two men holding Sedgely refused to give up their guns. Pointing their weapons, they pulled the reverend backward toward the trees. Tape covered the minister's mouth, and his hands were tied.

"Release him and put down your weapons, now!"

Shots were fired. The men holding Sedgely fell to the ground.

Three men approached Lea. "I'm sorry about this," one said. "We had no other way of grabbing the agents without the possibility that you might be injured."

"You must be CIA. How did you find me? Was it Rolf, Inspector Youngmark?" asked Lea.

The man didn't answer.

Lars worried she would give away too much information.

"No! Wait, don't untie the minister," Lea shouted. "He's a Stasi agent."

It was too late. The tape had been removed and the rope holding the minister's hands, cut.

Rolf started to climb out of the hole. "Inspector, they're CIA. We've got to get over there before Sedgely finds a way to kill Lea to stop her from talking."

Something wasn't right. "No, don't move." It was unusual for Americans to use the word hooligan, but in communist circles, a very common term. It was the hoax he expected. Lars grabbed the younger man and pulled him back down. His words were louder than intended. Lars braced himself for a confrontation, putting a hand on his shoulder weapon, but no one paid them any attention.

The detective pointed toward the tree line. "They're all KGB. The show is for our benefit." It was also the break Lars waited for, the best chance for Rolf to escape. "Get to the water. Find their transport. The Western agents will be on board."

"But Lea."

Before he could say anymore, Lars put a hand on the younger man's shoulder. "Trust me."

The detective counted eight KGB men on the beach. He guessed there were more waiting for orders. Lars handed Rolf a knife to strap around his leg. "Find the captives. Make sure not KGB!" He gave Rolf the verbal question to ask the prisoners. "This is the plan…"

Rolf crawled out of the hole and moved away from the group into the scrub trees. After losing the protective cover of the tall brush, he crawled on his belly across dirt and rock toward the water. Almost there, he spotted two men walking toward him. Flattening out his body, he virtually slithered into the waves to avoid detection. He lifted his head to look for their boat. It was farther out than he expected. Away from the shallows of the coastline, it was a long swim to reach the craft. Heaving himself over the backside, Rolf banged full force into an outboard engine.

"Aah!" Blood spurted out of his foot. Reaching into his pocket, he pulled out a wet handkerchief, mopping the deck around his feet before tying the rag around his ankle. *Can't afford to leave a trail of blood*, he thought, although he doubted anyone would see it. There weren't any running lights on the deck. The bright spotlight on top of a spire concentrated its narrow illumination toward the beach.

"Shit! This can't be it."

The boat couldn't accommodate more than four or five people. It was an open runabout without a cabin. It was logical the KGB used a submarine then transferred to this small craft. He had passed two large rubber rafts pulled up on the beach. The rafts would have been used to paddle the rest of the way to shore.

Time was wasting and Lea's life was at stake. He had to get back. "Trust me," the inspector had said. Rolf looked at his watch. He would give it another minute.

Lars had warned him not to use logic. "If it makes perfect sense, be careful of a trick."

On his knees, Rolf searched the bottom of the boat, keeping his palms flat against the deck. If he missed something, he had to find out, and fast.

A noise caught his attention, then a throbbing under his hands. He followed the tremor until his ears picked up a soft mechanical hum directly underneath.

The pull to the hatch was hidden under a length of coiled rope. Standing, he would have missed it. Slowly, Rolf raised a hinged cover and listened. The motorized sounds were louder, but still no voices. The space was small, only enough room for one person to pass through. Lars had been right! Rolf tied off the rope to a metal bar he found on the inside of the hatch. He lowered himself, landing with a thump next to a large generator. The outboard engine was a fake. This is what powered the craft.

That old fox, he thought to himself. Without his insistence, Rolf would have fallen for the sham.

Dim ceiling lights gave off enough illumination to allow a look around. The area below was much larger than topside. The deception was remarkable to anyone spying the boat above the waterline. He walked in a narrow hallway with rooms on both sides. Signs using the Cyrillic alphabet made clear the sub was Russian. Rolf strained his ears to catch any sounds as he moved past each door. He heard nothing. At the end of the corridor, he spotted a shaft of light.

Through the crack of an open door, he could see a man sitting at a communications station, headphones on, looking at charts. Ten men were chained together on the floor with hooded masks over their heads. Stacks of ammunition and explosives were packed around the men and against the wall.

Slowly opening the door, Rolf picked up a revolver from a desk, crept behind the man and cracked his head with the gun butt. He looked around for rope. Pulling the wires and cord from the headphones, he had enough to hogtie the man's feet and hands together. Quickly moving to the group on the floor, he removed each man's hood and the tape from their mouths. He wouldn't go any farther until making sure of their identity by using the agreed password.

Inspector Youngmark had discovered one of the captured agents was a native of Sweden's Västerbotten County. Unless Ivanavich was well-versed in pre-World War II cinema history, neither he nor his men should know the answer to Rolf's question.

"Who is Johan Olund?"

"Warner Oland, better known as Detective Charlie Chan," replied the man. "I'm Agent Arnesson."

"Rolf Sundren. Inspector Lars Youngmark, Swedish Police, sent me to get all of you out." Rolf noticed the key in the padlock and reached down for it.

"No, don't touch it! It's hooked to the explosives. Move that key and we'll all go up. I'm Michael Collins, by the way, and glad to see you," said the man closest to the lock.

"Cut red first. Find the blue. Carefully push it to the side. Look for the green and white wire. Cut it." With Collins giving him the sequence, Rolf cut the wires with a knife taken from the unconscious man. He had just finished pulling off the chains and unlocking the shackles when voices were heard topside.

"Quick. Get down," Collins ordered.

The men piled back on the floor, pulling the chains over them.

The ten men entered one at a time. One bent down to look at the chains.

"Now!"

The fight for control of the boat was quick, surprise being the controlling factor. Collins searched each of the Soviets and found a copy of the identity cards the ten captured Western agents wore around their necks. The intruder's physical features were similar to the agent they were there to replace.

The group of Soviets was bound, mouths taped shut, and the black head masks slipped over their heads. Agent Collins hooked the last of the explosives to his clone and attached the wires to the key in the lock. Everything was back in place.

Arnesson quickly smothered the radio man Rolf had knocked out. He removed the wires binding the operator's hands and feet and reconnected all but one wire to the headset. He then placed the man back in his chair. Collins found a bottle of whiskey on the shelf, poured it over the body, and set the empty flask at the man's side.

Arnesson smiled at Collins. "When Ivanavich returns, he'll have a surprise waiting."

"Who has a mobile?" Rolf asked. "This is the frequency to connect with Inspector Youngmark,"

Each man grabbed their gear from the clones.

"Done," said each man with a unit.

Rolf described the situation to the agents.

"Three men are holding a woman and a man on the beach. Inspector Youngmark is hiding there," he pointed out the detective's hole on the beach and repeated the instructions from Lars.

"One agent with communication stay one hundred feet from Lars's position. All others scatter in different directions. Those in the woods search and silently take out any KGB agents. The others, when signaled, make increasing amounts of radio and phone chatter. It has to look like a large sea action off the coast. The inspector wants the Soviets nervous."

Rolf glanced around, making sure everything looked the same as when he arrived. He replaced the gun back on the desk before slipping in the water with the others.

"I am not a Stasi agent or any other kind of spy," Sedgely insisted. "My name is Reverend James Sedgely. I'm a minister and counselor to this young woman."

The men turned to listen to the reverend.

"Forgive her ravings. This has been a difficult time for Lea. I recently found out her mother and father were murdered by communist agents trying to gain a diary showing the location of the Amber Room treasure. When they were unsuccessful, they turned their attention to her."

Lars's heart sank as he listened. Sedgely, under the impression he was speaking to the CIA, spoke of Lea's ties to the Amber Room.

"Unfortunately," the minister continued, "I found her too late to stop the drugs. To make Lea talk, a Stasi agent gave her a poisonous concoction. The effects to her mind…" his voice trailed off as he looked at Lea.

"There are times she's lucid. But increasingly, she has become paranoid and delusional. The woman is combative, a danger to herself and those around her. Frankly, I doubt she'll ever recover. The episodes have gotten worse. It's impossible to believe anything she says."

"He's a liar. Don't listen to him!"

The men ignored her and continued speaking to Sedgely. "So, Reverend, it is the Stasi that are responsible," asked one of the men.

"No! That was the intended appearance. Ulrik Orensson, a man working for the KGB, was in charge. I met him on an overnight ferry from Denmark to Sweden. The fellow had had too much to drink and started to speak about the Amber Room and how he planned to gain this lost treasure. I listened, but discounted his story to alcohol…until he talked about Lea Reardon.

The minister waited for a comment or questions, but there was no reaction from the group of men. He continued telling his story without interruption until he mentioned Ulrik's death.

"You caused the death of a KGB agent?" challenged one of the men.

James was annoyed at the tone of disbelief, and began his explanation of how he came across two men in a tavern cellar.

"I spotted Ulrik entering the underground room, heard noise of a struggle and followed the sound. From their conversation, it was more than a simple fight.

"When my eyes adjusted to the dim light, I realized Ulrik had managed to over-power the other fellow. I watched Orensson pour something over the man, pick up matches. I was hesitant, but if I didn't do something…When Ulrik spotted me, he pulled a knife, came at me.

"We struggled. Orensson tripped, fell, hit his head. A fire started. The smoke was thick, choking. I grabbed the other man, pulled him outside. I tried to go back for Ulrik but the door had shut. I couldn't get it open. My eyes burned, my throat was on fire, my fingertips blistered. A gypsy wagon stopped. The last thing I remember was two men picking me up. When I came to, I was sprawled on the ground in a section of woods. My wallet was empty, my watch gone. I don't know what happened to the other man. Now, please, let me give this poor woman her medication."

"Don't touch me!" Lea jumped at the minister, her fists pumping into his stomach. The two men struggled to pull her off, holding her arms to keep Lea from Sedgely.

The minister didn't try to protect himself from her blows. His face reflected pity at her outburst. "You see what a state she's in. Hold her down and let me help her."

Hearing the minister, Lars pulled out his gun, straightening his arms to a firing position.

James took out a small black case from his pocket. Opening it revealed a syringe. "I just need to give her a small dose, it will calm her down. She's been through so much." Sedgely took the syringe out and started to move toward Lea.

"Stay away from me." She tried to pull back from the two agents, but they held her tight.

Lars had no doubt the liquid would kill the woman. Taking careful aim at the minister's head, he waited for Lea to move. The gun range was at its maximum distance. He needed a clear shot. To his advantage, the boat light made the man an easier target.

Before he could fire a protective shot, Lea managed her own. Using the men holding her for leverage, she jumped and kicked out, landing a painful blow to Sedgely. The minister howled. The syringe flew out of the reverend's hand and cracked when it hit the ground. The contents spilled into the dirt. The Soviets were amused. Lars lowered his arms and holstered his gun.

A man came up to the group inserting himself between the minister and Lea. By the differential stance of the others, it was obvious he was the leader.

"I don't believe the lady wants your help." Bending down, the man picked something up from the ground. "This is yours, Reverend?" He held a ring up to the light.

"Yes, a family piece. It must have fallen from my case."

"The gypsy must have missed this when you were robbed. How lucky for you."

Sedgely quickly put the ring on his finger and shoved the case in his pocket.

"Thank you. I'm James Sedgely. I'm grateful for the CIA's help." He held out his hand to shake, but the civility was ignored.

"Reverend Sedgely, by chance do you know the location of the Amber Room? From what I heard you say, everyone who knew about the treasure is either dead or," turning toward Lea, "mentally scarred."

James wondered why the CIA agent was asking about the Amber Room and not the *Hitler Document* from the diary cover. Then realized the CIA would have dealt only with Ulrik. No matter. He could play the game with the best.

Lars recognized Ivanavich's voice, but his crude, hesitant speaking of English had disappeared. The detective smiled to himself. Without realizing it, the minister's words had saved Lea from the Soviet's interest.

"I don't know the specific location of the Amber Room, but I believe I can figure it out. With your help and God's, I'll find it. The communists won't get this one," declared the reverend.

"We're anxious to hear what you have to say. And of course, if you're successful, you understand our nation will be very generous," Ivanavich replied.

"I won't go with you." Lea had seen the minister's ring and realized how similar it was to her own. Is that what Sedgely wanted from her? Putting her hands to her throat, Lea felt the chain to make sure the locket was still inside her shirt.

"Miss Reardon," Ivanavich used a comforting tone. "No one will harm you. If you're concerned about the minister, he will not be permitted near you. Your friends have been worried. They should be contacted. Let us help you."

"No! Leave me here," Lea insisted.

"She must come with us," Sedgely exploded.

"Why, Reverend? From what you said, the woman can be of no help. I'm beginning to think you're not telling us everything," Ivanavich mused.

Rolf stood up in the water to judge his location. He intended to work his way back toward Lea and the inspector. Her safety and rescue were his only concern now.

"The woman is a distraction to our conversation," declared Ivanavich. "Take her down the beach and back a distance. Stay with her."

Lea dropped to the ground. "Please, give me a minute to re-tape my ankle." She unwrapped the stretchy bandage and tightened it.

Ivanavich held out his hand.

"I can manage." Slowly, Lea got up, trapping the small gun that dropped from Sedgely's case, under her shirt.

Rolf was surprised to see two men with Lea. He dropped back in the water and watched as they passed close by. He followed them at a safe distance. Why were they taking her away from the beach?

With the leader's nod, both men flanking the minister grabbed an arm and walked toward the water.

"What are you doing? Don't handle me like that!"

"Youngmark, you are here," asked Ivanavich.

Lars climbed out of the hole. "I am."

"We have what we came for. There is no reason to give you the ten agents," stated Ivanavich.

The inspector reached for his weapon, making sure Ivanavich noticed his slight movement.

"Your reflexes are slow, old man." The Soviet grabbed the gun.

"The agreement was for the ten agents."

"I made a change. Your life and the woman's for the murderer of Ulrik Orensson. Yes, Minister, you made a critical error. We are Soviet."

37

KARLEVI RUNESTONE, 1989

"No, stop! I am Ulrik Orensson!" Sedgely shouted. Ivanavich turned to the reverend.

The minister removed colored contact lenses. The silver-colored hairpiece was next, then the beard and glasses. Taking off his coat, he reached inside and pulled out large pieces of rubber. The person who emerged was slim, blue-eyed, clean-shaven, with graying blonde hair.

Like Ivanavich, Inspector Youngmark was stoic. Using a critical eye, Lars looked at Ulrik without his costume. From the intelligence he gathered, he knew Benjamin Farmer had the same physical makeup as Ulrik, including dentures. The burned corpse in the cellar hadn't a tooth in his mouth. The dead man was likely Farmer, murdered by Orensson so he could be used as a body double, a doppelganger.

The plot was brilliant. Ulrik had lulled everyone into his net of deception. But this time, the spider would be caught in his own web. Lars would make sure.

"Don't you understand? Reverend Sedgely was a cover, my way to gain information on the Reardon family without suspicion."

Ivanavich didn't comment.

"Youngmark can tell you who I am. We've known one another for years." He didn't ask why Lars was there. It didn't matter. The detective was an honest man, no guile, no deception. He grabbed Lars's hands. "You know it's me. Tell them."

Orensson talked about the jobs the men had worked together, memories they shared. "Do you remember all the missions for Swedish security? And when you left the department, I left as well. What about the holidays we celebrated together?" He showed the ring to Lars.

"Do you remember this?" Ulrik tried to hand the ring to Lars.

"Stand back!" Ivanavich slapped Ulrik's arm away.

The detective shrugged. "I remember."

"Do you also recall the difficult days after Hulda's death? Who took care of you and Margretta? Who cooked for you? Who notified the department of your loss? I helped pick out a cemetery gravesite. I was there when you buried her. I helped you then, Lars. Help me now!"

As an agent, he had learned much from Ulrik, although Lars was never able to master the detachment, the lack of emotion and compassion which had been the older man's style.

Ulrik had said, "You are too soft, Lars. Understand your enemy. Use their greed, their lies, to your advantage. Once you have your opponent cornered, show no mercy."

This time, Lars would follow his old mentor's advice.

"His facts are correct, Ivanavich. Without a doubt, this man is Ulrik Orensson," he said the words without feeling.

"Ivanavich will not call you a liar, Youngmark. I will just say you are misinformed. Any agent could have found the information this man spouted, including the circumstances surrounding your wife's death. Everything was listed in your private file. I also have a copy of your complete set of notes concerning the death of Ulrik Orensson. A very interesting sentence you wrote, Inspector. It included a short description about hands. 'Ulrik Orensson's heavily scarred hands were covered by white gloves…'

Ivanavich turned toward Ulrik. "Show me your hands, Minister!"

The men holding Ulrik pulled his arms out straight. Ivanavich took out a small, flashlight to examine his skin.

"Nothing."

"That's easily explained. My skin was fixed years ago. Without scars, I was able to obtain information from the Reardon family as Reverend Sedgely, and then slip into the role of Agent Ulrik Orensson by removing the padded suit and wearing a pair of white gloves. It was a simple but effective way to gain a dual personality. I am Ulrik Orensson! Let me prove what I say!"

"You will have your chance." Ivanavich pulled out the paper Lars had included in the drop.

"Are you familiar with this, Reverend Sedgely? It's a letter proposing terms for surrender to Swedish authorities and specifying what document this person is willing to trade for money and guaranteed protection. It is, of course, Hitler's list of deceptive turncoats that the author is referring to. And the information on this document is something the Soviet Union would be very interested in acquiring."

Ulrik barely glanced at the paper. He couldn't admit to the letter. The wording clearly indicated the author was a double agent willing to sell out the Soviet Bloc. It was the reason he printed the offer and why he refused to sign it. If he was surprised Ivanavich had the letter, he didn't let on.

"The letter is printed. Anyone could have put those words on paper."

Ivanavich nodded in agreement. "That is true. But it is a question I will ask you again, later, when we know one another better."

He took a second sheet of paper from the envelope, carefully unfolded it, pressing out the creases. "And this," he said, holding up the paper. "This is a Stasi directive that we recently acquired. The signed name is Agent Gerstaub. It is addressed to Per Knudsson, and orders the agent to assassinate Ulrik Orensson and Rolf Sundren. I tried to locate Agent Gerstaub, but it seems there is no such person. This communication is fake."

The KGB had examined the order as Lars had hoped. When he first pulled the Stasi communication from Knudsson's briefcase, something about it seemed familiar. Then he remembered that when he first looked at the inn register and noticed the writing of the reverend, it reminded him of someone else. When he went back to check a second time, it was clear the order from Stasi Agent Gerstaub, and the signature of Reverend Sedgely in the Kalmarsson guest book, were written by the same person. That person was Ulrik Orensson. Ulrik hadn't bothered to disguise his handwriting when he signed as Reverend Sedgely. To be certain, Lars compared it to several sentences that Ulrik had written while he sat with the detective and Lea Reardon in his office at the police station. Lars had kept the paper in his briefcase. It was the first mistake Ulrik had made.

Orensson had always been very careful never to leave anything in his handwriting. In the past, even personal letters to Lars had been typewritten. Besides the signature in the inn register, and the order written as Agent Gerstaub, the only other example of Ulrik's handwriting was the paper he had written comparing the diary script and the rune alphabet for Lea Reardon. Lars destroyed it. Without that paper, no one would ever know that Reverend Sedgely, Agent Gerstaub, and Ulrik Orensson were one and the same person.

Per Knudsson had been set up. And since the man now resided in the morgue, he could not be questioned by either side. It was obvious, Per's briefcase was never meant to leave Sweden.

If as Orensson planned, Swedish intelligence had opened the case, the practice sheet of the Hitler document would have stopped all interest in the diary. The Stasi order of assassination would have proved conclusively that the body in the tavern cellar was Ulrik Orensson. Per Knudson would have been found guilty for the murders of Ulrik and Rolf Sundren.

East and West covert organizations would have written Ulrik off the books. There would be no Western veil of protective custody waiting for Orensson. No living in constant fear that the KGB or Stasi would hunt him down and find a way to bring the renegade spy back to the Soviet Union. As Reverend Sedgely, Ulrik would be a free man. Anyone with the slightest possibility of challenging his new identity was already dead or would be, soon.

Ivanavich spoke, breaking into the detective's thoughts.

"It is unfortunate, Inspector, so many people handled the papers. The fingerprints are smudged, useless. But the KGB found another way to gain information." Ivanavich held up the Stasi directive. "The signature of Agent Gerstaub was analyzed and compared to another piece of writing. The results are…"

A man ran up and handed Ivanavich an envelope.

"Inspector, I think you know Agent Peter Anatov. He has been serving as your aide," said Ivanavich.

Turning toward Lars, the Soviet pulled out a photograph showing the inn guest ledger. "Peter had no trouble accessing information, including this, Inspector." He handed the photo to Lars.

"This page illustrates your signature, Reverend James Sedgely."

The Soviet took the picture from Lars and handed it to the minister along with the Stasi communication.

"I have been informed by our specialists that these two signatures, Agent Gerstaub and Reverend James Sedgely, were written by the same individual. That person is you, Reverend James Sedgely, or may I call you Benjamin Farmer? I think that's your real name. Either way, there is no error. You are responsible for the death of Ulrik Orensson. The young Stasi might have been in the tavern cellar with you, but you committed the murder.

"As for the *Hitler Document*, we would like to see the names of those who made money selling supplies to the Third Reich, those traitors who smiled and shook hands as our allies. Ah, but I digress.

"Ulrik spent years searching for that book and the Amber Room. You knew the prize was the Hitler paper hidden in the diary's cover. Once Ulrik found the journal, you killed him. You know nothing of the Amber Room," said Ivanavich.

"No, you're wrong," exclaimed Reverend Sedgely. "I am Ulrik Orensson. Let me explain."

"I dismiss your explanations, Minister. Let's look at facts and fingerprints."

Ivanavich reached into the pocket of Sedgely's discarded coat and pulled out a pack of cigarettes.

Lars held his breath until he saw the brand.

"These are the Chesterfield cigarettes Benjamin Farmer smoked. When one of our agents searched outside the rental house of Agent Ulrik Orensson," Ivanavich held up a cigarette pack, "this was found. Again, it is Farmer's brand. I also know, Inspector, that one of your men found a cigarette butt of the same type inside the house. At the murder scene of Gunnar Johansson, a pack of this brand was found in a corner of the garden shed." Ivanavich turned. "Why did you kill Gunnar Johansson, Reverend? Did he see you without your disguise?

"It was careless of you to leave so many of your cigarettes behind. But then, as Reverend James Sedgely, you didn't smoke. You weren't concerned what cigarettes were found. That was a mistake."

The Soviet took out a tattered pack of British cigarettes. Lars recognized the pack as the one he pulled from the tavern cellar. Lars had left the pack, his notes on Ulrik, and the report from the tavern cellar hidden in his secret space. With help from one of his officers, the detective had counted that Peter would find the stash in his office under the floorboard.

"Youngmark, did you forget to tell Benjamin Farmer that this English brand of cigarette is what the real Agent Orensson smoked? It must have taken you by surprise, Inspector, to discover Orensson smoking, since the man had quit years ago. For some reason, Ulrik picked up the habit again and that was something you hadn't planned on."

"How did you find this information?" asked Inspector Youngmark.

Ivanavich smiled at the detective's reaction. "Are you surprised? It was very helpful for the KGB that you kept such detailed notes in your office. Although, I must congratulate you on your ingenuity. Your briefcase taped under the desk at Kalmarsson Inn was easy to find. But my agent only recently discovered your cache of information beneath the loose floorboard under a dog dish. It wasn't the fierceness of the animal that kept people away but the putrid smell of rotting meat.

"Ah, but I didn't mention fingerprints, did I?" chided Ivanavich. "Benjamin Farmer's prints were lifted from several items, including the assassination weapon found in the tavern cellar."

Ivanavich looked again at Ulrik's hands. "I see no blistering. Isn't that what you said, Reverend? Your fingertips became blistered from the tavern cellar fire. A good excuse to explain your injured fingers and lack of fingerprints, but not the correct one.

"The KGB uses acid injections to remove print ridges. I suspect you had your fingertips altered by this method, very recently. The change is immediate, but there is a life-lasting effect on the finger pads." Ivanavich shined his light on Ulrik's fingertips. "Like this."

He held up the minister's hand.

"The tips become red and distended. When we become better friends, you'll tell me who did your work. So examining your fingerprints and matching them to Benjamin Farmer's is impossible. What is left? Two things. Number one. Compare your writing with Ulrich Orensson's. That is not likely. Like any great KGB spy, Orensson left no examples of written text. I received that information from our Soviet intelligence office. And number two, check Farmer's physical appearance. From your conversations with Swedish intelligence, Inspector, it was learned that no photographs of Benjamin Farmer were found. The CIA made sure they were destroyed, eh, Youngmark? But we do know Benjamin Farmer is slim, has blue eyes, faded blond hair, and..." Ivanavich turned to one of men holding the minister. "Open his mouth and remove them. Benjamin Farmer has false teeth," said Ivanavich. The man opened the reverend's mouth and held up the teeth before pushing them back into Sedgely's mouth.

"Listen to me, you fools!" The Reverend barked. "I am Ulrik Orensson. Reverend Sedgely and Ulrik Orensson are the same person. I am not Benjamin Farmer!"

The men didn't listen. Things were happening fast. Lars sneaked a look at his wrist. It was a motion he had made a few times, but this time Ianavich finally looked at his watch. Lars knew the Soviet felt pressured for time. Ivanavich had followed the road Lars had set, but if he was given more time, the Soviet would find questions the detective couldn't easily answer.

Ivanavich picked up the bulky rubber inserts Ulrik had removed and stuffed them back into his coat. He placed the wig back on Ulrik's head. "Benjamin Farmer and his alter-ego, Reverend James Sedgely, is a talented man. Most probably a deep undercover CIA agent. His assignment, to recover the *Hitler Document* hidden inside the Reardon diary. It must have been difficult to perform husbandly duties to both women for so many years as two different men." The Soviet looked over at the reverend. "Then again, I've heard American women are not as physically demanding as our Russian ladies."

Ivanavich's men laughed.

"After years of searching, Ulrik finally obtained the diary. You murdered him to acquire the document. You, Benjamin Farmer, then abandoned your wife, Brenda. She and Susan Sedgely have been found dead at the hotel, from poison. Their use to you was over. You left behind traceable evidence and disappeared. And that was the plan. Benjamin Farmer would never be found. But why, Inspector? What was the point in continuing this ridiculous masquerade after you gained the document inside the diary?"

Lars shrugged his shoulders.

"No answer, Detective Youngmark? Let me help you with the details. With your knowledge of Ulrik Orensson, you were able to coach Benjamin Farmer in Ulrik's dress and mannerism. You contacted me for a trade. Was this exchange using Sedgely accidental, a set of sudden circumstances? Or was this swap of the reverend for the ten agents the primary mission from the beginning? I believe the trade, using the minister, was the original plan. You, Lars, a past Swedish intelligence agent, would make a credible contact.

"Once the KGB arrived at Karlevi, your mission was to make sure we concluded Benjamin Farmer was Soviet agent Ulrik Orensson. After giving you the ten agents, this man would be brought back to the USSR. Masquerading as KGB Ulrik Orensson, Farmer would have easy access to Soviet classified information at the highest level. Once he gained our superior intelligence, he would be smuggled back into the United States. He would put on his padded suit and take up his disguise as Reverend Sedgely, without his cumbersome wife.

"Ah, but this is a great day for the Soviet Union, and I should not be harsh with you, Youngmark. I can't fault you for trying to convince me of this charade; I would have done the same. But if this is an example of Western capability, we Soviets have little to worry about."

Ivanavich was pleased with his success, but Lars knew the man didn't stay to boast or reveal his plan of operation. The Soviet wanted something else and the inspector was ready to give it to him.

Carefully, Lars pressed down the button on his phone, opening the line. If Rolf was successful, Ivanavich would begin to hear radio and phone noise. Lars hoped the agent that would play in the next part of this drama was in place and ready.

The Soviet glanced again at his watch. "However, there is a way for you to come out of this with a small prize. I am still willing to exchange the ten agents for something I want. Are you interested, Inspector?"

"I am."

"You have the document from the diary cover."

Lars had to be careful. Ivanavich was no fool, and Peter had given him all the information.

"Swedish intelligence already has a copy of the *Hitler Document*. It is no good to you," declared Lars.

"To the contrary, Detective! My agent tells me the paper has been in your possession the entire time. Didn't even trust putting it in the safe or your depository under the floorboard, eh, Youngmark? Swedish intelligence does not have a copy, nor have they read the paper. I believe you are carrying the document, or it is hidden nearby. I could have you forcibly searched and tortured."

Lars steeled himself to show no fear.

"Contrary to your Western expectations, we rarely use such vulgar tactics. Only in special cases." Ivanavich smiled. "Your ten agents are surrounded by explosives, Inspector. If you agree to this exchange, they will survive. If not, well…Do you care more about the men or a paper? Decide now!"

"I cannot trust your word, Ivanavich."

"I doubt you came alone, Youngmark. Call out your man. He and Comrade Sessitch will release the agents together.

"Sessitch, come here," Ivanavich called out to one of the men holding Sedgely. Did you contact our ship by radio?"

"There is trouble transmitting," Sessitch said. "There must be problems with the wires. I need to check. But I heard…" The man spoke softly to Ivanavich, pointing over the water.

Lars smiled.

"There is no time left. Youngmark, it is up to you. The raft is waiting on the beach and I will not expect the document until you see and identify your agents. What do you say?"

"Give me your radio until the men return. Maybe the wires are down, maybe not," Lars said.

"Agreed," Ivanavich said.

Lars spoke into his phone. "Agent, this is Inspector Youngmark. You are to come out, now!" If Rolf had gained entrance to the Soviet craft to free the Western agents, someone would answer him.

A man crouched behind bushes near the shoreline stood up and walked to the group. "I'm Officer Collins." He hoped the Soviets wouldn't recognize him as one of the prisoners, but they paid his appearance little attention.

"You see, we do think alike." Ivanavich nodded to Lars. "We will wait together."

Lars watched the two men run down the beach. He understood the gamble and still didn't know how this would end. If the KGB agent discovered the switch of men, if any of the ten captured Soviets managed to alert Ivanavich, those were risks he and the agents were willing to take. But he would not jeopardize Lea's life or continue to put Rolf in harm's way.

He knew Sundren planned to rescue the woman. Lea had been taken farther down the beach by two of Ivanavich's men. He couldn't see her. Retrieving the group of captured men from the boat would center attention away from Lea and give Rolf time to find her. Lars was confident Rolf or one of the Western agents would silence her captors and get her to safety. He looked over at Ulrik. Lars thought there would be a reaction to the situation. He saw nothing.

The two men walked over to one of the rafts and paddled swiftly to the boat. Collins waited for Sessitch to lead.

"Down here." Sessitch opened the hatch cover and tied the rope. The two slid down. Sessitch gave a cursory look to make sure nothing was out of place. If Ivanavich had not been in such a hurry to get the document and leave, he could be more thorough.

Their comrades should have made the switch by now. The Western agents would be locked up in engineering and ten KGB agents would have taken their place. Sessitch had to admit Ivanavich was brilliant. The Soviets would gain much from this trade.

The ten Western agents would be sent to Lubyanka prison, and their Soviet impersonators would spread much disinformation before the CIA, or some other Western covert agency, realized the truth and captured the KGB agents. A very important document would be in Soviet hands, and the murderer of Soviet agent, Ulrik Orensson, would be treated to KGB hospitality.

Sessitch wanted to open the door to the engine room and make sure the Western prisoners were there, but it would make Collins suspicious.

Both men entered the radio room of the sub where the ten men were chained. Sessitch spoke to his friend, the radio operator, Posmovitch. Head down, the man appeared unconsciousness. Sessitch pulled out a pistol.

"You will not move."

Collins stood perfectly still, but he had already aimed his own weapon at Sessitch on the chance the KGB man discovered the truth.

"Poso, what's wrong?" Using his nickname, Sessitch shook the limp man with no reaction. He picked up the empty whiskey bottle. "Wake up, you fool!" He dropped the man back into the seat. Picking up a broken wire, he knew the reason Ivanavich had trouble transmitting. Reconnecting the set, Sessitch whispered in the man's ear. "Poso, when Ivanavich sees this, you will be a dead man!"

Collins heard the exasperated outburst, understood the language, and smiled. Comrade Sessitch had no idea how right he was.

Sessitch turned to Collins. "The wires hooked up to your comrades are ready to blow. I will give you the sequence; you cut the wires and release the chains."

Collins snipped the wires and opened the shackles. One man started to move.

Sessitch quickly rapped him on the back. "You! Stand up." Putting his hand in the man's shirt pocket, Sessitch pulled out his identity card and examined it. He had helped copy the original cards and knew his own work. Everything was correct. These men were KGB. Sessitch handed the card to Collins. "It is accurate?"

Collins looked at the card, shook his head in agreement, and handed it back.

"Your men will be lashed together. If one is foolish, he will be thrown overboard. Of course, the rest of the group will drown as well." Taking a rope and a roll of tape from a shelf on the wall, he threw both to Collins. "Tie your friends with enough lead that each can climb out of the hatch. Use the binding tape on their hands as well." Sessitch kept his gun leveled at Collins as the man corded the length of rope and taped their hands.

"I'll take off the hoods so the men can see." Collins knew he took a risk offering to remove the masks. If Sessitch accepted his offer, the KGB agents would manage to alert him of the switch.

"No! They go as they are."

Sessitch went topside. Collins stayed below to make sure each Soviet agent's hands were trussed, mouths securely taped, and hoods stayed on.

The climb up the rope was slow until the first man hitched himself on deck. After that, they were able to pull the rest up quickly. One by one, as Collins gave each a push, the men jumped down into the raft. They paddled back to shore. Once the raft beached, Sessitch and Collins got out. The group of ten remained in the raft.

Lars and Ivanavich walked down to the water. The man holding Ulrik stayed back. With his head hanging down, Lars was suspicious of Orensson's docile behavior.

"Check the identity cards yourself, Youngmark," Ivanavich said. "Give the man a light, Sessitch."

Flashlight in hand, Lars searched several pockets of the captured men to pull out ID cards and showed them to Collins. "Are these your men?"

Lars noticed Ivanavich had reached into his jacket.

"They are," said Collins.

The Soviet's hand was again visible. "Tie their feet. I don't want any of them to move.

"My side of the deal is complete, Youngmark."

"It is," agreed Lars. He reached into his shirt, pulled out the *Hitler Document*, and handed it to the Soviet agent.

"If I had known the paper was in easy reach, this discussion would have been over long ago." But Ivanavich smiled as he unfolded the paper shining a light on the document to see what he had bought. The Soviet said nothing, but his large grin indicated pleasure.

"An important paper, I admit." Ivanavich held up the document again to scan the sheet. "Normally, I would suspect a trick. But with your time constraints, Inspector, there would not have been enough hours to make a credible forgery."

"It is done then." Nodding to Collins, the detective gave the signal to increase the phone and radio chatter. It was time for the Soviets to think they would soon have company.

Ivanavich looked nervous as he put his phone away. Pulling a gun, he pointed to the hole Lars had dug. He threw rope at the detective. "Tie your man's hands. Tie them tight, Inspector. Put this tape on his mouth. Good!" Ivanavich pushed Collins into the pit. "Turn around, you're next, Detective." Tape went over his mouth. Lars's hands were tied and he was pushed in with Collins.

"Go get Farmer, Sessitch. Put him in the raft. We must leave now! Goodbye, Inspector. We will do business again."

Ivanavich looked toward the water. He had used his handset to call the agents holding Lea.

"Bring the woman with you. Tape her mouth, and meet the men holding Benjamin Farmer. They are waiting a mile down the coast." He had decided to take her along for insurance. If everything went well, she would be released unharmed. If not, well…there was always a cost to doing business.

"Hurry, Sessitch! Cover them with the tarp." Ivanavich was nervous. He did not want Western company.

From a distance, Lars could hear Ulrik curse and yell claiming to be Ulrik Orensson. He wasn't sure how much time the man had left to live. The KGB might wait until they returned to the Soviet Union to interrogate Ulrik. But if the process started immediately, to avoid torture, Ulrik could snag a button from his shirt that was a fast-acting poison. He would have no more than ten minutes to live. It was more choice than he had given Hulda.

Crouched behind a tree, Rolf saw the men tape Lea's mouth. It was obvious the KGB were not going to let her go.

"Good evening," Rolf said the words before he barreled into the two men, knocking Lea from their grip.

Surprise had given him a small advantage, but he had to stop one of the agents quickly. Pulling his knife, he plunged it deep into the chest cavity of the larger man and ripped the blade downward. Without a sound, the Soviet dropped to the ground, bringing Rolf with him.

The second agent grabbed Lea by the arm while trying to get a shot off at Rolf.

"Oh, no, you don't." Lea twisted enough to jab her elbow up into the Soviet's face, breaking his nose. The gun under her shirt dropped to the ground. Rolf dove for the weapon.

Hands slippery from blood, the two men wrestled for control of the pistol. A silencer muffled the sound when the gun discharged. Both men were still.

Ripping the tape from her mouth, Lea pulled the agent off Rolf. "Rolf, talk to me!"

"What do you want me to say?" he asked Lea with a smile.

38

KALMARSSON INN, 1989

The detective sat in Sigrid's small upstairs office penning his resignation from the police force. He had been commended by his superiors for his success, but they hadn't argued his decision to quit. Lars knew the department questioned his loyalty. His oldest friend, Ulrik Orensson, was proven to be a double agent. Many in the organization wondered if Lars had been involved in Ulrik's scheme.

His direct superior did not spare words when he phoned.

"Lars, it is apparent you did not listen to my earlier warning. You did not follow protocol. You disobeyed direct orders and you created your own operation without authority. I can say it is for the best you chose this time to resign from police work."

The detective knew what the agency suspected. Was he trying to save the ten agents as claimed, or was his mission a cover-up to hide his partnership with Ulrik and Sedgely. None of this speculation surprised Lars, and he had no regrets.

He had stayed with Sigrid for a week after his resignation. While admittedly a competent woman, it was obvious after what happened, she needed support and what the bonds of friendship offered; and truthfully, so did he. With little coaxing, Lars had committed to weekly dinners at the inn. It was time to relax and enjoy life.

The detective had already given a verbal and written report. "What we need from you, Lars, is a barebones account of the action, nothing more."

His supervisor in Kalmar was not interested in details, or how he interpreted evidence to reach the conclusions that ended at Karlevi. That, he was told, would be left for experts. He understood the meaning. Every word he said on the operation would be weighed and questioned. And because he was now an outsider, there would be little future intelligence from the agency. Lars had removed Ulrik's practice sheet of the *Hitler Document* and given it to Swedish authorities. He never said how he acquired the paper, and no one asked. Hearing the knock at the door, he considered ignoring it, changed his mind and put down his pen.

"Come in. Come in, Collins, or as I understand it, CIA Agent Collins. How are you?" The detective smiled.

"Fine, Inspector. It is good to see you under better circumstances. Lars, you remember my fellow prisoner, Agent Arnesson of National Security Service, counterintelligence."

"Yes, my contact from Västerbotten County. I knew you would be able to answer my security question on Johan Olund. You certainly played an important part in the operation, Agent Arnesson."

The men shook hands. "Inspector Youngmark, Lars, I'm here to thank you again for your contribution. But there is another reason for our visit. We would like your input on the working report."

Lars nodded.

"Good. Experts in various fields combined their skills, and have studied, what is now classified as the Karlevi Incident. However, there are still a few more questions that would help us."

"Yes, of course."

"First, the paper labeled 'practice sheet.' That document was turned over to Swedish intelligence by you and tested. The paper and ink were authenticated as original to the time period of Nazi Germany. We assume the document taken by Ivanavich of the KGB will test the same."

"That is correct."

"Those who examined the Nazi practice sheet and diary concluded it was most likely Ulrik who authored the *Hitler Document*, the practice sheet, and the diary."

"You believe he wrote the documents and the diary?"

"We know from his background that Ulrik had the means and ability to do such work. And a small bundle of blank paper rolled up in a watertight skin was discovered in the sink drain of his rental house. It chemically matched the practice sheet. If Ulrik had that paper, it was logical he had access to vintage ink, blank journals, and other goods from that time period. Under Western protection, he could have used that paper to make more phony Nazi documents."

"I understand." Lars didn't agree, however. He had guessed Ulrik meant the bundle of paper to be found. It was added evidence to prove the diary a fake. Why make more forgeries as Ulrik when the Amber Room was within reach as Reverend Sedgely?

The detective had known about the bundle. When Lars directed his man to search Ulrik's house hoping to find the ring, he specifically told the young officer to search the sink drain. It had been a favorite hiding place of Ulrik's in the past. When the officer reported a small, rolled-up bundle of paper, Lars told him to put it back, intending to check the house himself. When he returned after Karlevi, the paper was gone. Swedish intelligence had talked to his officer.

"But let's get back to the *Hitler Document*, the practice sheet, and their effect. It would have been difficult, if not impossible, for those World War II neutral countries, banks, and corporations that were listed on the document to repudiate charges of conspiring with the Nazis, whether guilty or not, without the practice sheet exposing the forgery.

"As you know, Ulrik would have received a large amount of cash and Western protection for that Nazi document. So why keep a practice paper proving the document a worthless forgery?

"We thought of various possibilities, but only one seemed logical from Ulrik's vantage. In the beginning, the prize of the diary was the supposed location of the Amber Room. The Nazi documents were known only to Ulrik. But in case Reverend Sedgely found out about the papers before Ulrik's defection, the existence of a practice sheet would give leverage. Stealing the *Hitler Document* was useless with the practice sheet still in circulation. Collins, please continue."

"So who is Reverend Sedgely? The CIA did a background on the man, Inspector. We can trace him to 1979 when he acquired the assumed name. Before then, we have no history. The man was skillful in covering his true identity.

"In 1979, a Reverend Theodore J. Sedgely left a small country church in Indiana. A note left behind asked for forgiveness from his congregation and alluded to an affair with a married woman. For his grievous transgressions, the minister could do nothing else but leave God's service. With no more correspondence and no way to reach the man, the elders hired another to take his place.

"That information was never in the public records because Reverend Theodore J. Sedgely had no family and was never reported missing. A Reverend James Sedgely arrived in Evanston, Illinois, soon after.

"Our best guess is that Reverend Sedgely was a high-ranking Stasi or KGB agent assigned to keep a close eye on Ulrik. Those two agencies would have had the most interest in what Ulrik was selling. The man was a genius at targeting his market. The Stasi and KGB would do anything to acquire the Amber Room, while the Western markets dismissed the diary and its treasure map as myth, and salivated at the thought of gaining the *Hitler Document*. We dismantled the minister's room at the inn, but there was nothing to find. It appeared that he never used the place."

"What about Per Knudsson?" Lars inquired.

Swedish Agent Arnesson took over the explanation. "Swedish intelligence tracked him as a runner, a low-ranking Stasi agent assigned to help Ulrik as needed. Though the question remained, how did the Reardon family become involved with the diary and a double agent in the first place?

"As you are aware, Lars, counterintelligence has had a continuing problem with leaks. Over time, we checked everyone in the unit. It is possible that when Ulrik realized he would be monitored, he smuggled the diary out of Sweden in a box scheduled for auction in the United States. He then traced the sale to Lea Reardon's grandmother."

Collins continued. "When the CIA went over the police account and medical examiner's report regarding the grandmother's death, what appeared as a heart attack then is now considered murder. Ulrik must have been hiding outside the Reardon home waiting for a chance to search for the book when Lea was attacked by Bradley Farmer. Believing all the family members outside, he slipped into the house to locate the diary and the grandmother surprised him. Forced to deal with the old woman, Ulrik lost too much time and had to leave without the book.

"What did seem strange to Central Intelligence is that with ties to the State Department, why didn't Mr. and Mrs. Reardon give them the *Hitler Document* paper hidden in the diary?

"With a closer look, we realized that the couple had only been back from Europe a day when the grandmother was killed. That was 1978, and there's doubt the book was even mentioned. Before her death, the grandmother probably stuck the diary in one of the multiple bookcases located in the home, and it sat unnoticed for years.

"We believe during that period the only ones who knew about the diary and its worth were Ulrik, Sedgely, the Stasi, and the KGB. As a known operative, Ulrik couldn't stay in the area. Even using Sedgely in his role as minister, there would have been only limited opportunities to search the house for the diary.

"This is pure speculation, Inspector. We don't know when Mr. and Mrs. Reardon found the book, but we think it was very recent. Something also must have tipped off the couple that they were being watched. Not knowing what to do or whom to trust, the mother wrapped the diary, addressed it to Lea, and put it in the bedroom bookcase. This would have been right before their last trip. Who knows what the Reardons would have done with the book had they lived."

Collins told a plausible story, Lars thought to himself, but he knew it was wrong. Ulrik did find the diary the night he murdered Lea's grandmother. What he didn't have was the missing page. At first, Ulrik must have thought it was only the parents who had the answer. But Lars had learned that Ulrik's alter-ego, "Reverend Sedgely," was present at one of Lea's nightmares during her "summer service" year, and commented on the few words of a rhyme she spoke. That had to be when Ulrik realized Lea unconsciously knew what was on the missing diary page.

After the couple's death and right before Lea's trip to Öland, Reverend Sedgely put the book in a place she'd be sure to find it.

"Okay, Inspector," Collins said. "For the record, I want to make sure I have the timeline right. Lea told you that she discovered the package among her parents' things the night before she left for Europe and that she took the package with her."

"That is correct."

"However, she didn't open the package until she was here on Öland, specifically, alone in her room at Kalmarsson Inn. The break-in to her room occurred the evening of Midsummer Fest. After your investigation that night, she arrived the next day at your office and showed you the book. That was the first time you saw the diary. Lea didn't leave the book, but brought it back for the meeting with the three of you, Lea, yourself, and Ulrik. Is that the way it happened?"

"Yes, that is what took place."

Collins was a good man. He wanted the official record to show that there was a question whether Lars had anything to do with Ulrik's forgeries.

"Let's go back to the parents again. Getting tired of the game, the Stasi kidnapped Mr. and Mrs. Reardon during their last trip. From your evidence, Inspector, in the form of letters and notes that you discovered in Per Knudsson's house, you found proof Knudsson administered a toxin to the couple, likely an attempt to force the real location of the book. We checked with the hospital in the States. Whatever he used is unknown.

"We concluded that after Lea left for Europe and the house was empty, Ulrik and Reverend Sedgely had time to make a thorough search for the book. Finding nothing, they followed the woman to Sweden. Agent Arnesson, do you have something to add?"

"It is certain that Per drugged Lea at Midsummer Fest. Again, you provided the photo evidence, Lars. And the break-in to her room was certainly an attempt to find the book. However, it wasn't until the meeting at the police station that Ulrik gained possession of the diary. Left on his own in your office, he had time to remove the *Hitler Document* and practice paper from the journal. He needed both in order to cement his multimillion dollar bargain with Swedish intelligence.

"The diary Ulrik created was extraordinary," Agent Arnesson commented. "The complexity of the graphics makes it among the best samples of cryptography I have ever seen. But then he had to make sure that anyone closely examining the book before he removed the documents concluded that the pages were the prize, not something hidden in the book's cover. By making the diary pages so intricate, and including the piece of amber, Ulrik made sure the simple cover was overlooked and ignored.

"To your knowledge, Lars, from the time the woman arrived in Sweden to her visit at the police station, those few minutes in your office were the only time the diary was out of Lea Reardon's possession," asked Arnesson.

"Yes."

"I won't lie to you. There are a few in the agency concerned you purposely left Ulrik alone, then managed to get Lea out of your office to give him a chance to retrieve the documents." Arnesson paused to let Lars comment.

The inspector was silent.

"Let's continue with what happened next. This is when events seem to accelerate. Because there was no ability to speak personally to Reverend Sedgely, a rational profile of his actions was created by our people in partnership with the CIA.

"By the time the reverend learned about the concealed Nazi documents and that the papers and diary were forgeries, Ulrik had made his deal with Swedish intelligence and leaked to the communists that Sedgely was his partner.

"Hunted by the Stasi and KGB as a traitor, the reverend didn't know the *Hitler Document* had been turned over to your office until after Ulrik's murder. His only chance to stay alive was to find the practice sheet.

"To give himself time to search, the reverend kidnapped Lea Reardon to stop her from any more meetings with you and Rolf Sundren. It was too risky to kill you, Lars, but Sundren would be dead if you hadn't seen through Per's disguise and managed to shoot first.

"But in my opinion," Arnesson said, "your finest effort occurred when you realized the writing on the Stasi assassination order matched the reverend's written signature from the inn registration, proving Sedgely ordered the murders.

"The reverend had already killed his brother-in-law, Benjamin Farmer, and used his personal effects and fingerprints to paint the man as the killer of Ulrik. He also poisoned sisters Susan and Brenda. But the murder of Gunnar didn't seem to fit until our agents went back to the tavern and interviewed the bartender.

"The man recognized Gunnar when he stopped in to buy a bottle. Our thinking," Arnesson commented, "is that Gunnar might have seen the reverend enter the cellar with Ulrik. The minister killed him to eliminate a possible witness.

"Reverend Sedgely made sure the murder was not difficult to uncover. He understood that with numerous killings in such a short time, Swedish authorities would dedicate manpower and resources to stop his brother-in-law from committing more murders, leaving him alone to complete his plans.

"Now," Arnesson said, "getting back to the documents, Ulrik gave you the *Hitler Document* to hold for intelligence. Is that correct, Lars?"

"Yes, he did," Lars agreed.

"It would seem logical that he gave you the practice sheet at the same time. That way, all of the important documents would be kept safe and away from Sedgely while you negotiated Ulrik's defection. You were used, Lars," Arnesson chided.

"To stop your reporting the existence of the practice sheet to Swedish intelligence, Ulrik played on your strong bond of loyalty, years of friendship, and the help he gave you after Hulda's death. Do you want to say something about this, correct the impression of what happened, give your explanation?" Arnesson was frustrated at the detective's silence. He tried again on a personal note. "Lars, I can't help without some words from you."

The detective shook his head. "There is nothing."

Arnesson added, "So it must be formally noted you held both documents, the *Hitler Document* and the practice sheet Orensson used to perfect said document. In addition, you knew policy on this matter would be to turn both papers over to Swedish intelligence immediately. You knew and recognized that one was a practice sheet. You also knew the value of both documents."

"Yes. That is correct."

"This is from your report. You stated after hiding the practice sheet at the inn, you created a trap for Sedgely at the Karlevi Runestone. You contacted KGB agent Ivanavich and arranged the trade of the Nazi document and the reverend for ten captured agents. This was done without involvement of the Swedish police or Swedish intelligence. Instead, you chose a civilian to accompany you. And even though your and Collins's reports stated Rolf Sundren did a credible job in difficult circumstances, you took great risk with many lives at stake. Is there anything you want to add or change in this section?"

"No. Nothing."

Arnesson held out the written report for Lars to sign.

The inspector read over the report, signed, and put his pen down. "Arensson, can you tell me what will become of the diary, Ulrik's practice sheet, and the communist agents?"

"The CIA has been given the practice paper and the ten KGB agents. While the KGB are aware the ten Western agents escaped their submarine, they have no knowledge the *Hitler Document* is a fake. The Soviets will have an unpleasant shock when they try to use that paper against a nation or corporation. As for the ten Soviet agents taken from the boat, most have asked for asylum, and each will be used according to their talents. The others have families in the Soviet Union. When this operation comes to an end, a trade will be arranged."

"Good."

Arnesson continued, "The diary has been returned to Lea Reardon. She was told by Agent Collins the CIA did not believe her parents were involved in this matter, and no more information on the incident could be given. We didn't interview the woman because she had no knowledge of the *Hitler Document*. While the Nazi paper is controlled by the communists, this action isn't over. We can't afford to draw attention to the forged paper taken by Ivanavich. From what you said, Inspector, Lea Reardon never knew about the paper hidden in the cover, so I don't believe there's a problem. Any other information she might have is not relevant to the case."

"And Rolf Sundren?" Lars asked Collins.

"Sundren was questioned only about his part on the submarine, and his CIA contacts. He didn't volunteer any opinions about the reverend or the diary. If he was curious why we didn't ask more, he didn't comment. There was nothing else said on the matter. Rolf Sundren and Lea Reardon will receive copies of the official death inquiry. In this uncertain climate of politics, it's too dangerous for the couple to know more."

Agent Arnesson took out a paper. "Inspector, this is the 'official' account of the deaths of Reverend and Mrs. Sedgely, and Mr. and Mrs. Farmer. Swedish and American authorities collaborated on the statement. Considering the sensitivity of the subject matter, and the covert agencies involved, as long as this case remains open, the actual facts will remain limited, and viewed 'as needed.'

"The sisters died in their hotel room. The autopsy will state that Brenda Farmer had a piece of food lodged in her throat and suffocated. The pathologist will report that Susan Sedgely likely suffered a fatal heart attack while struggling to help Brenda. No trace of poison will be found in either sister.

"The bodies of Reverend Sedgely and Benjamin Farmer will be discovered washed on shore, badly decomposed. Wallets, among other items, will make certain their identities. A small craft will be discovered snagged on rocks. Food, drink, poles, and bait will be found in the boat. Among the effects retrieved will be hotel identification cards from both men. The boat's owner logbook will identify the craft as one rented to a 'Reverend Sedgely.' Only a very few know the truth of what actually happened."

Lars nodded.

"We have already notified Bradley Farmer of the deaths of his parents, aunt, and uncle using this story," Agent Collins said. "The young man threatened to bring the matter to court in the form of a lawsuit. However, upon news of a large cash settlement from a travel insurance policy taken out by both parties, he had a change of mind and signed off on everything without asking more questions. He was told their bodies were already cremated and the remains would be sent to him in the United States for burial. He declined the offer and gave us permission to scatter the ashes over the Baltic."

Agent Arnesson commented, "Lars, this is news for you. A man's body was recovered from the Baltic yesterday. We think it might be Sedgely. Unfortunately, the deterioration was extensive or I would have had you view the remains. A clear identification was impossible. This was found in the pocket of the corpse. Do you recognize it?" Arnesson handed the ring to Lars.

"This is the ring Sedgely wore the last time I saw him."

"Are you sure, Lars?"

"I am positive."

"Then Reverend Sedgely's file can be closed for now, unofficially. Because of who he was, the circumstances of his escape, and the impossibility of identifying the physical remains, there will always be uncertainties. This body will be tagged as 'unknown.'"

Lars noticed the ring still on his desk. "Wait, gentlemen, you forgot the ring."

There was no answer as the two men walked out of the room.

He looked at the ring. Interesting how things turned out. No matter how the Karlevi Incident resolved itself, he understood there would always be questions about his role in the action. Was he a traitor or a hero? The conclusions from the experts were well thought out, not correct, but the departments were satisfied.

Lars knew the importance of the ring. He was uncomfortable possessing it. If it was his decision, the ring would be destroyed.

Lea had the diary. He knew the agencies were intrigued by "Ulrik's forgery," and he was surprised they gave it back so quickly. Probably made a copy, but it didn't matter. Without the rhyme and two rings, they had nothing.

He looked down at the ring in the palm of his hand. His wife would have said it was fate that brought the rings together again, and maybe he agreed. Lars would give the ring to Rolf. If it was the couple's decision to find the Amber Room, they would have the tools. No one but himself knew that Reverend Sedgely and Ulrik were the same person. No one ever would.

39

KALMARSSON INN, 1989

Lea and Rolf sat in the garden. The inspector joined them.

"Where is Sigrid?" Lars asked.

"Registering new guests."

"Miss Reardon, Sigrid tells me you're ready to leave Öland."

"It's time to go home, Inspector."

He wondered if her life would include Rolf, but he would never ask such a personal question.

"Now that it's just the three of us, I have something for you, Sundren."

Lars took out the raven ring he was given, and handed it to Rolf. "Agent Arnesson informed me a body was recovered from Kalmar Sound. The person had this ring. I confirmed it was the one I saw on Reverend Sedgely. The agency didn't consider the ring important to the case, and left it behind with me. I'm giving it to you."

"Why, Lars?" questioned Rolf.

"It is up to you and Miss Reardon to decide what to do with the rings," he explained.

"That was quite an experience, Inspector. I'm sure Swedish intelligence was impressed by your handling of the case. I doubt any of the official agencies could have pulled it off. You're a remarkable man, and they are lucky to have you."

"For once I agree with everything Rolf said." Lea smiled.

"That is very generous praise."

The couple had no idea that Swedish authorities suspected he was involved with Ulrik and Sedgely and forced the detective into permanent retirement. There was no reason to tell them.

"So the reverend is dead." Lea shook her head. "Then it's done. It's over." She took out her locket, removed the intricate ring, and handed it to Rolf. "Reverend James never knew I had the matching band. When the KGB captured us, I saw his ring and knew they were a pair."

Rolf took both rings and put them together. "You can see they are a perfect fit, the eagle and the raven. These colors you see marking the different symbols," he held the two rings so Lea and the detective could see, "these will be a match to others on Karlevi. If I'm right, it will reveal the hiding place of the Amber Room." He said the words without conviction. "Excuse me. I have to go upstairs and make some business calls."

Lars waited while Lea followed him up to her room. "What's wrong, Rolf?" she asked.

"I don't know what you mean," he evaded. But he did know. It took self-control on his part not to use the rings to discover the message on the Karlevi runestone. He wanted the challenge of solving the Amber Room puzzle.

"What's wrong?" she repeated.

"Lea, how do you feel about finding the Amber Room?"

"When I hear the words, *finding the Amber Room*, I think about my family and all the people who died. I remember the treasure hunters, the greed, and the governments who want to use an art work for political leverage. In my opinion, the treasure should never be found."

Rolf wanted to agree with her but was silent. With the opportunity in front of him, he understood the lure of the golden Amber Room. He also knew it was a temptation to walk away from.

They planned to go back to the beginning, where the story began; the place where a World War II submarine was scuttled and a young girl died. They would return to Ragnar and Inga's house the following morning.

Lea walked into the kitchen and smiled.

"Inspector, I see Mrs. Kalmarsson is teaching you how to cook." The kitchen had the distinct odor of cooked cabbage as the two friends worked together wrapping cabbage leaves around a meat filling.

"I'm retired," said the smiling inspector. "I have to keep busy. Fishing and my daughter and grandson will help. But I think it's time to start other things as well."

"Somehow, Inspector, I don't think you're talking about learning to cook," Lea said cheekily.

After dinner, Rolf and Lea walked upstairs in the inn to her room.

"Why so quiet?" he asked.

"I'm just thinking again of everything that happened…" She turned to look at him. "Are you sure you agree with me that the rings should be destroyed?"

"Until the rings are demolished to a state where there is no possibility they can be read, there will always remain a chance that someone will find the eagle and the raven and understand how to use them."

Lea woke early the next morning. The fresh cup of coffee on her nightstand and note from Rolf had her hurrying into the shower. After dressing, she picked up the rings and diary and put them in her purse, ready to join him and the inspector. After Ragnar's house, they would be on their way home.

She found Inspector Youngmark and Rolf in the kitchen finishing breakfast.

Sigrid set another place at the table and motioned Lea to sit.

"Just coffee please."

Sigrid shook her head. She had hoped to get a decent meal into the girl before she left.

The suitcases were packed and put into the car trunk.

"Mrs. Kalmarsson. You've taught me Swedish recipes, dressed me for a ball, and worried about me when I was late. You've become my Swedish grandmother. I will miss you so much." Lea hugged the innkeeper.

The men waited while Lea and Sigrid said their goodbyes.

The ride to Ragnar's house with Rolf and the inspector seemed to take forever. Lea stared at the pages of the diary, thinking about the journal and rings, and the unhappiness and death associated with them.

The two men hardly spoke, except for scant comments about the local soccer team.

Reaching the house, the three walked to the shoreline. The sky was sunny and the waves gentle. Lea picked a few flowers and placed them on Inga and Ragnar's grave. She then took the diary, purposely ripping every page into small pieces and scattered them to the wind.

Putting the rings on the ground, she stepped hard on each one, grinding her foot down to bend the metal and render the symbols unintelligible. She picked them up. "Is there anything left?" She handed the twisted bands to the inspector.

"I see nothing." Lars handed the rings to Rolf.

Rolf looked at the scratched symbols with all color removed. "Everything is gone." He gave them back to Lea.

She handed one ring back to Rolf and threw the other out into the water as far as she could. Rolf followed her example. Last to be thrown in the waves was the small piece of amber that had been attached to the diary. Everything associated with the Amber Room and the journal was given back to the sea.

Lea thought of the young girl who wrote in the journal. "I hope this brings you peace."

The three got back into the car for the ride back to Kalmarsson Inn.

Lars rode with Rolf and Lea over the bridge to Kalmar and said goodbye.

"I look forward to your return for next Midsummer." Lars shook their hands and waved as the car pulled away from the station house. It was time to empty his office.

Lars filled boxes with his police manuals, personal logs, and garden journals. One of his officers would bring Knute later. A younger station dog had been requisitioned. When the boxes were closed and taped, he was ready to leave. His car was parked outside.

"Inspector, may I help you carry?" the young officer asked.

"I would appreciate the assistance. I forgot how much was stuffed into this office." It had taken him all afternoon to put things in boxes and stack them at the door.

"This place will not be the same without you," the officer continued speaking. "We have a meeting next week, everyone in the station. I happen to know no one has been picked to take your place yet."

Downstairs, ready to say goodbye, Lars shook hands with the young officer.

"Inspector, it has been a privilege to serve you. Oh, this message came into your office while you were packing. Do you want it, or should I put it away until the next chief is settled in?" He reached in his pocket for the yellow slip of paper.

"No, I will take it." It might be something that had to be dealt with immediately. He could do that much for the department before he left.

The paper was nothing more than an update on deaths around Öland from the past week. One death caught his eye. It confirmed what Agent Arnesson had said. "White male, age fifty years plus. Facial features unrecognizable. No teeth. No fingerprints. No identification. Unclaimed."

He walked down the steps to the morgue one last time. The body was kept in one of the drawers.

The radio was loudly playing a Swedish polka as he walked in looking for the attendant. He found everyone busy at the cutting tables and asked the pathologist about the victim.

"I was informed a body was found in Kalmar Sound."

"Yes, Inspector. The person you want is in drawer five. He will be the next post. The report will be ready tomorrow."

Lars nodded and walked into the room. He felt no sadness in Ulrik's death. The man was responsible for countless murders that Lars knew about and certainly numerous more that had not been documented. And why? All for room ornaments made of fossilized tree scabs. He stood in front of the slab but didn't open the door.

He spoke softly. "I hope you can hear me, Ulrik. The Amber Room is lost to you and anyone else searching for it. Every clue has been destroyed. The boxes will never be found."

Lars waved goodbye to the pathologist and walked back up the stairs. He made arrangements for the remainder of his boxes to be taken from the station house and shipped to Öland. Thinking of Sigrid, he stopped in a confectionary for a box of chocolate to bring as a thank you for dinner.

"Samuel, I need help with this body." The pathologist called his assistant. The unidentified male found in the water was large with bloat, but he had been a very hefty man in life as well.

References

Ross, John F. (1993, January). Treasured In Its Own Right, Amber Is A Golden Window On The Long Ago. *Smithsonian.*

"Runic alphabets". *Omniglot.* Ancient Runes. Ager, Simon. 1998-2014

"History of Russia," Andy Young, http://historyofrussia.org/stalins-purges.